WHY COURTS DON'T WORK

WHY
COURTS
DON'T WORK

Richard Neely

McGraw-Hill Book Company

New York   St. Louis   San Francisco   Bogotá   Guatemala
Hamburg   Lisbon   Madrid   Mexico   Montreal   Panama
Paris   San Juan   São Paulo   Tokyo   Toronto

1 2 3 4 5 6 7 8 9 0 F G R F G R 8 7 6 5 4 3
ISBN 0-07-046152-X
      0-07-046151-1 {PBK}
LIBRARY OF CONGRESS CATALOGING IN PUBLICATION DATA

Neely, Richard, 1941-
Why courts don't work.
1. Court administration—United States.
2. Judges—United States. 3. Justice, Administration of
—United States. I. Title.
KF8732.N43 1982   347.73'1   82-25893
ISBN 0-07-046152-X   347.3071
ISBN 0-07-046151-1 (pbk.)

Book design by Roberta Rezk

To my wife, Carolyn, who has sacrificed much to permit me the time to write this book and has lovingly and cheerfully encouraged most of my endeavors

Contents

Preface

MOST of this book discusses the behind-the-scenes machinery of the courts to explain that machinery's lackluster performance. However, the courts *do* work—at least they work sufficiently well that there has never been a concerted citizen drive to change their structure. But at the same time, our courts do not work as well as we want them to work. We have very high standards of acceptable performance for both our institutions and our machines. Our telephones and other public utilities, for example, are the best in the world, and when our courts fail to perform as efficiently as our utilities, we conclude that they don't work. In comparison to every other country in the world, our courts work superbly. Even in England, where the titles, robes, wigs, and general decorum of the courts give the impression of a professionalism unmatched elsewhere, there is not the access to judicial relief that prevails in the United States. Japan has almost no court system at all, and in continental Europe, court procedures are even more cumbersome than they are here.

Our courts have more power vis à vis other private and governmental institutions than courts elsewhere. An American court has a higher capacity to rectify individual injustices, and while the courts in other nations may be efficient in handling certain routine matters like the trial of criminal cases, our courts undertake to give more relief under more diverse circumstances.

My first book, *How Courts Govern America*, explained why the courts are taking over more and more governing functions from the other branches of government. It addressed itself to the role of the courts as political policymakers. The most dramatic instances of this type of lawmaking in recent years involve the 1954 decision requiring school integration, the 1964 decision requiring reapportionment of both houses of state legislatures on the basis of one person, one vote, and the 1973 decision striking down state statutes prohibiting abortion.

All of these cases were decided by the Supreme Court of the United States and affected the entire country. However, state courts are often engaged in similar policymaking. In New Jersey, for example, the state supreme court required that the legislature enact an income tax in order to provide a "thorough and efficient system of free schools" as required by the state constitution. When courts make broad policy, it is usually by interpreting either the state or federal constitutions.

At another level, however, the courts supervise both state and federal administrative agencies under a body of law known as "administrative law." The Nuclear Regulatory Commission, for example, cannot decide to build a nuclear power plant without an ultimate appeal to a federal court with the power to reverse the commission and substitute (at least in effect) the court's judgment for that of the commission.

While it is difficult to summarize here all of the occasions where courts intrude themselves into the political process and, in effect, make law, the problem of government by court rule is very much on the minds of the American public. In many regards, *How Courts Govern America* was a conservative book; it attempted to establish principles by which courts, lawyers, and the general public can decide whether courts should intrude themselves into specific political areas ostensibly assigned to coordinate branches of government. In essence, the book tried to distinguish between legitimate court government arising from the infirmities of other institutions and bare power grabs. In the main, however, that book was positive about the court's contribution to American government, both in circumstances where the courts are "legislating" and

2

in other circumstances where they are supervising the activities of the executive branch.

In being positive about courts in the context of their broad governmental functions, I was required constantly to remind the reader that I was talking about courts in their political capacity, not about courts in their routine, day-to-day dispatch of ordinary civil and criminal matters. While, indeed, grand political issues necessarily reach the courts in the context of specific lawsuits, these test cases must be separated from the bulk of the courts' work that involves nothing more than doing justice for individual parties.

Unfortunately, when people go to court with routine civil matters, the courts do not work very well. At the simplest level, for example, people who have contested domestic matters, such as those involving either the terms of divorce, the collection of alimony and child support, or the award of child custody, are seldom satisfied with the way they are treated in court. On the criminal side, the courts and their supporting agencies seldom seem to be effective in getting felons off the street. Juveniles appear to be able to vandalize property and intimidate their elders with impunity, and in most places none of the vice laws is enforced with even a modicum of enthusiasm.

This book, then, is an analysis of the courts as they plod through their daily docket of largely pedestrian civil and criminal cases. It excludes from its purview any analysis of the courts as policymaking bodies. Nowhere will there be a reference to such phenomena as the federal court's taking over the school system in Boston, the state courts' dictating educational policy, court-ordered busing for racial balance, court decisions about pornography, or the court ban of prayer in the schools. This book is concerned with the routine prosecution of murderers, rapists, robbers, burglars, and thieves, and such issues as the way the minor traffic and magistrate courts work, the way prosecuting attorneys work, and the economics surrounding the use of the legal system.

I have not intended this book to be a scholarly presentation of any particular body of law. In a way, many of the problems of the courts are related to an excess of specialization that narrows our focus to a discrete set of problems. Yet it is counterproductive to view any one problem of the courts in isolation. This book is a horseback ride through the entire criminal and civil court system so that we can understand the relation of specific problems to a total structure. The purpose is to explain the court system's problems to a wide audience who can add their political strength to local programs for improving the courts.

In the course of writing this book I have received the invaluable assistance of many people. My preeminent thanks go to my administrative assistant, Pauline Jenkins, who has prepared draft after draft of typescripts. Pauline, however, has done much more than process my words; she has been responsible for correcting egregious misspelling and making sure that everything makes sense. The problem with lawyers is that as they get older they become more accustomed to legal jargon; it often happens that eventually they can no longer tell the difference between that jargon and English. Pauline has been responsible for flagging all deviations from English and rewriting them. My secretary, Betty Price, has also worked nights and weekends to meet chapter deadlines and has contributed both her knowledge of language and her cheerful good humor to this project.

Several of my excellent law clerks have contributed to the writing, editing, and researching of this book during the last two years. Without their help, in light of the other demands on my time, I would never have been able to finish the project in any reasonable period. In addition, they have brought to this book diverse personal experiences that have helped infuse life into what is potentially terribly dull material. I am indebted, more than I can adequately express, to Stephen Moorhead, James Dorsey, Matthew Slater, and Sheldon Whitehouse.

As this book was being written, several chapters were serialized in the *Atlantic*. Since the style of a magazine and the style of a book are entirely different, much material needed to be edited, rearranged, or supplemented. Often the editors of the *Atlantic* would find gaps in my reasoning or arguments that needed further support to be convincing. The material was unfailingly improved by the *Atlantic*'s incomparable editing. I have incorporated much of their superior wording and organization into the book. William Whitworth, the editor of the *Atlantic*, James Fallows, the *Atlantic*'s Washington editor, and Corby Kummer, the Boston editor assigned to my work, all made significant contributions to this volume.

This book would never have been written without the encouragement and support of my editor at McGraw-Hill, Cynthia Merman. Besides editing the typescript to simplify the language, Cynthia's constant good humor and encouragement urged me on to greater efforts. Furthermore, she quickly solved all of the administrative problems that inevitably arise in the course of writing a book for a large publishing house. Finally, I am indebted to my friend Professor Cecil Lang of the University of Virginia, who methodically read page proofs to eliminate errors in usage and to excise the last vestiges of jargon and other lapses into non-English.

What courts should do—and what in fact they do—is regularly the subject of ill-informed and mostly thoughtless speculation. Questions about the role of courts in a democratic society seldom receive the attention they deserve. However, an occasion for serious inquiry into these issues arose in May 1982 in St. Louis at a conference on the role of courts, which was assembled to consider the Discussion Draft of the Council on the Role of Courts. From the opening address of Thomas Schelling of the Kennedy School of Government at Harvard to the concluding general session, the more than one hundred participants asked questions not often asked (and less often answered) and thought the hitherto unthinkable. It was a stimulating experience that provided me with many new insights. Accordingly, some of the thoughts expressed in this volume, including a few that may at first seem outrageous, came from, or were reinforced by, this conference.

There is very little that is entirely original in this book. To the extent that I have relied on particular works I consider exceptional or original I have tried to give credit in a footnote. However, there are scores of scholars and commentators who have done significant work in this general area who have not been mentioned either because I am unfamiliar with their work or because what they have said has now so thoroughly entered the collective consciousness of lawyers and judges that citations to their work pointing out agreements and disagreements would be distracting to the general reader. Yet any book like this stands on the shoulders of ages of scholars who have shown the path down the right roads and excluded many wrong roads. To all of them I am very grateful.

Fairmont, West Virginia
December 7, 1982

If the priests and barons who set their names to Magna Charta had been told that in a few centuries every swineherd and cobbler's apprentice would write and read with an ease such as few kings could then command, and reason with better logic than any university could then practise, the priest and baron would have been more incredulous than any man who was told in 1800 that within another five centuries the ploughboy would go a-field whistling a sonata of Beethoven, and figure out in quaternions the relation of his furrows.

Henry Adams

The Deliberately Broken Machine 1

NOT LONG after I began practicing law, it dawned on me that courts don't work. When I was in law school no one told me that courts don't work, but small-town practice quickly showed me that when a litigant went to court he was usually a loser even if he emerged a technical winner. An old country lawyer summarized it all: "When I was young I lost a lot of cases I should have won. Now I win a lot of cases I should lose. So overall justice is done."

There are times when I am embarrassed to be a lawyer and a judge because on many occasions the machine I am supposed to control does not perform competently or even honestly. Sometimes in magistrate or traffic courts, justice is for sale, and even more often it looks that way. At another level, felons go free because prosecutors are too understaffed to prosecute. Judges encourage plea bargains in criminal cases where the accused is obviously guilty because they don't have the time or staff for trials. Delays in administrative rulings stop everything from highways to power plants to new factories. However, all proposals for reforms predicated on the supposition that expanding personnel, streamlining procedure, or increasing the number of courts will cure the courts' problems are naive and doomed to failure. The fact is that courts don't work because at some point in the system most people consciously, and deliberately, do not want them to work.

Today's court system reminds me of medieval cities like Florence, whose modern configuration is dictated by the happenstance of fourteenth-century cow paths, bogs, and streams. Our court system's organization has changed little since the Middle Ages. We have merely superimposed twentieth-century problems on a medieval structure for handling them. In order to make any major improvement in the way courts perform, it is necessary to think creatively about some entirely new designs, not about bigger and better versions of our current obsolete design.

Of all major business and governmental institutions, the courts are alone in having no administrative hierarchy. Each judge is independent administratively, and while some states have made lackluster efforts to establish some central management system, the higher courts everywhere can do almost nothing about trial judges who are either lazy or incompetent or both. Courts are organized on a decentralized basis where each trial-court judge has his or her own independent fief. In the federal system, judges are appointed for life, and no matter how lazy or incompetent a judge may be, even the chief justice of the United States can do nothing about it. The organization of the best court system in America might cause any business executive to roar with laughter.

Consider what happens when a power plant is announced, a superhighway designed, or a shopping center proposed. Protestors flock to the courts with everything from environmental objections to zoning challenges. At that point everything stops. If the courts are backlogged or if the judge is indecisive or confused, matters can be delayed for years during which inflation makes the financing arrangements and projected costs of construction obsolete. When I was chief justice of West Virginia I was powerless to do anything about this disorder. I could not direct that a particular case be given priority, nor could I shorten the time it took to litigate serious cases involving thousands of jobs. The pace and organization of the litigation were dependent on the quality of the judge in the lower court where the case was initially brought. Although I was chief executive officer of the entire state court system, I had no power to hire or fire anyone. No central system functions to establish priorities and allocate resources in our courts, and

8

since the political process is paralyzed by a web of vested interests, many of which profit from the current disorder in the courts, it is probable that none will ever be created.

I have spent more than ten years as an appellate judge trying to make courts work. If I had been more successful I would not have written this book; I would have been out repairing courts instead of talking about them. The consolation prize for not being a more successful man of action is the ability to explain why my own success rate has been downright dismal. The one thing I have learned from beating my head against stone walls is that the conventional explanations are all resoundingly wrong because the questions being asked are consummately silly. These questions almost invariably are predicated on the erroneous assumptions that: (1) most people want a court system that works; and (2) the new system should be merely a better working version of the old system. In order to frame the correct questions, it is necessary to abandon any vision of courts as simple decision makers and to understand them for what they are, namely, the most terrifying governmental force in the United States.

While decentralized control and medieval procedure may seem easily remedied by the traditional American expedient of throwing money, people, and know-how at the problem, the current antiquated and overloaded structure is a political advantage to many groups. Furthermore, as will become apparent throughout the rest of this book, these political advantages are not necessarily unjust. The court system, evolving as it has through hundreds of years of history, is characterized by measured straining in opposite directions. Unlike modern business organizations, the court system was not designed from scratch with a coherent vision. Whenever there has been a particular egregious problem, the judges have jury-rigged some contraption to fix it. Thus the system is a hodgepodge of inherited, medieval ways of doing business with an overlay of modern repair work. For example, the boundless discretion that the system reposes in a jury to award damages for pain and suffering in a personal injury case is deliberately intended to offset the delay any plaintiff has in getting his or her case tried and moved through the appellate process. It is the terrifying specter of ridiculously high awards if a case finally gets to a jury that forces insurance companies to offer reasonable settlements fairly promptly. If we change one element, say, delay, which helps establish balance in the current system, then we must also change others such as jury discretion, or we will never have a proposed reform that will survive interest-group attack in the political process.

By far the greatest factor bearing upon court performance is our society's lack of consensus about what we want courts to do. When I lobby the state legislature for such a simple thing as clerical help in the magistrate courts, conservative senators tell me outright that they do not like me or my court and that as far as they are concerned, society would be better off if someone killed all the judges and lawyers. Not all legislators are quite so candid or undiplomatic, yet even among progressive legislators there is a grave suspicion of the power of courts and great reservation about the intelligence with which courts perform their functions.

The way courts are organized—number of judges, delay, appeals procedures, and technical rules—has a decisive effect on the ultimate outcome of lawsuits. Therefore, lack of a concerted effort for improvement merely reflects general contentment with a system that does not work very well. For example, when courts work efficiently in civil litigation, the net result is that plaintiffs as a class prosper to the detriment of defendants as a class. Silly as it may sound, the world as a whole breaks down into groups like injured workers, who are usually plaintiffs in civil cases, and groups like insurance companies, which are usually defendants. In cases between working people on the one hand and insurance companies, employers, or business people on the other, it is fair to say that courts are in the business of redistributing the wealth. When the machinery breaks down, no wealth is redistributed; this is obviously an advantage to insurance companies, slum landlords, and fly-by-night businesses.

The layperson usually envisages the court system as a neutral institution that applies preconceived, scientific rules. In fact, the courts are not neutral; the rules are not preconceived through a wide spectrum, and law is only partially a science. Much of law really reflects the political judgments and emotional passions of the judges. Consequently, political battles rage in the courts about the same issues that engage the executive and legislative branches. It is rich versus poor, black versus white, male versus female, business versus consumer, developer versus environmentalist, and employer versus union. One way to decide many issues is to make the courts ineffectual so that no decision is given—*vive* the status quo.

The reason that the paralysis in the courts is so frightening is that as the courts take on more and more responsibilites, decisions about income distribution, the pace of economic development, and civil liberties are being made unconsciously, haphazardly, and randomly through inattention to questions of overall design. Superimposing twentieth-century problems on a medieval structure for handling them means increasing deterioration of the effectiveness of the courts. The question of overall design implies new ways of handling old controversies that may affect their outcome—winners may become losers. It is for this reason that there is so little innovation. If the courts become more efficient, and therefore benefit one group, then adjustments must be made in the design to compensate other groups that had derived advantages from inefficiency.

An efficient criminal court system implies less time between arrest and trial, less plea bargaining, more certain prosecution, less technical error, and less probation based exclusively on lack of jails and prisons to house dangerous felons. But certain groups have a higher likelihood than others of running afoul of the criminal law, and these are not only common professional criminals but also tax evaders, unscrupulous businesspeople, and the organized criminal elements.

When laypeople speak of the courts they often mean just that, the courts with their judges and attendant judicial staffs of clerks and secretaries. However, the term *courts* must be expanded when we talk of criminal law to encompass all of the supporting agencies that feed criminals to the judges and receive them after conviction. Without prosecuting attorneys, for example, it is impossible for a criminal court to operate. Without adequate police to gather evidence, it is impossible for prosecutors to present their cases. Finally, once a person is convicted he cannot be sentenced to prison if there is no prison fit to receive him.[1]

1. A word on third-person pronouns. In this instance the use of the masculine pronoun is statistically accurate, because male inmates outnumber female inmates twenty-three to one in our nation's prisons. However, in this book I shall use masculine pronouns on occasions when there are no such underlying factual justifications. I am acutely aware of the important positions women currently hold throughout our judicial system, and I intend neither to hide nor to ignore

11

When the courts are thought of in this expansive way, it becomes clear that improving them carries a big price tag. However, criminal courts and their supporting agencies—unlike most government operations—actually generate revenue. At the simplest level, traffic courts make more money from fees and fines than it costs to operate them. When state or local business regulations are enforced, the fines augment the treasury. Moreover, low crime rates contribute to a desirable climate for industry, commerce and housing, which in turn means higher property values and a stronger tax base. Consequently, lack of funding for courts must be something more than just a reflection of overall budget constraints; while budget considerations do play a part, underfunding is often deliberate, purposeful, and unrelated to the budget.

One simple example illustrates the point. Cheating on federal and state income taxes is pervasive in all classes of society, and except among the compulsively honest, cheating usually occurs in direct proportion to opportunity. Waitresses do not report all their tips; the fellow with a chain saw who sells the odd cord of wood in the winter never reports the fifty-six bucks you hand him in cash; businesspeople deliberately set up small corporations to facilitate illegal tax deductions of personal automobiles and club dues; and doctors and lawyers routinely receive cash payments they never "remember" to run through their business accounts. Cheating is not limited to individuals or small businesses; state tax commissioners seldom audit a large corporation without discovering a substantial underpayment of complicated state business taxes.

Why, then, do we not expand the Internal Revenue Service and its state counterparts since every new revenue agent will pay his or her salary and overhead at least eight times over? The answer is that we do not really want Rhadamanthine enforcement of the tax laws. As long as the IRS is overworked and understaffed, everyone except the scrupulously honest will accomplish his or her own personal tax-reform program. The IRS's understaffing guarantees that all but the most un-

their contributions by the use of masculine pronouns. Nonetheless, there are situations in which neutral pronouns such as *person*, *someone*, and *they* are simply more awkward than *man* or *men*. Additionally, I find the use of such constructions as *him/her* and *s/he* to be distracting. Therefore, I would hope that the reader will interpret the word *man* in its generic, as opposed to its restrictive, sense. Similarly, *he* and *him* should be read to include *she* and *her*.

abashed evaders will escape with a payment of back taxes and possibly a civil penalty. Furthermore, when it comes to questionable deductions such as the corporate automobile used exclusively for personal pleasure, every businessperson knows that the IRS appellate division will exclaim the Santa Claus "Ho! Ho! Ho!" at settlement conference and give the government's case away.

Overworked United States attorneys simply cannot spend their time arguing every questionable deduction in tax court, and the IRS appellate division knows that. The mediocre enforcement of the tax codes stems not only from the IRS's lack of staff but also from a lack of U.S. attorneys, U.S. district-court judges, and court-of-appeals judges. Without an increase in the personnel of supporting agencies, there is a limit to the effectiveness of new IRS agents, but there is no question that such an increase will bring in far more money than it costs.

Since more rigorous enforcement will inspire a higher level of "voluntary" compliance, it must be obvious that many out there in politics land do not want better enforcement. I am probably one of them. I actually do pay every cent I owe in taxes, and since I am a public official, I get audited about every four years. Notwithstanding my sense of offense at those who cheat, I don't want to be audited more than once every four years, because it is a nuisance. It takes two days of my own, my staff's, and my accountant's time (the latter sending me, not the IRS, a bill for same), and there is always the specter of someone having made a mathematical or other innocent error resulting in the need to pay additional, unexpected taxes. Frankly, I prefer to let my neighbor cheat a little rather than be bothered with a yearly descent of IRS locusts.

While it is easy to calculate the cost:benefit effectiveness of more revenuers, it is more difficult to calculate the economic benefit of more police and state criminal courts.[2] Nonetheless, the cost of crime in the United States every year is over $150 billion. Shoplifting alone accounts

2. There is one notable exception to the general rule that the costs of upgrading the court system are inconsequential in comparison to the anticipated benefits from such upgrading and that much of the time better criminal law enforcement actually pays for itself by directly generating revenue for the treasury. This exception is the cost of prisons, which obviously must be available to receive convicted criminals unless we are to change our entire approach to criminal law sanctions. For example, in fiscal year (FY) 1980, there were 24,268

13

for between 3 and 7 percent, depending on the location, of all merchandise purchased for sale by chain stores like J. C. Penney's, which means we all pay 3 to 7 percent more for our routine dry-goods purchases.

Furthermore, money alone does not adequately measure the personal inconvenience of replacing stolen jewelry, silver, or television sets; the pain and suffering from personal injuries; or the grief caused by the death of a loved one. In urban crime control there is one easy, irrefutable, and provable correlation: where police strength is increased crime goes down. Ask any resident of New York City's ritzy and well-patrolled Upper East Side why he or she feels safer there than in other parts of the urban jungle.

Most potential victims would prefer paying another few hundred dollars in taxes to being mugged or having their houses ransacked. Furthermore, while most people probably feel as I do about forgiving their neighbor's tax trespasses in return for minimum personal harassment by Uncle Sam, a similar philosophy of live and let live does not exist about violent crime. Most male urban dwellers would be willing to submit to a daily

inmates in federal prisons, and the budget of the Bureau of Prisons, which runs the institutions, was $333,244,000. That amounts to about $13,700 per prisoner annually, enough to send them all to Harvard, Yale, or Princeton. In 1977 the costs of keeping one of the more than 250,000 prisoners in state prisons averaged $7,000. Capital outlays for prisons and jails for that year exceeded $400 million. The costs of building one maximum-security cell in 1978 averaged $50,000. To meet the minimum standard of sixty square feet of living space per prisoner urged by penologists would cost $8 to $10 billion.

Obviously the costs of prisons are high and the resemblance to social service great (a theme taken up later): inmates are given (at the very least) food, clothing, and shelter at taxpayers' expense. And while prisoners do generate revenue (e.g., Federal Prison Industries had sales of $116 million in FY80), they do not pay their own way. But once a serious crime has been committed, what alternative is there? The literature indicates that various treatment and rehabilitation methods have been no more successful at reducing recidivism than has a straight lock-up prison regime. I am not convinced that rehabilitation programs outside of prisons can't work, but they are still expensive. Also, there are very few, if any, voices calling for the abolition of imprisonment when it comes to violent crimes against the individual. But this is not a book about prisons, and in any case I am not in a position to write one. Whatever alternatives there may be to imprisonment for various crimes, there appears to be no alternative to high levels of expenditures for corrections in general.

polite and unobtrusive "stop and frisk" if they knew that everyone else would be required to do the same and that their personal safety would be significantly enhanced. Few of us object to the nuisance of airport security. Why, then, do we not double the number of police and courts?

The reasons are financial and ideological. The primary victims of crime pay the lowest taxes. As one small-town cop once explained it to me, "Crime happens where the criminals are at." Most crime victims live in ghettos or declining working-class neighborhoods, and they work at low-wage jobs in places such as all-night diners or gas stations, which are easy to knock over. But the taxpayers who would bear the cost of better protection for these victims are seldom themselves victims. They are large corporations that have retained private security forces or are middle-class taxpayers who live in well-protected neighborhoods and send their children to safe public or private schools.

The political questions tied to the consequences of a better criminal-justice system—more police, swifter court action and so on—extend beyond simple tax concerns. Police, in my experience, are by nature bullies as well as heroes, and the smaller the police force, the more police officers tend to exhibit the characteristics of heroes rather than of bullies. The more personnel cracking down on crime, the greater the likelihood that individual citizens will suffer abuses of their civil liberties. Work in any bureaucracy tends to expand to fill the time allocated to do it, and if police are not busy with serious crime, they may meddle in citizen activities like private poker games, where no one wants their help. Consequently, a silent alliance exists between pro–civil liberties liberals, who want small police forces for ideological reasons, and conservative, large taxpayers, who do not want to pay the upfront costs of what, from their point of view, amount to social services for others.[3]

3. A similar explanation is given for England's late development of professional police forces of any kind. Well after the Star Chamber was abolished in 1641, memories lingered of the political uses to which its extensive powers were put by the monarchy. The gentry recognized the potential for centralized power and abuse that a police force entailed and they were not about to allow a repetition of Star Chamber's abuses to be visited upon them through that mechanism. Hence they prevented the establishment of a police force of any substance until the mid-eighteenth century. Instead, they chose to rely on capital punishment for all serious crimes as a supposed deterrent rather than rely on a police force.

As long as we are talking only about criminal courts, the questions are comparatively simple. As soon, however, as civil courts enter the picture, all bets are off. For while improved funding of the criminal courts would return economic dividends to the public, improved funding of the civil courts has mixed income effects. In fact, civil courts can be calamitous to local governments, businesses, unions, landlords, and even tenants. It is here that we really enter the never-never land of lack of consensus among different groups or classes in society about what courts are expected to do.

My favorite example of how financially threatening a working court system can become involves New York City, which is notorious for its long court delays. In the abstract, most New Yorkers would like an efficient court system so that criminals would be sent away. To the casual observer, New York's felon problem would appear easy to solve: expand police, prosecutors, and courts.[4]

The hitch, however, is that a New York trial-court judge is empowered to hear criminal *and* civil cases. If the number of criminal judges is increased, those judges will also be available for civil cases. Of 25,589 civil cases concluded in New York City in the first forty weeks of the 1979–80 fiscal year, 5,523 were brought against New York City itself! New York City has been on the verge of bankruptcy

4. According to a detailed study by the staff of the *New York Times* in January 1981, hardly any of the persons arrested on felony charges in New York City are ever prosecuted and convicted as felons. (A felony is a serious crime that can result in imprisonment in a state penitentiary. A misdemeanor is a minor crime for which the penalty is either a fine or a year or less in the local jail.) The statistics of the Police Department showed that the chance of a person arrested for a felony being sentenced to prison was one in one hundred eight. While many cases can be explained away by "overcharging" on the part of the police, the largest number of avoidances of jail sentences come from the prosecuting authorities' willingness to permit felons to plead guilty to lesser charges. The prosecutors pointed to lack of staff and failure of the police to follow through and secure lists of witnesses or other essential items of evidence. In 1979 there were 104,413 felony arrests, of which 88,095 cases were dismissed and 16,318 indictments secured. Of those indicted 56 percent pled guilty to felonies, 16 percent pled guilty to misdemeanors, 12 percent were dismissed after indictment, only 13 percent went to jury trial, and 3 percent resulted in some other disposition.

since 1975, and the policies of the Reagan administration portend even greater financial strains. The potential liability for New York City from the civil suits currently awaiting trial runs to billions of dollars. New York City cannot afford an efficient court system because it would be bankrupt beyond bail-out if all these suits got to trial in one or two years.

While New York is an extraordinary example, elsewhere legal-aid and other public-interest lawyers are bringing suits challenging the condition of mental hospitals, prisons, schools, and other state and local facilities. When courts take action in these humanitarian areas, it can mean new local government expenditures of millions, or even billions, of dollars that were never budgeted. In West Virginia, for example, the supreme court of appeals struck down the entire legislative scheme for handling juveniles and forced the state to create and fund new agencies. In New Jersey the state supreme court ordered the legislature to enact an income tax to support the public schools. This required the reallocation of state money away from projects governors and legislators wanted in order to support projects judges wanted.

The moral of these sorry sagas is that the costs of creating more courts, along with attendant supporting staff, are but the tip of the fiscal iceberg in terms of the total amount of money that more courts will eventually disgorge from the unwilling guardians of any given jurisdiction's failing treasury. Traditionally, the entire judicial branch of government takes less than 2 percent of any state's budget. In New York City, therefore, the cost of doubling the number of judges, prosecutors, city attorneys, courtrooms, and supporting staff is small in comparison to the cost of paying judgments the new courts would render against the city.

In other parts of the United States there are powerful private interests that are in the same position as New York City and are not in the least interested in improving the efficiency of civil courts. If, for instance, litigation against an insurance company takes eight years to complete, the company has the use of its money for eight years, which it can invest during that period at between 9 and 15 percent. Furthermore, delay alone is a powerful force to inspire settlements for low amounts. When the amount of money judgments throughout the entire judicial system runs to the scores of billions of dollars, the income effect of the use of free money becomes substantial. Since most state and federal courts consist of unified criminal and civil tribunals where any judge can hear both types of cases, the positive net income effect of improved criminal courts on the general public is almost always offset by a negative net income effect through the civil courts on those who have the most political power. As is usual in these matters, the general public takes its accustomed beating.

It is always tempting to ascribe the imperfections in the operation of government to the machinations of evil-hearted vested interests. Yet, as I indicated earlier, I am not as condemnatory of insurance companies for their love of delay as might appear warranted to the casual observer. Without delay, there would be no encouragement to reasonable settlements. Much of what appears as corrupt and self-seeking political action is nothing other than a battle for survival. This returns me to the point that we cannot tinker at one part of the system without tinkering at the whole system. To do otherwise would not be an exercise in neutral reform but one-sided advocacy for particular economic or social classes.

Often the institutions or individuals that find themselves opposed to court reform are, like New York City, benevolent in intent but forced by circumstances to oppose the side of the angels. It is a simple fact of life in general and of government in particular that things do not work the way they were intended or are expected to work. Every system of government is composed of two separate systems—a myth system, which is how people expect government to operate, and an operational system, which is how government actually operates.[5]

The myth system is the product of political theory, idealism, and a healthy fear of human lust, avarice, aggression, and self-seeking. The myth system has a salutary effect upon the operational system by providing criteria by which, no matter how imperfectly or unrealistically, the operational system can be judged. Like religion, the tenets of the myth system are jealously protected, and any direct attack upon them is punished, very much as religious heresy was punished in the Middle Ages. The natural tension that exists between New York State's desire to provide a good court system and its need to keep New York City

5. I purloined this analysis from W. Michael Reisman's *Folded Lies* (New York: Free Press, 1979).

solvent provides the perfect example of conflict between the two systems.

The operational system's departure from the myth system comes from lack of money as well as from the nature of the raw material of which it is composed, namely men and women. Lust, avarice, aggression, and self-aggrandizement are inherently part of the makeup of people, and these qualities are reflected throughout the operational system. Furthermore, even if natural human vices could be bred out of the personnel, there would still be architectural defects in the design of the myth system, making it impossible to engineer an operational system according to the myth system's plan. In the case of New York City, the myth system puts forth the following axiom: for every injury there shall be just and adequate compensation according to an impartial jury determination. The operational system, however, asks the pedestrian question: Where you gonna get the money at? And the only answer—from either myth or operational system—is a deafening silence.

As with equal justice, support for the tenets of the myth system is held in the abstract, while pressures to corrupt these tenets in the operational system manifest themselves in organized, concrete political action, frequently from individuals or institutions that in all regards reflect the highest qualities of honor, integrity, and good citizenship. The New York City example is grandiose, yet the same phenomenon of irreconcilable values is experienced in slightly different form everywhere in both civil and criminal courts.

Down at the barbershop, for example, where the boys like to rehash last night's rerun of "Kojak," the atmosphere changes dramatically when a customer's college-going son gets busted for selling marijuana to high-school students. The whole law-and-order mentality that usually dominates the conversation noticeably abates as everyone searches his list of contacts to discover how he can get to the prosecutor, probation officer, or judge to help a friend.[6] The ties of politics and friendship

6. The day before I wrote this chapter a former West Virginia sheriff called me to ask if I could intercede for a friend of his who was being prosecuted in federal court on a firearms rap. From what he said I concluded that this defendant was in a big jam, and while I declined to help him, nonetheless the sheriff had

in the operational system outweigh more nebulous, abstract principles of equal justice. In fact, throughout the entire court system, abstract principles are tugging for equal justice while practical politics urges so many exceptions that the exceptions have been known to eat up the inadequately defended abstract principles.

It is at this point that the decisive, paralyzing effect of lack of consensus becomes most obvious. Even when the basic issue does not involve money, every effort at court improvement has, from the perspective of some political interest group, positive and negative components. No action on the part of government moves in only one direction. An increase in the number of police means more protection to some, more bullying to others. If the staffs of prosecuting attorneys are increased so that they can diligently prosecute armed robbers, murderers, and dope peddlers, they will also be available to ferret out consumer fraud, antitrust violations, and political corruption. Since prosecuting attorneys are usually elected and, therefore, are lawyers with political ambitions, they will be tempted to play to the press by prosecuting white-collar crime. While the political establishment in most places is genuinely against murder, armed robbery, and dope peddling (although the latter is frequently the source of enormous graft), that same establishment is less enthusiastic about prosecuting consumer fraud, antitrust violations, or politicial corruption, because they are often involved in these activities themselves.

Even firebrand political reformers use questionable tactics at election time, and the prospect of an elaborate enforcement bureaucracy falling into enemy hands is horrifying. Efforts to increase staff for the prosecution of violent crime, a universally well-regarded undertaking, become impaled on the well-justified fear that the same prosecutorial staff that can do a number on the longhaired denizens of the underworld can also do a number on all our well-manicured country-club friends who engage in an occasional payoff, rigged election, or a little consumer fraud. It is not possible to rely on sound prosecutorial discretion to

tried. The irony is that when this particular man had been sheriff he had run for Congress in the 1972 Democratic primary on a law-and-order platform. From my brief conversation it was obvious that the person he was trying to help was a genuine, 24-karat bad hombre, and he knew that as well, but influence in elective politics is not limited to the law-abiding.

provide a solution to this problem because all of the incentives to the politically ambitious prosecutor encourage country-club prosecutions at the expense of robbers and murderers.[7]

The newspapers get bored with run-of-the-mine violent crime, but

7. A classic example of frivolous white-collar crime prosecution took place recently in Pittsburgh. A county commissioner, who was also the county Democratic Party chairman, was charged with theft of services during his tenure as county coroner. At that time, in addition to being coroner, he owned a private laboratory that did pathology and toxicology testing. It was alleged that he brought tissue specimens from his lab to the morgue, where they were processed by morgue employees on the county payroll, thereby "stealing" $115,000 worth of county services.

The investigation and trial took nearly two years and involved ten investigators and seven lawyers from the district attorney's office at one time or another. The trial itself lasted six weeks, and the whole affair cost the county about $1.5 million, more than ten times the value of the services said to have been stolen.

The case had all the trappings of a political trial. The defendant, Cyril H. Wecht, was highly placed in county politics, so prosecuting him would bring much publicity: adverse for Wecht, angelic for the prosecutor. Wecht had political enemies even within his own party, and some of them were involved in initiating and developing the investigation. Others used the investigation and trial to force him to withdraw from the party chairmanship. And the district attorney responsible for the prosecution, perhaps trading on the publicity it generated, was running for the state supreme court bench at the same time.

Political or not, theft of government services is not a trivial charge. But it is rare that it merits a $1.5 million, seventeen-person investigation, and this case certainly was not one of those occasions where efforts of this magnitude were warranted by any cost:benefit analysis of the public good. Fortunately for Wecht, he was able to hire nationally known trial lawyer Stanley Preiser to defend him. Preiser succeeded in conveying to the jury the defenses Wecht had made throughout the investigation: Wecht never attempted to hide what he was doing; the work done was part of an educational program for pathology residents studying at the morgue; his private lab performed free tests for the county on a reciprocal basis; and the private work was never done to the detriment of public work, but instead it enhanced the skills of the public employees. Pathologists from across the country and Europe testified that Wecht is a world-class forensic pathologist and that he had upgraded the quality of the county morgue (in part through the residency training program) to the extent that it had a worldwide reputation. Preiser and the experts argued that the county got they go into ecstasy over the prosecution of the humblest white-collar criminal. The reason is simple: it is entertaining to prosecute white-collar crime because its prosecution is a middle-class morality play that assuages the newspaper reader's personal sense of unrequited merit. Those who equate white-collar and violent crime, however, are usually the residents of neighborhoods where crime is a rarity. In Miami, for example, where in January 1981 the likelihood of being murdered exceeded either the likelihood of being killed in an automobile accident or of dying from cancer, people are a little more rational in their perception of the proper hierarchy of crime and of the urgency of its prosecution in different categories. The police estimated that in 1981 a significant proportion of the violent crime in Miami emanated from the multi-billion-dollar drug traffic, which, in terms of gross revenue, dwarfed every single legal industry in Florida, including tourism. Compared to this, a little political corruption, tax evasion, or consumer fraud must recede from an intelligent agenda. That is the political price demanded in order to achieve any positive movement away from the status quo.

COURT reform requires the active support of political institutions, and if there are areas of broad agreement, such as a universal desire

the better of the bargain. Moreover, Preiser offered, but was not allowed, to prove that private work was routinely performed by public employees, even in the district attorney's office. After six weeks of exhaustive testimony and with thirty-two cartons of documentary evidence, the jury deliberated for ten hours and acquitted Wecht.

Ironically, the district attorney also was trounced in the primary elections the same day, so apparently not even all the publicity from the Wecht trial could get him elected to the supreme court. If he did not get anything out of the case, did the public? Clearly not. The $1.5 million could have bought almost forty prosecutors for a year at an annual salary of $40,000, and each of them could have been prosecuting fifty violent crimes and property crimes such as murder, rape, arson, armed robbery, and larceny, the ones that affect the average citizen's life.

It appears that the district attorney's office in Pittsburgh is relatively understaffed and underpaid. Despite that fact, excessive time and effort were spent on a comparatively trivial alleged crime. The public is wary of giving more staff and money to prosecutors; they fear that instead of pursuing more prosecutions of serious, violent crimes, prosecutors will look for prosecutions that will advance their political careers.

to reduce violent crime, then it is necessary to create institutions that will work only in that agreed area and not elsewhere where there is a political lobby against enforcement. That is not the way the myth system teaches us things should work, but that is the way things do work. The solution is hard to engineer, because no one is likely to say publicly that he or she is in favor of enforcing some laws but not enforcing others. Frankness is not a highly rewarded quality in this society; virtuous members of the American middle class are taught to cultivate sincerity and its twin, hypocrisy. It is easier and safer for politicians to be against all augmentation of enforcement on budgetary grounds than it is to explain their fears of certain types of enforcement.

My favorite illustration of the diverse alliances that oppose improvements in the criminal justice system is the failure of a bill that is perennially introduced in the West Virginia legislature. The bill, which is introduced at the request of the state attorney general, would give the attorney general statewide prosecutorial powers. Under the current system, each West Virginia county elects a prosecutor who has absolute discretion concerning what crimes will be prosecuted in his county. The attorney general handles criminal cases on appeal, defends the state's interests in federal habeas corpus proceedings, and represents the state's agencies in civil litigation. However, the attorney general has no power to initiate prosecutions at the trial-court level in the fifty-five counties. Why should there not be a statewide prosecutorial agency, particularly since many local prosecutors are reluctant to enforce the law against their political friends?

The answer is simple. The position of attorney general has historically been a stepping-stone to the governorship. Since 1936 four out of ten governors were attorney general immediately before their election as governor. Since the demise of well-organized political machines in the wake of civil service, radio, and television (the latter two providing a one-on-one relationship between voter and elected official), high elected office has tended to go to media stars rather than to organization politicians. Only certain types of political antics, however, attract media attention. Crusades against political corruption and white-collar crime have all the attributes of a religious revival. Everyone who is actively involved in business or government is aware of the public relations

23

value of an anticorruption crusade, yet even the consummately honest prefer not to be bothered. Zealous investigations demand the production of documents, testimony by employees on company time, and a costly disruption of normal business operations. None of these costs is borne by the government; all must be borne by the private sector. More important, however, is the fact that there is less than universal support for the enforcement of most laws, from consumer fraud to drug use, and that lack of consensus is reflected in the legislature's failure to establish a statewide enforcement agency.

For example, in West Virginia's four northern panhandle counties, the population is composed largely of the sons and daughters of Italians, Greeks, Poles, Hungarians, and other non-Anglo-Saxon peoples. The biggest illegal gambling institutions used to be the churches themselves which held regular, illegal bingo parties and raised significant revenue that way.[8] Other social and religious institutions similarly enhance their coffers through slot machines and football pools; it is a way of life different from the predominantly Anglo-Saxon, fundamentalist life-style of the southern part of the state. Local prosecutors in the panhandle are elected by citizens who expect a conspicuous policy of nonenforcement of the gambling laws, at least as they relate to churches and social clubs. The last thing on earth they want is a statewide strike force destroying their churches and clubs.

When John D. Rockefeller IV became governor in 1977, his new chief of the state police attempted to enforce the gambling laws in the northern panhandle. Within a month the state police were instructed to back off. Continued enforcement would have incurred the ire of every member of the legislature from those counties, and in retaliation those legislators would have torpedoed the governor's legislative program.

When we investigate the entire issue of court reform, we must always bear in mind that there is hardly any piece of the complex law-enforcement mosaic whose reinforcement does not invite a strong, adverse

8. Such bingo games are no longer illegal. In 1980 the state constitution was amended to allow the legislature to enact legislation permitting charitable organizations to sponsor bingo games and raffles. In 1981 a bill was passed permitting charitable bingo. But both the amendment and the subsequent law declare that any county, through special elections, may disallow charitable bingo games in the county.

political reaction. The very courts themselves are threatening. Everywhere the courts have extensive political power, and they are perceived as malignant meddlers by all the other actors in the political process—legislators, governors, mayors, and administrators. Local school boards hate courts almost as much as they hate Communists and dirty books.

The best way to reduce court intervention in political matters is to keep the number of judges so small that the work load will force them to devote their efforts exclusively to trying criminals and hearing automobile accident and domestic cases. That way judges' spare time to run departments of welfare, schools, or mental hospitals will be at a minimum. The ultimate application of this theory comes from South Carolina, probably the most conservative state in the Union. Traditionally, South Carolina has had one of the most powerful legislatures in the United States, which is reflected in its leisurely pace of development. Furthermore, from my observations, the South Carolina legislature has no intention of sharing any more of its power than necessary with the judiciary.

For a population of almost three million people, South Carolina has only thirty-one trial-court judges empowered to handle important cases, which means that they are very busy and, sure enough, have little spare time to make political trouble. The South Carolina theory of judge control is based on the simple observed phenomenon that judges do not enjoy working any more than do professional posthole diggers. Since political involvement is largely discretionary with the judiciary, while criminal, tort, and domestic cases are not, overworked judges will reduce their work by eliminating political cases first.

Judges can decline to hear certain types of political cases where the plaintiffs are seeking to break new ground, and they can arrange their own dockets so that grandiose political cases, like the ones involving schools or hospitals, languish for years from judicial inattention. Judges quickly telegraph what cases will sustain their attention, and those are the cases the lawyers bring. While judges must always hear routine criminal, tort, and domestic cases or suffer vociferous public outrage, they can be unimaginative in the political area and dismiss every case they do not want to hear on procedural grounds. While obstructionist trial-court tactics of this variety can always be the subject of an appeal, appeals are long and expensive. Where the lawyers know that seeking social change in the courts will be an expensive, time-consuming, uphill struggle, all but the most radical or dedicated give up. Political cases take lots of judicial time, and overworked courts hate to see them coming.

The judiciary, including all its nonjudicial officers, is the most carefully scrutinized institution in government. The reason is that the courts offer the prospect of an alternative government, a government independent of and superior to elective politics. Courts are the final arbiters of what the federal and state constitutions mean, and since every conceivable political question can theoretically be stated in constitutional terms (usually within the confines of the vague "due process" or "equal protection" clauses), courts essentially can define their own role in the political structure.[9]

Courts are not asked to decide only disputes between individual private entities or between the government and its citizens. Since courts are much cheaper and far more accessible than legislatures, litigants come in increasing numbers asking the courts to change society. And it is exactly these social cases that cause courts to become a terrifying political force to a host of vested interests. The executive branch is constantly frustrated in its efforts to govern because the courts not only initiate change in some directions but also block change in other directions. Every organized group from welfare clients to strip miners come to court at the first sign of adverse government action. There, *horribile dictu*, the litigation can often last longer than the administration seeking to make the change. It is unlikely that today either the Tennessee Valley Authority or the Interstate Highway Program could have been established because of the volume of litigation the courts now would both permit and even encourage to surround such major undertakings.

Courts accept invitations to meddle in politics in direct proportion to their available time and support staff. The primary limitation on the courts' capacity to create a supervisory government is lack of manpower. It is one thing to enter a court order and quite another to enforce that

9. I have devoted an entire book to the exploration of this proposition. See *How Courts Govern America* (New Haven: Yale University Press, 1981).

order. The federal judges, for example, who have taken over school systems (as Judge Paul Garrity did in Boston) or who have taken over mental hospitals (as Judge Frank Johnson did in Alabama) have found that they must develop large staffs to supervise the enforcement of their orders. Since their own government-supported staffs are not large enough, they must rely on either volunteers, the prevailing litigants themselves, or some combination of the two. Judges quickly get bored hearing formal arguments about how many rolls of toilet paper should be placed in school bathrooms or about the wattage of light bulbs in recreation rooms of mental hospitals, so courts avoid large-scale political undertakings when they know that they lack the staff to manage effective enforcement of their orders. The first rule of being a trial judge is never to enter an order you cannot enforce. That, by the way, is why judges are so careful in entering injunctions in labor disputes.

There are only approximately as many federal and state senior appellate judges as there are representatives and senators. This means that Congress is intimately familiar with federal judges, and the state legislatures are even more familiar with state judges. Elected politicians and their policymaking appointees form a small society; everyone knows everyone else. This is particularly true at the state level because a sizeable number of part-time state legislators are practicing lawyers. Accordingly, courts are not perceived as impersonal institutions by the people who can actually do something to improve them; the courts are personified by the individuals occupying judicial office, and these judges are either friends or foes to legislators in the most intense, personal sort of way.

Legislators and other power brokers easily become concerned over the actual decisions of the courts, but personal hostility can as well be generated by the mere participation of judges and their staffs in politics. In many states judges run for office and this means they must be members of political parties and political factions within the political parties. The lower the level of the judge and the shorter his or her term of office, the more intense his or her political involvement tends to become. By far the most political of all judges are lay magistrates (sometimes still called justices of the peace), who preside in the lowest level of courts that hear minor civil and criminal cases. They receive comparatively high salaries, social prestige, and rewarding work without being required to have extensive academic qualifications. In many locales this lay judiciary forms the most effective political machine in the area.

Political judges not only get involved in their own elections but in those of legislators and governors as well. As Chapter 3 explores in depth, it requires the bad will of only a few well-placed legislators to torpedo pro-court legislation, and the nature of elected politics makes it inevitable that at least some legislators will have an ax to grind against particular judges. For years, for example, a powerful state senator from Lewis County, West Virginia, despised the local circuit judge who had committed numerous political and social affronts against him. This particular senator was a senior member of the Senate Finance Committee and an ardent enemy of higher judicial salaries because of his antipathy for one judge. He had a few friends elsewhere in the state who were judges, but his obligations of friendship in that regard never completely outweighed his desire to punish his offending hometown judge. The result was that from 1970 to 1980 judicial salaries increased less than the salaries of any other group in West Virginia state government. This senator was defeated for reelection in 1980, and in the next session of the legislature, both trial and appellate judges were awarded an average salary increase of 20 percent.

As long as governments are run by human beings and not by computers, I suppose that little can be done about the personalization of the judiciary by other actors in the political process. However, personal antipathy alone is not an insurmountable obstacle if we can develop a consensus about what we really want from our courts. In this regard it is important to be conscious of the hidden agendas of all the various constituencies that have veto power over proposed changes in the existing way of doing business. The most significant problem is probably that opposition to court reform is so intensely selfish. Universally the real objections to change must be camouflaged by other more respectable objections. Movement in any direction is frustrated by the simple fact that the status quo usually achieves more of the objectives of powerful interest groups than any alternative. Crime victims, it should be noted, are not an organized interest group, although they should be.

It is worth returning for a moment to the issue of white-collar crime. White-collar crime runs the gamut from bank embezzlement to violations of pollution abatement laws. While certain types of white-collar crime, like embezzlement, are distinguishable from street crime only by the absence of violence, other types of white-collar crime are essentially political. Anglo-American law has always made a distinction between natural-law crimes (crimes that every civilized society has held to be inherently evil, such as murder, robbery, and rape) and positive-law crimes (crimes that have become crimes exclusively because some group has lost a political battle). Violation of environmental laws are positive-law crimes, and the fight over enforcement is viewed by the offending industries as a legitimate battle for survival. The real fight is a political battle over income shares. How long shall polluters have to clean up their processes? Who pays for the cost of pollution control? As long as enforcement is slack, the income share of polluters and their employees rises because existing plants can still be used. No polluter would willingly permit augmentation of enforcement personnel. More to the point, it is easier for dirty industry's minions to scuttle enforcement appropriations than to scuttle the pollution abatement bills themselves, because appropriations are hidden in the interstices of the complex and largely invisible budget-making process.

Long ago, in my days as a legislator, I learned how to manipulate the budget process to defeat the goal of legislation passed by a majority. The budget-making process is incomprehensible to the outsider and Byzantine to the insider. Even the press can't figure out the "who struck John?" of appropriations. So, if you happen to be a polluting industry, you do not give up after you have lost an environmental battle at the stage where the pollution-control bill was passed, because you get another bite at the apple in the appropriations process. When it comes to gutting enforcement, you go after all the agencies—inspectors, prosecutors, *and* the courts.

The bottom line for the serious court reformer is that there is an ongoing guerrilla war in which people who do not have the votes in Congress or the state legislatures on issues that are well publicized try to minimize their losses in the back rooms of appropriations committees. It is for this reason that just throwing money and people at the existing court structure will never be a viable political program. Lots of people for lots of reasons do not want a bigger and better model of what we have. Before a new and efficient court system can be designed, we must answer the basic question, What is it we want a court system to do? Since there will never be a consensus, courts will continue to be inefficient because they will continue to be a battlefield.

There are certain parts of the courts—the parts that decide whether to build a power plant or a highway and the parts that prosecute violent criminals—where there are signs of some broad agreement. Five years ago the public mentality was different. More recently, Americans have been responsive to arguments in favor of investment, new jobs, and a changed attitude toward industry. More agreement is emerging on the advisibility of quickly concluding cases involving development projects, regardless of results. Hard-core environmentalists who encourage delays because delay in and of itself destroys projects are dwindling in number and force. Furthermore, everyone wants violent criminals prosecuted and the streets made safe. During the 1960s and 1970s, numerous programs were inaugurated that attempted to get at the root causes of crime—slums, broken families, unemployment. While we have not abandoned these efforts, there is an increasing awareness that we do not have the resources or scientific technology to solve the violent crime problem exclusively through preventive means.

Since we have a growing consensus on litigation involving large-scale business or government projects and the prosecution of violent criminals, a little careful engineering ought to create new structures that do only these two things, leaving ordinary courts and their supporting agencies a large terrain for continued guerrilla encounters. While limited solutions to specific, egregious problems hardly handle everyone's dissatisfaction with the poor performance of courts, this particularized approach at least has a hope of political acceptance. Furthermore, it will solve the two biggest problems the current broken-down system presents.

This book is not intended as a blueprint for court reform since my career in practical politics instructs me that revolutionary reform never occurs in American society. It is sufficient from my point of view if the interested reader obtains a better grasp of the overall problem so that he or she can tinker successfully at his or her own state courts. Furthermore, I am acutely aware of my own limitations as an observer: I am intimately familiar with the courts of one small state and have paid careful attention to discussions of problems elsewhere when they have arisen at national meetings or judicial seminars. Nonetheless, there are fifty separate state court systems plus the federal system composed of twelve separate circuits. While violent crime may be the major problem in the urban areas, in the western rural states the urgent problems may be entirely different. No two states share congruent economic, geographic, ethnic, social, or political configurations.

In West Virginia, for example, the general-jurisdiction trial courts and appellate courts (but not the low-level magistrate courts) are lavishly funded because the drafters of our Constitution provided that the Supreme Court of Appeals, rather than the legislature, could establish the budgets for these high-level courts. While the legislature must approve the creation of new general-jurisdiction judges, it cannot determine the number or the salaries of supporting staff. Consequently, West Virginia is particularly concerned with mechanized systems for expediting business, such as computerized transcription of court records (where the court reporter types shorthand notes directly into a computer that automatically translates them into full text copy), while other states are struggling just to get courtrooms, typewriters, and secretaries. Our biggest problem in West Virginia is not the funding of the current system, but designing new systems that make courts more efficient.

In Massachusetts, on the other hand, the legislature has been so parsimonious in its appropriations to the courts that proceedings in district courts in the areas surrounding Boston are impeded just by lack of courtrooms and office space. In 1976 I asked Archibald Cox, who was back at Harvard after his sojourn as Watergate special prosecutor, what conclusions he had drawn about criteria or systems for evaluating the cost:benefit effectiveness of certain types of judicial personnel and court programs. At the time he was Harvard's leading expert on court reform, and he told me that cost:benefit analysis of new programs had never seriously engaged his attention because his frame of reference was Massachusetts, where the subject was academic. There was so little money, he said, for Massachusetts courts that the problem of how to spend money wisely never occurred to anyone since the needs were so overwhelming that money could be spent usefully anywhere.

The pervasive problem that all action to improve courts has both beneficial and detrimental components has been the primary subject of this chapter and must figure into all the calculations of any serious court reformer. It is applicable, in differing degrees, everywhere in America.

Its introduction here is intended as a forceful illustration of the central argument of this book—that in general, the poor performance of courts emanates from complex political causes, which are but dimly understood, and not merely from the symptom of those causes, inadequate staff and funding.

While the rest of this book does not attempt to develop a program to be lifted from its pages and implemented in any particular jurisdiction, it gives a comprehensive overview of all the hidden problems. My purpose is to create a common language through which laypeople as well as lawyers, judges, and scholars can analyze the current court structure in any given jurisdiction in order to formulate practical, politically achievable improvements.

The people who write about government or teach the subject in universities are usually not the people who run government. Consequently, a great deal goes on in any governmental institution that is obscured from public view because it cannot be discovered in recorded statistics or even in exhaustive interviews—the basic tools of political science. When all of the answers in the area of court reform are to questions having little bearing on the real problems that confound the system, it is little wonder that improvement is slow. The rest of this book sets forth most of the correct questions along with a few tentative answers. The reader must evaluate the issues presented in terms of his or her own state and its peculiar problems, cutting and pasting ideas from here and elsewhere until he or she comes up with modest proposals that might actually be implemented.

Flanneled Fools 2
at the Wickets

IF AN ARCHITECT or engineer with sensitive measuring devices stands in the nave of the great cathedral in Salisbury, England, he or she can discover that the tip of the cathedral's spire is exactly 3.2 feet off dead center in the direction of the southwestern prevailing winds. Someone unfamiliar with the prevailing winds and the flexibility of structures built from stone and medieval mortar might conclude that Salisbury's builders were sloppy craftsmen; yet it is the deviation from theoretical perfection, a concession to reality, that has permitted the spire to survive in all its splendor hundreds of years of punishment by the elements.

Medieval cathedrals like Salisbury don't sustain our attention and draw us back time and time again because they achieved spectacular heights or supported incredible stresses. Any modern architect can design and execute a cathedral with the proportions of New York's World Trade Center supporting a load several hundred times the weight of all parts of Salisbury combined. What is amazing in Gothic architecture is the effect, in terms of upward thrust and exhilarating proportions, achieved with primitive materials. The flying buttress is not itself beautiful; it is a beautiful concession to nature's physical laws of outward force.

Greatness in architecture is not achieved by creating a good structure from superb materials; it is achieved by creating a superb structure from mediocre materials. The same general criterion applies to government. At any particular time the quality of people in government service is a given. While discrete hirings and firings may solve specific problems, the statistical average will remain about constant. Success or failure depends on how we organize the material in order to improve overall statistical performance.

The popular literature on courts tends to concentrate on the quality of the men and women who are judges. This approach looks to individuals, selecting the least competent for censure, instead of looking at the statistical average. Critiques focusing on the personal and intellectual failings of judges provide something concrete that the lay public can understand. Certainly there are egregious cases of incompetent judges, yet reducing problems to the level of personal failings is just a commercial journalistic technique to provide entertaining copy.

The inefficiencies of courts are systemic, and the personal failings of judges are merely one small piece in the total system. Much as the ability and educational level of government personnel has improved since Simon de Montfort's day when the priests and barons who first began banging out an English legal structure could barely read or write, we may be able to look forward to general improvements in the quality of judicial personnel as society as a whole progresses. That process can not be rushed, but other changes can be accomplished immediately. Serious court reform would imitate the builders of Salisbury by designing the system in such a way that its tilt would exactly compensate for the forces of nature and the imperfections of the material.

Yet, before analyzing the design, it is necessary to explore the quality of judges and the judicial selection process, since journalists dwell almost exclusively on these subjects. Although exploration of personal vices and perceived incompetence per se ends in a blind alley, it will lead to the much more rewarding exploration of the way judges, on statistical average, respond to a unique institution. For it is the interaction of the personnel with the structure of courts that produces many of the most intractable problems. The point is not that human failings play a central part in the breakdown of the courts but rather that courts as an institution tend to breed many of the observed failings.

Certain personal vices are not remarkable in people employed outside the judiciary (immediately arrogance and indolence spring to mind). And if the people appointed to the bench had exhibited various qualities in excess before their appointments, they would not have been selected. It is in the nature of the judiciary, with its life tenure or long elected terms, that it can encourage arrogance and indolence, just as the occupation of salesperson tends to mask them. What follows, then, must be understood for just what it is—an exploration of the nature of building materials as that nature relates to a particular design.

During the 1970s, a popular television commercial featured a cartoon character known as Charlie the Tuna. Year after year, Charlie conducted a campaign to attract the attention of Starkist by demonstrating that he was a tuna of "good taste." He took up golf, drank Perrier, read scholarly books, learned tennis, and even began to jog. He was never tapped by Starkist, however, because, as he was told at the end of the commercial: "Sorry Charlie, Starkist wants good-tasting tuna, not tunas with good taste." Almost all judges in the United States are selected by the same basic criterion. Yet as much as our system of political selection lends itself to the popular lampoon, it is not accidental. Political appointment achieves many valuable goals, preeminent among which is political acceptance.

Judges don't conform to any particular profile. They range from the aging and elegant jurists who sit on the United States Supreme Court to the twenty-one-year-old who may be elected magistrate in a rural county. The higher the judicial office, the greater the scrutiny given to the candidate to determine whether he or she is qualified. Outright hacks like Harrold Carswell, a Nixon nominee for the Supreme Court in 1970 who was rejected for his racial views and later disgraced by a sex scandal, and Francis Morrissey, a potential Kennedy nominee in 1961 for the Federal District Court in Massachusetts who was a family friend of the president but without any experience as a trial lawyer, are miraculously screened out most of the time.

The whole concept of "qualified" refers to the possession of certain minimal skills without which it is thought a judge cannot function. In the federal system judges are appointed through the political interaction of the president and the Senate, with participation from assorted other political actors, depending on the political structure of each state. A

35

federal judge cannot be appointed unless he or she is nominated by the president and confirmed by the Senate, and since the Senate still acts like a social club on judicial appointments, disapproval by a senator from a nominee's home state automatically forecloses appointment. When the president and the majority of the Senate are from different political parties, trades are made.

With regard to all federal judges, the question of qualification is passed upon by a number of outside institutions, preeminent among which are the Department of Justice, which is required to make a background investigation and provide a recommendation, and the American Bar Association. Both of these agencies look for obvious personal and intellectual flaws and they frequently make negative reports that inspire senators and the president to look elsewhere. The screeners search to determine whether a nominee has a temperate disposition, has previously been courteous, is willing to work, has performed acceptably as a lawyer in some capacity, and, finally, whether his or her personal life is such that there is little likelihood of scandal.

Inquiries are not generally made into a nominee's interest in the law as an all-consuming passion, his or her understanding of the social and political issues that the courts must decide, or his or her dedication to an energetic career on the bench rather than early retirement. Finally, no inquiry is made into a nominee's ability as an administrator in the judicial system, which is an entirely different quality from being a good judge of individual causes. Numerous lobbying groups, from the NAACP to the local manufacturers' association, also involve themselves by endorsing or contesting specific nominations. Their interest is in a judge's philosophy—is he or she pro–civil rights, pro-business, liberal, conservative, of the proper race or sex?

The ironic conclusion to which we must ineluctably be drawn is that if inquiries into quality as opposed to qualifications were undertaken, no two investigators would agree on how to weigh the criteria or even whether the criteria were met by a particular candiate. In fact, the whole notion of quality gets blurred by the far more urgent concern of philosophy. The lack of consensus about what courts should be doing guarantees utter lack of agreement about what makes a good judge. Any concept of merit selection—that is, selection based exclusively on objective standards rather than politics—is chimerical. With the possible exceptions of courtesy and willingness to work, the qualities that make a good judge are subjective. In the final analysis, interest groups are not looking for brilliant lawyers, they are looking for lawyers who will decide cases in their favor. Certainly blacks and women do not want judges measured by either academic performance or number of years at the bar; they want black and women judges. The corporation bar does not want qualified black and women judges; they want narrow-minded Republicans, preferably as stately and stupid as possible so that they can subtly influence them at country-club cocktail parties. Under these conditions the political process probably handles selection about as well as any other.

Basically, there are two paths to political power—the "lion path" and the "fox path." The classic lion goes out as a young man into the elective foray, first in the county commission, state legislature, or city council, and then as far as he can propel himself, ending as a congressman, governor, or United States senator. The classic fox finds an energetic and competent young lion, hitches his wagon to the lion's star, and waits for the lion to make the big time. When and if that occurs, the fox is entitled to either a cabinet or subcabinet level job or a federal judgeship. For lawyers, a federal judgeship is the jackpot, and judgeships are usually passed out to influential machine politicians, superb fund raisers, or the childhood buddies of governors, United States senators, or presidents.

Lions, in general, do not take foxes very seriously: most big-time politicians look upon the courts as tiresome administrative agencies whose highest political use is to supply patronage. When my grandfather was U.S. senator in the 1930s, he "created" a federal judgeship for one of his friends. It was not until the 1950s that this roving federal judge sitting in both the northern and southern districts of West Virginia worked more than a few hours a week.

With the demise of political machines in the wake of civil service and television campaigns, presidents and senators frequently resent the need to select federal judges. As one senator recently defined his problem, "All you get out of that mess is hundreds of enemies and one ingrate." It is the hundreds-of-enemies problem rather than any urge for good government that inspires increasing retreat to merit selection committees composed of the mandatory members from business and labor, along with blacks, women, Hispanics, and any other interest groups in the area. In small states where patronage still makes a difference to politicians, senators keep control of judicial appointments.

I have been talking about federal judges because they are the judges everyone hears about. However, most of the judicial work in this country goes on in state courts. The overall proportion of state appellate and general-jurisdiction trial court judges to federal judges is at least seven to one, and in many places it is substantially higher. This ratio does not even take into consideration all of the state justices of the peace, magistrates, and limited jurisdiction district court judges who dispose of the millions of traffic offenses, municipal-ordinance violations, landlord-and-tenant cases, and consumer credit claims. When we try to figure out why courts don't work, we must think about the state, not federal, courts, because the state systems do the bulk of the routine work, particularly in criminal law.

Most social theories are primarily the autobiography of the theorist. This book is no exception because my election to West Virginia's highest court instructed my understanding of how politics makes judges. I became a supreme court of appeals judge at the age of thirty-one primarily because between 1922 and 1958 my grandfather had served both as governor of West Virginia and U.S. senator. I inherited both his numerous friends and his extensive positive name recognition among older voters. When I was elected judge I was a state legislator who three years before had been an unemployed army artillery officer. I was nominated and elected as a Democrat through statewide elections where the skills required for success were entirely political.

Upon graduating from law school in 1967, I had gone immediately into the army. Earlier, as an undergraduate, I had studied some economics, so when the army sent me to Vietnam, they made me staff economist for about a quarter of South Vietnam and legal officer for the group doing civil operations in that area. I came home from Vietnam in April 1969 and opened a one-man law office in Fairmont, West Virginia. At that time my uncle was judge of the criminal court, and he had a fair political following in the local area.

I had never aspired to be a practicing lawyer, except to the extent that practicing law would earn me a living, give me a certain credibility and respectability, and provide something for me to do when I lost elections. While I actually enjoyed practicing law, my overriding interests were the economic development of West Virginia and government in general. I wanted to be a United States senator and had no intention of waiting. I decided to run for the Senate against West Virginia's incumbent senior senator, Jennings Randolph, in the 1972 primary election. To do that I needed a base and visibility; so I mounted a strong and successful campaign for the lower house of the state legislature in 1970.

In January 1971 I went to the state legislature, where I immediately began to run for the U.S. Senate. I hired my own press staff and gave speeches everywhere. When the legislature concluded in March I began an almost full-time campaign for the Senate race, making a formal announcement in July 1971. I practiced some law, but I devoted most of my total working time that year to politics. My biggest chore was raising money to feed my staff and purchase advertising during the coming primary campaign in 1972, which would run from February to the first week in May. In the meantime, incumbent Senator Randolph had spoken to a number of people about possible retirement. I never believed that he would really retire, but since others did, I took advantage of the uncertainty to obtain entrée whenever anyone was looking for a relationship with his possible successor. I actually raised some money and used it to travel, send out press releases, and write thousands of personal letters.

Everything went well indeed until December 1971 when Jennings Randolph announced his candidacy for reelection, at which point I received my first practical lesson in politics: it is hard to defeat an incumbent. A stone wall went up in front of my efforts, and I quickly realized that Senator Randolph was about to beat me like a drum. I began to consider some face-saving options that would avoid the loss of an election and potential political oblivion. Two members of the West Virginia Supreme Court of Appeals had unexpectedly left the court earlier that year, one through death and the other through retirement. Furthermore, the governor was a Republican who had appointed unknown Republicans to serve until the next election, and in West Virginia, with a strong Roosevelt tradition, lackluster Republicans were easy for Democrats to beat.

It occurred to me that I could knock off a seat on the supreme court,

39

hide there amid an atmosphere almost completely devoid of controversy, keep my name and presence alive, and bide my time until a Senate seat opened that I could win. Furthermore, this strategy was no secret and was enthusiastically endorsed by the voters. I discussed it openly and never promised to serve out my twelve-year term as judge.

While my political organization and financial resources were inadequate to beat a good, incumbent U.S. senator, I knew they would be like the atomic bomb to any ordinary lawyer or local judge who entered a statewide election for the supreme court. So I took my inherited name recognition, my political friends, and a considerable sum of my own money and entered a low-stakes game, one I won handily. The secret was that nobody cared a hoot who got elected judge; positive name recognition alone was basically enough to convert any unobjectionable person into a winner. Most of the rank-and-file political leaders were not lawyers, and they knew enough about my educational background to infer that I would do a competent job. They considered it perfectly fitting for a young politician who was aiming at a major office to use a lower state office as a training ground. They drew no distinction between the state supreme court and jobs like secretary of state, state treasurer, or attorney general.

This brief personal history might not be persuasive if I did not add that at the same time that I was elected, the other seat on the supreme court was won by James M. Sprouse, who had been the Democratic candidate for governor in 1968, losing by fewer than thirteen thousand votes. He got fifty thousand more votes than I did for the supreme court in 1972, for the same reasons that I beat all other candidates—he was a big-time politician who had gone into a low-stakes game because he could not have defeated John D. Rockefeller IV in that year's Democratic primary for governor. Jim Sprouse was waiting, too, although when he did run for governor again in 1976, Rockefeller beat him in the primary. Yet the judiciary saved Judge Sprouse once more from the tedium of private law practice. No sooner had he lost the governorship again than he was appointed to the U.S. Circuit Court of Appeals for the Fourth Circuit. Other members of my court include Sam R. Harshbarger, who once ran unsuccessfully for state attorney general; Darrell V. McGraw, who ran unsuccessfully for Congress; and Thomas McHugh, who had been active in Sprouse's 1968 campaign and ran successfully in 1974 for the trial court in the state's largest county, before running statewide for the supreme court in 1980.

This political aspect of the judiciary is not peculiar to West Virginia. In every state a judge needs to be some kind of politician. The methods for staffing the states' judiciaries break down into about five different patterns. In many states, as in West Virginia, the judges are nominated in partisan primary elections or in party conventions and run for office under the aegis of a political party in the general election. The constitutions in these states usually call for certain qualifications for running for judicial office, typically including membership in the bar for a certain number of years and a minimum age, such as thirty. In some states, as in Illinois and Pennsylvania, the judges are initially elected on a nonpartisan ballot and then run at regular intervals in retention elections where the only question on the ballot is: "Should Judge Wossname be retained in office?" Only if a majority votes against retention of an incumbent judge is a contested election scheduled for his position. In other states, such as Colorado and Nebraska, judges are first appointed and then run in retention elections. In Connecticut and Massachusetts, judges are appointed until a retirement age. And in Virginia and Rhode Island, judges are elected by the legislature.

Furthermore, within any given state, there is not necessarily any consistency in the way high-ranking and low-ranking judges are selected. Frequently, the lowest courts are elected, while the general-jurisdiction trial courts or, at least, the state's highest court are appointed. Since twenty-two states have virtually an entirely elected judiciary, at least in those states judges must start out as elected politicians. Where judges are appointed by the governor or elected by the legislature, there will be the same type of political interplay that exists in the federal system. In states where the legislature elects the judges (a sort of compromise between popular election and appointment), the best way to become a high-level judge is via the state senate, where years of accumulated personal debts can be cashed in for a judgeship.

Frequently, therefore, judgeships become consolation prizes for those who fail in big-time elected politics, and this phenomenon is not limited to high-level appellate courts. In the local trial courts it is usually local, rather than state or regional, politicians who are elevated to the bench. Many trial-court judges are former elected prosecuting attorneys or, in

41

large cities, senior assistant prosecutors. Others come from service in city councils, state legislatures, county commissions, or party hierarchy. When we finally descend to the level of justice of the peace, magistrate, or small-claims court, where the judges may be laypersons, we find all types of local politicians, some of whom are just attractive young people with political ambitions who are using these minor judgeships as entry-level jobs.

That judges are former politicians is not to say that they are inferior; it merely implies a type of judge different from those found in England, where senior barristers are elevated to the bench after distinguished careers of practicing law; or in France and Germany, where the judiciary is a separate branch of the legal profession. In my experience, politicians are both smarter and more humane than their counterparts in industry, commerce, law practice, or academia. I suspect that the low esteem politics as a profession is generally accorded comes not from the quality of its men and women but from the fact that the demands on government cannot all be met with government's limited resources. Yet even if we allow that politicians are as good as or better than their counterparts elsewhere with similar education, training, and income, the fact that judges are politicians has broad implications for the workings of the American judiciary that are unrelated to the inherent quality of the people selected as judges. In many states, the mere fact that judges must run for office at comparatively frequent intervals makes them an integral part of the rough-and-tumble political process.

While the political background of judges does not imply inferior qualifications, it is true that most judges get their jobs by accident. Either a person is elected to the job as a consolation prize or he is appointed because his particular lion came in first at some point. In either case, elevation to the judiciary is almost entirely dependent upon politics; consequently, no person can ever be sufficiently confident that he or she will become a judge to prepare for the judiciary as a career. The people who most want to be judges rarely achieve the office, while people like me become judges easily because we aspired to something else. This is the "Charlie the Tuna" phenomenon.

Success in every other branch of the legal profession, as well as in most other professions, involves years of training in a speciality. For example, the great law firms of New York City never trust inexperienced counsel to try cases on behalf of important clients. A large firm will frequently send its promising litigators to the office of the United States Attorney for the Southern District of New York with express instructions to make all their trial mistakes on the federal government's time and then come back to the firm. Since the government has thousands of cases, young people get substantial responsibility immediately. It is the ideal training ground.

Yet in the judiciary men and women are taken from business and narrowly specialized law practice and overnight are made powerful judges. Some people, of course, become judges and then embark on their own educational program in order to become good judges. This is particularly the case with judges who assume the bench in their early forties; however, the normal age for appointment to senior judgeships is the early or middle fifties, and by then a person is usually no longer ambitious. Just being made a judge achieves his or her ambition. It made a great difference in my own career that I became a judge at thirty-one rather than fifty-one.

Open-mindedness, enthusiasm, and a willingness to experiment are qualities associated with young, ambitious people. A majority of the court systems' managing judges are of comfortable middle age, remarkably contented, and accustomed, like the British Army on the eve of World War I, to a way of doing things which, if not entirely wrong, is only partially right. For the judiciary attracts two types of people— those of good quality who have earned or inherited enough money to supplement their salaries and those for whom a salary of forty-five thousand dollars a year is attractive compared to what they made practicing law. Furthermore, once a person becomes a judge, he or she is usually terminal. Ambition as a tool of upward mobility is useless; after all, there are only nine seats on the United States Supreme Court.

There is some truth in the assertion that experience in general trial practice is good preparation for the judiciary. Yet practicing law basically involves taking the system as it exists and manipulating it to achieve a favorable result for a client. Good former trial lawyers work well within the existing judicial system; they are usually careful and can usually achieve equitable results in specific cases. Yet in general the vision, imagination, and enthusiasm of judges are inadequate for any creative or reforming role. This may be harsh, and there are nu-

43

merous exceptions to the general rule, but there is a pervasive and unwarranted contentment among judges.

Frequently judges are intelligent but devoid of ambition, and as frequently they are ambitious but devoid of intelligence. Ambition without intelligence is far more dangerous than intelligence without ambition. Since judges can blame the court system's failures on others—on society's lack of consensus or society's parsimony in funding supporting services—there is no gnawing sense of shirked responsibility on the part of the judiciary. This is a convenient attitude; a gnawing sense of inadequacy would suggest a great deal of very hard work. Furthermore, the pervasive lack of ambition that is a function of old age and terminal status chills any receptivity to invitations to hard work not required by daily routine, including creative thinking about administration and design.

Since a judgeship is often a prelude to retirement, and since being a judge fulfills personal needs for leisure and prestige, judges themselves resist any new design that might reduce their prerogatives. While the appellate judges who run the court system are lawyers trained to decide individual cases, the majority of them were not trained to master problems of overall design. Certainly the judicial associations are constantly offering proposals that imply a bigger and better model of what we already have, but committee work of that type is pedestrian at best. As subsequent chapters explore, making the courts perform efficiently implies a radical departure from the mind-set our sitting judges have had since law school and, more important, a commitment to hard, nasty, administrative work. Unfortunately, ambitious judges who experiment with new types of systems rather than bigger models of the old system are perceived by their complacent colleagues as a menacing, disruptive force.

The hard, nasty work that new designs for the judicial system would entail is difficult to exact from sitting judges because they signed on to avoid hard, nasty work. There are four personal advantages a professional job can offer: income (including all fringe benefits); power; prestige; and leisure. A fifth may be intrinsically interesting or worthwhile work, but I would subsume this under the category of power since any other approach makes my examples too subjective. A top-ranking business executive has excellent income, significant power, acceptable prestige, and no leisure. A college professor has months of leisure, acceptable prestige, mediocre power, and little income. A White House aide has enormous power, considerable prestige, mediocre income, and no leisure. The same person is likely to accept any of these jobs since, in some grand psychological equation, the advantages and disadvantages of each about balance out.

It is the sad fact of the judiciary that the preeminent attraction of the judging business is its leisure.[1] I can hear the agonized screams of outrage from my colleagues across the country, so I should probably put the leisure issue into perspective. Work has two dimensions: length and intensity. If we compare judges to postal employees, assembly-line hourly workers, plumbers, or college professors, judges work hard. However, if we compare them to successful trial lawyers, they have an easy life.

Lawyers must watch cases meticulously to make sure that time periods do not run out; lawyers must be prepared to give up a vacation or weekend if they receive a notice on Friday afternoon to be in court on Monday morning; and often, just as a lawyer sits down to dinner, looking forward to a good football game later on, the telephone rings with a client on the other end who is either in jail, on the verge of bankruptcy, or in the midst of a violent domestic quarrel.

A trial-court judge has almost complete and unfettered control of his own court. He can schedule hearings, arguments, and motions for his own convenience. If a judge wants to take a long weekend, go squirrel hunting, or put up hay, he can just decide to do it. While judges cannot take six months off at a time or establish a schedule where they work only three hours a day all year, they generally have greater discretion in the use of their time than other executives earning comparable

1. Bear in mind that most of the work of the courts goes on in state courts and not the federal courts. Being a federal judge has very, very high prestige, comparatively high pay, good working conditions, and the best retirement plan in the world. Few of these characteristics apply to state judgeships. The state courts, unlike the federal courts, cannot pick and choose among the best lawyers in the country. Frequently, given the salaries offered and the larger number of places having to be staffed in the state systems, there are insufficient numbers of qualified lawyers willing to serve as state judges, even when the appointing authority is genuinely looking for merit, whatever that means.

salaries. Furthermore, they can be sick and laid up for years at a time with no loss of income—an attractive feature to a middle-aged lawyer in poor health. This contrasts sharply with the practicing lawyer, who is always at the mercy of judges, other lawyers, clients, and his own physical stamina.

All of these observations are merely a sketch of a general mode. Every lawyer knows judges who try to place the convenience of the lawyers first and are conscientious about not imposing upon lawyers for their own convenience. There are judges who voluntarily accept long and complicated cases that require strenuous five- to ten-week trials. The point is not that all, or even most, judges abuse their positions; it is that judges have options about how they will use their time and how hard they will work.

The second benefit that comes with black robes is lack of pressure. This may sound absurd since obviously judges make decisions about child custody, sentencing of criminals, and political matters like busing and integration. Certainly there are pressures of a sort that would be burdensome to anyone not used to practicing law. But if the pressure of judging is compared to that of law practice, the difference is really quite remarkable. The practicing lawyer is involved with every type of decision that concerns a judge; however, the lawyer's responsibility is to make sure the judge decides the case in favor of his client. If a client wants her children, the lawyer must agonize with the client through the custody fight and listen to her if she loses. If a lawyer's client is to be sentenced, the lawyer must make sure he gets probation instead of ten years in the penitentiary. Furthermore, in many cases, such as those involving personal injuries, the lawyer gets paid only if he wins; if he loses he is out hundreds of hours of working time plus thousands of dollars in unrecoverable expenses.

A lawyer's income and his reputation depend on how many cases he wins. A judge's salary arrives promptly on the first and the fifteenth of each month, regardless of whether he is good, mediocre, or abjectly incompetent. While the judge who takes work home, diligently prepares himself, and works hard in the writing and reasoning of his published opinions may be marginally better regarded than his lazy colleagues by the bar and other members of the bench, nobody else knows or gives a damn. Some judges actually do devote as many hours to judging as a good lawyer devotes to practicing law; however, their pressures are internal rather than external, which makes a great deal of difference with regard to many things, including life expectancy.

Most of this discussion has focused on the one-judge court that actually hears evidence and makes the initial decision in all litigated cases. In general, these same observations apply to appellate courts consisting of three-, five-, seven-, or nine-judge panels. While the need to sit as a group does imply less individual flexibility in the scheduling of court work, appellate courts typically schedule arguments for only one day a week or one week a month, which leaves roughly 75 percent of the judges' time flexible. Furthermore, appellate judges are generally accommodating to one another, and an appellate judge can always get a colleague to sit in for him if he wants to go away.

Probably fewer than half of all general jurisdiction trial judges and appellate judges come from the ranks of successful litigators. The average trial judge makes forty-five thousand dollars a year (federal judges make twenty-two thousand dollars more, while some states pay a lot less), and although that seems like big money to most Americans, it is very little money for a good lawyer. In recent years, a new phenomenon has occurred: federal judges, who in general were the better lawyers, have been resigning these lifetime jobs because they cannot continue the life-style they enjoyed before they became judges.

It is worth noting that the skills of a successful practicing lawyer and a good judge are not entirely congruent. I've known fine judges who were mediocre practicing lawyers because they did not have an instinct for going for the jugular. Yet the courtesy and humanity that kept them from being big income earners at the bar made them excellent judges, particularly if they were bright and possessed an academic interest in the law. Good lawyers and good judges do have two things in common: willingness to work and a better-than-average intellect.

Since it is obviously not money that attracts good lawyers to the judiciary, it must be something else. Usually, for high-quality lawyers, it is some combination of prestige and leisure. But the relationship between the leisurely life-style of judges and poorly functioning courts is not direct.[2] The indirect effect of the leisurely life-style is a fear that *any* administrative innovation or change in overall design will ultimately result in a time-and-motion-study mentality. Such fears are frequently well founded since reformers always like to start by making judges work harder. Furthermore, the leisurely life-style in and of itself attracts a particular type of person to the judiciary, and this returns us to the whole question of ambition. Sitting judges have comfortable and rewarding lives; they perceive any effort at innovation or new design as personally threatening.

Finally, many successful practicing lawyers have purposely fled to the judiciary at an enormous sacrifice in income in order to escape the tedium and constant pressure of law practice. They hated working fourteen hours a day; they hated firm pressure to overlawyer and overcharge; frequently they despised their clients; and, more frequently, they despised their law partners. These people were once compulsive workers, but at age forty-five they want out.

The political nature of judges and their leisurely life-styles do not alone distinguish the judiciary from other American institutions. Senior officials in the executive branch are former politicians placed in office

2. With the exception of some outrageously lazy judges, I don't believe that it is possible to work judges substantially harder than they are working now without sacrificing many of the good qualities of the current system. It is possible to require judges to organize their schedules to compress litigation time, but I doubt that a majority of the judges could handle a greatly expanded total case load. During the last twenty years the work load of almost all courts has more than doubled, without commensurate increases in the number of judges, but the judges have not been working substantially longer hours. Instead they have delegated more responsibility to their law clerks, special masters, and (in the federal system) magistrates. While I have a high regard for young law clerks, life-and-death issues in the criminal field or multi-million-dollar controversies in the civil field should not be decided by young people with almost no practical life experience.

Judicial work is both boring and strenuous. While it is not in toto as hard as a lawyer's work, it quickly drains a judge of his reservoir of creative energy. Though the words *deliberation*, *consideration*, *research*, and *evaluation* are frequently used as excuses for outrageous judicial delay by the laziest and most incompetent judges, even fast, competent judges need time to think. The real craftsman in any field cannot be treated like an assembly-line worker.

accidentally, and it is not possible to say that judges are more wedded to leisure than state or federal legislators. What makes the personal attributes of judges so critical is that these attributes are combined with a unique institution.

Courts, it must be remembered, are essentially medieval in origin, and they evolved—they were not made. The most important medieval quality which persists into the twentieth century is that courts are decentralized both within and among jurisdictions. We usually accept the inherited structure of the courts as if it were an inevitable feature of any court system, but in fact it is merely a historical accident. American courts followed in direct succession the English model that existed in the colonies without ever missing a stitch. After the American Revolution the development of American and English courts diverged, leaving American judges with substantially more political power than their colleagues across the ocean, but many of today's courts' strengths and weaknesses can be traced directly to their medieval roots.

In the England of Henry II (d. 1189) the royal judges were the preeminent force of the central government. The aim of the Norman kings from the conquest onward was always to reduce the power of the local, landowning nobility, centralize authority in the crown, and provide a uniform taxing and legal system throughout the country. The agency chosen to effect this legal and administrative transformation was the judiciary, whose members were sent out from London clothed with awe-inspiring power. These judges were surrogate sovereigns: they could issue orders and require local lords to attend the king's court personally if the lords refused to cooperate with them while they were sitting in the local area.

The local judge is still a surrogate sovereign. A general-jurisdiction trial court judge today is clothed with all the power of the legislature and the executive in deciding any individual case (until reversed by a higher court). In every local county seat and U.S. district courthouse there is a person who can cut through red tape, require bureaucrats to respond to citizen demand, and forbid all types of outrageous government activity. Furthermore, that person need not ask anyone's permission to do any of these things; there is no chain of command before the fact.

For our purposes, English judicial history has had two important consequences: a tradition of judicial autonomy and a lack of an administrative hierarchy. These were the consequences of having a collection of independent courts. Since each court was legally independent, there was no place for an extensive administrative system. Each court was a discrete unit so, except to prohibit a court from hearing certain kinds of cases, one court had no reason and no business telling another court how to conduct its affairs.

In the United States we have a collection of court *systems*. Each system has retained within itself the consequences of the English *nonsystem* rather than having developed appropriately systematic control. Modern courts are decentralized because their organization predates the Industrial Revolution. Consequently, courts look unlike other modern institutions.

Until the beginning of the nineteenth century and the dawn of the mechanical age, mankind had neither experience organizing large groups of people nor the logistical support needed for an industrial or commercial undertaking. The only previous experience in large-scale organizing was in the military. In general, the structure the Industrial Revolution produced everywhere imitated the military and was hierarchical, with a chain of command starting with the chief executive officer and extending all the way to the lowest employee. Regardless of how decisions were made at the top—whether by one person, a leadership commitee, a board of directors, or after extensive consultation—once a decision was made everyone down the line was expected to follow orders or lose his or her job.

We see this pattern in government (but not in the courts) even today. While there is much fashionable discussion among political scientists and sociologists about how the president and the state governors have no power because they can't control the bureaucracy, this theory of lack of power misses a very important point. The *power* to control the bureaucracy is there; what is lacking is both the time and the motivation. Notwithstanding civil-service rules about discharge, a recalcitrant civil servant who fails to follow a direct order can be fired or, better yet, transferred to Lawton, Oklahoma. In both business and the executive branch of the government there is total administrative control within bureaucracies. Not only is general policy set at the top, but if there is sufficient motivation and manpower, senior officials also determine the budgets, staffing patterns, priorities for the dispatch of business, allocation of resources among departments, and with certain broad bounds established by either civil-service commissions or labor unions, the actual people in charge and on line. None of this happens in the courts.

When Henry II's courts began developing, the lack of transportation and communication precluded strong central control. The object was to provide a powerful representative of the crown at the local level, and that model has continued down through the centuries. Even in American states where there has been a concerted effort at judicial reorganization, the local judges retain much of their historical feudal autonomy. For example, West Virginia has one of the strongest unified court systems in the United States. The supreme court allocates all the money for the lower courts and has the power to promulgate rules and regulations for the behavior of judges. Every year the position of chief justice rotates among the five members of the supreme court, and in 1980 I served as chief justice. Although, allegedly, I was chief executive officer of the unified court system, in reality I was the proverbial wingless fly in the hands of small boys. The system was still so decentralized that the chief justice could have but little influence on its total performance.

In the system I was supposed to administer there were sixty general-jurisdiction trial court judges, all of whom had been elected on partisan ballots for eight-year terms. In addition, there were 150 nonlawyer magistrates, each elected in a particular county by a particular constituency, and while the chief justice is empowered to move judges around to handle extraordinary problems, judges generally serve primarily in their own counties. Consequently, as chief executive officer I could not hire, fire, transfer, or discipline any of the officer personnel under me. While violation of the *Code of Judicial Conduct* might have provided grounds for a complaint against a judge, ultimately resulting in discipline, the judge's conduct had to be outrageous before this procedure could be invoked. And in any case, it takes about a year for the wheels of the judicial discipline machinery to grind out a decision. Mere laziness or incompetence is beyond sanction. During my ten years on the bench only one general-jurisdiction judge has been disciplined through the formal procedure used to enforce the *Code of Judicial Conduct*, although a few magistrates have been forced to resign through fear of formal sanctions.

51

WHY COURTS DON'T WORK

The West Virginia system is typical of many states but better than most. Each general-jurisdiction trial court judge appoints his own secretary, court reporter, and magistrate court clerk. Each magistrate appoints his own magistrate's assistant. The only people whom the chief executive officer of our courts can hire or fire are his personal administrative assistant, secretary, and law clerks. Out of almost eight hundred people in the judicial system, the chief justice controls four. Believe it or not, the Chief Justice of the United States controls only about the same number of people.

In those states where some effort has been made to achieve centralized control, as in West Virginia, the administrative power has been placed in the hands of the state's highest court. An appellate court, however, is actually a five-, seven-, or nine-judge committee, and in most states the chief justice is elected by the entire court. The rotation principle for the office of chief justice is merely a voluntary rule, like the seniority principle in Congress, to avoid internal power struggles. In the federal system the chief district-court judge of each district and the chief judge of each circuit court of appeals are selected exclusively by seniority. That offers greater potential for leadership if the senior person is competent and has a vision of what needs to be done. Yet, even in the federal system, the power of the chief judge is severely restricted. No chief judge or justice has the power of a president, governor, or chief executive officer of a business; he cannot change policy without the acquiescence of a majority of his court of equals. And even if there is a consensus on policy, enforcement is cumbersome without threat of discharge or transfer.

Leadership, particularly leadership of small, voluntary groups of equals, requires at least two qualities. The leader must have a vision of what needs to be done, *and* he must possess personal, small-group skills in order to get the willing cooperation of his peers. A leader who has a vision of what needs to be done is usually also an egotist, strong-willed, and intolerant of his colleagues. These attributes, which only the consummately skillful can disguise, are not calculated to win affection or cooperation. Strong leaders in the court system usually inspire a serious program of passive resistance that undermines any self-proclaimed leader's effectiveness. In both business and the executive branch of government, leaders display the same unendearing personal qualities;

however, they have been put in charge and need not constantly struggle among equals.

Since most judges have a high opinion of themselves, strong leaders do not develop; judges who seek leadership are resented. An eighteenth-century commentary on Lord Bathurst, one of the least distinguished chancellors in England's history, attributed his elevation to the kingdom's most powerful judicial position to the fact that he inspired neither envy in rivals nor fear in enemies. The requirements for success have not changed much in two hundred years.

The result of the state courts' social dynamics is that power accrues to the judge without an agenda; it is the plodding, apparently unimaginative beast of burden who ultimately achieves preeminence because he is unthreatening and willing to do the mundane tasks that either lazy or more imaginative colleagues shirk. Things could be worse. At least the plodder guarantees that routine work will be accomplished with some degree of craftsmanship. Should he ever become inspired, he acquires an agenda and loses his power.

Courts operate at two levels: judicial and administrative. There is obviously a hierarchy of trial and appellate courts to decide specific cases. However, the hierarchy for deciding cases does not exist in administrative matters. No superior authority tells a judge how many days he must come to the office, how fast he should decide cases, or what priorities he should assign to different types of judicial business. Even where guidelines are established by a state's highest court, they are difficult if not impossible to enforce. In the state of New York, for example, the only effort to assure reasonably expeditious decisions is a requirement that trial-court judges report to the office of the chief judge's court administrator cases ripe for decision that have not been decided after sixty days.

Making correct decisions in individual cases, which is what the *judicial* hierarchy is designed to accomplish, is only a small part of what makes a court system effective. What if the decision is correct but the case took five years to be decided? What if the costs of litigation exceed the total value of the controversy? What if a court is so understaffed that it is snowed under with paperwork and cases simply disappear after they have been filed? These are the problems an *administrative* hierarchy would face.

53

WHY COURTS DON'T WORK

It is easy to criticize the courts' diffuse structure, and theoretically it is also easy to segregate administrative matters, i.e., priority of cases, speed of resolution, etc., from actual decision making in individual cases. However, tight administrative control also implies an ability to control the outcome of decisions. It is concern for the outcome of case-by-case decisions that fires the controversies over selection of judges. Outcome is where philosophy is all important. A superior authority that can set a judge's hours, authorize or withhold his vacations, or control the number of his employees and the logistical support for his office can also bribe a judge into line with a particular judicial philosophy. With administrative control like that, those who go along will get along. Certainly this would apply to a strong chief justice on a policymaking appellate court.

Since the courts are the most powerful force in government because they interpret all statutes, common law, and the state and federal constitutions, it is reasonably thought that all administrative power must be diffused. To repeat the point for emphasis, administrative power spills over into judicial power. Real people don't live in the world of grandiose adjudicative theory; they live by day-to-day, case-by-case decisions. The plaintiffs' bar is not interested in an adjudicative theory that is fair; they want a court that will redistribute wealth in the direction of plaintiffs so that they can get their cut. Administrative power that could spill over into the way cases are decided threatens the current balance. A chief justice with the wisdom of Solomon and the organizational ability of Franklin Roosevelt might work wonders, but it is as likely that the position would be held by someone who resembled Huey Long.

The advantage of entrusting the administrative power to a state's highest court or a committee of federal judges is that administrative power will be exercised in a way congruent with the judges' overall judicial philosophy—a philosophy that takes into consideration the value judgments of members who have been made judges to vindicate particular philosophical positions. While I, for example, am concerned by the delay the courts cause in administrative rulings, because I tend to favor rapid economic growth, I have colleagues who don't like business and have grave reservations about the value of economic growth per se. While my priorities might include immediate dispatch of cases involving large investment projects, some of my colleagues would disagree and choose to expedite personal-injury cases. With limited resources we cannot expedite all cases (otherwise there would be no problem), so some compromise must be reached. Usually the compromise is to do nothing and let the chips fall where they may. In the realm of philosophy there are no right or wrong answers; there are just political decisions that combine issues of fact or science under a heavy overlay of values.

In those areas where all the members of my court agree philosophically, such as priority for child-custody cases, concerted administrative action can be achieved. Child-custody cases have precedence over other appeals. Similarly, in the area of labor injunctions, a compromise was made in my court years ago between those who favored unfettered picketing and those who wanted to restrain union power. A trial court could issue a temporary labor injunction, but the court had to give a hearing to the other side immediately (so the issue could be appealed), even if that meant getting out of bed in the middle of the night, or else the court lost jurisdiction to enforce its injunction order.

The highest court of a state does have substantial power if it can act in a concerted manner. While it does not have the direct power of business executives, once a state's highest court decides to do something, it will usually get done. The problem is getting sufficient agreement in the committee to arrive at a strong, collective conclusion. The point to be remembered is that there is no "purely administrative" matter. Eventually, every administrative decision affects the outcome of important political and social issues. In this regard the judicial process includes not only the cases that are in court but all the cases that never get to court. These latter cases, which comprise the majority of disputes, are settled based on predictions about judicial caprice, judicial delay, and litigation expense.

I have never known an appellate court that did not have about as many philosophies concerning civil rights, redistribution of wealth, consumerism, and environmentalism as there were members of the court. Many appellate courts, in fact, are composed of men and women who not only differ philosophically but who loathe one another personally. On important courts, like the Circuit Court of Appeals for the District of Columbia, those appointed are smart, aggressive, opinionated, strong-willed egotists who clash all day long. That sort of internal dynamic is hardly conducive to the temperate generation of new approaches.

But more to the point, any new approach that is not carefully crafted through collegial analysis (and here I imply no irony) will effect a change in the current winners and losers. That is not a neutral change, and judges oppose changes that are not neutral.[3] This is not to assert that there should be no changes in the current winners and losers. Everyone has his or her own agenda for changing the outcome of classes of litigation. That, however, is a matter of philosophy at best and pure politics at worst. The purpose of this book is to outline how the mechanical workings of courts can be improved. Some reforms, such as better functioning criminal courts, cannot be neutral. Yet, whenever possible, a strict adherence to neutrality should be employed, or mechanical reform will be confounded by questions of wealth distribution, civil rights, and a host of other political questions. This confounding has actually occurred. Judges can't put their own agendas on the back burner while they discuss procedural reform.

DECENTRALIZATION within jurisdictions and the invitation that structure extends to uncooperative or obstructionist tactics results in inertia. Decentralization among jurisdictions, however, presents the type of intractable problems that keep big law firms profitably employed for years at a time and impoverish litigants. Each of the fifty-three separate court systems in the United States, including the federal court system, has its own substantive and procedural rules that are often in conflict with one another. Each side of any quarrel rushes to get the case started in the jurisdiction that has the laws most favorable to its side.

3. The typical reaction of those who oppose a change in winners and losers is not to attack new ways of doing things directly but rather to talk them to death. Reference to bar committees, research reports, and endless nit-picking discussion leading to lengthy delays ultimately wears down the proponents of new approaches. It is in this regard that I have mixed emotions about the pedestrian committee work of bar and judicial associations.

Even simple legal questions like the probate of wills or child custody can become nightmares because there are no easily understood rules concerning when a judgment by a court of one state must or will be honored by another. Cases involving the competitive assertions of jurisdiction by different sovereign entities quickly become like *Bleak House*'s *Jarndyce v. Jarndyce*. The only winners are the lawyers. While the federal Constitution requires the judgments of the state courts to be given "full faith and credit" in other states, the exceptions to this apparently uncomplicated rule are sufficiently numerous that litigation on the validity of out-of-state judgments can take years and cost millions of dollars.

By this time the reader may be wondering where Congress and the state legislatures are in this mess. It is to that subject that I turn in the next chapter, but suffice it to say here that the legislatures are even less competent to handle these problems than the courts. In the first place, legislators don't know very much about the courts, and in the second place, they don't care very much about them. Succinctly stated, in the legislative process the squeaky wheel gets the oil, and there is no organized, squeaking lobby for court reform. There may be a lot of bitching but no organized lobby to design programs and urge their adoption. Wherever some group does urge a plan, all the proponents of the status quo, like the insurance companies or the criminal bar, come out of the woodwork and mobilize sufficient force to kill the scheme. (In fairness, some schemes deserve to be killed.)

The mentality of the judges themselves may be the least impressive of the obstacles to be overcome in court reform; nonetheless, only the judges can provide the catalyst necessary to overcome the other obstacles. The judges can torpedo any program they do not like because they have political friends. As the next chapter demonstrates, it is a Herculean feat to pass anything in the legislative process and comparatively easy to defeat proposed new legislation.

Finally, the most intractable problems of the courts extend far beyond problems of lazy judges or even a decentralized structure. After a brief excursion into the way a legislature works, the remainder of this book deals with these questions. This chapter's discussion of judges and decentralization explains why apparently simple problems have not already been solved. Perceiving a problem, designing a solution, and engineering the solution's adoption are separate processes, accomplished by separate groups and obstructed by separate interests, often for entirely unrelated reasons.

The Anglo-American legal tradition has designed a system calculated to encourage conflict perpetuation rather than conflict resolution. Even if every judge in the system worked fourteen hours a day, six days a week, and the budget for supporting services were doubled, the courts still would not perform significantly better than they do now. It is necessary to catalog judicial life-style, backgrounds of judges, and the organizational structure of courts because those factors often appear to be the cause of the court system's problems. Certainly these are elements to be considered and, in appropriate circumstances, corrected.

However, building a court system is like building a road. The better the road, the more the traffic. A state highway department will measure the traffic going between two points and build a four-lane road predicated on the initial count. They often fail to recognize that as soon as it becomes possible to drive to a neighboring town in forty-five minutes instead of an hour and a half, the trip becomes more attractive, and people who had never thought about doing business, shopping, or just visiting friends in the other town decide to do so.

My favorite example of this principle as applied to the courts comes from a four-county, rural circuit in West Virginia, which includes the famous Greenbrier Hotel. Until 1976 these four counties had been served by one peripatetic judge, and when I came to the bar, the person occupying that position was competent and decisive. During his last year on the bench the case filings amounted to approximately sixteen hundred. In 1976 the incumbent judge retired, and the legislature created a second judge for that circuit. By 1979 the case filings had increased to twenty-four hundred a year although there had been no change in the economy or population. It was merely the prospect that cases would be heard quickly and disposed of conveniently (since there were more sittings each year in each county) that encouraged the greater number of filings. Since human conflict is almost limitless, I infer from my experience that given the current system, which encourages litigation, the volume of work will always press against the capacity of any existing judicial machinery to get the work done.

While it is not amiss to think in terms of getting judges to work more diligently and of establishing greater centralized control over priorities for judicial attention, those easy answers are chimerical if we do not simultaneously come up with new approaches. The ironic conclusion is not that judges are incompetent as judges but rather that they are not disposed to be systems engineers. If things worked the way they are usually expected to work, the system would be designed by others in the legislature through the political process. But the system doesn't work the way it is expected to, so the only available force for reform consists of judges themselves, and most of them do not know it.

Muddied Oafs at the Goals 3

BY this time the reader has inevitably arrived at two conclusions. The first is that if my analysis so far is close to accurate, the web of special interests that frustrate court reform is common knowledge. The second conclusion, following upon the first, is that responsible legislators must have been working on a scheme for overall court reform for many years. Both of these conclusions are entirely reasonable and substantially incorrect.

In the vocation of lawyering there is a low return on analyzing the entire system. The body of law is so enormous that little alternative exists to early specialization. The brighter and better trained lawyers tend to gravitate to large, established firms where they are encouraged to specialize almost immediately. Specialization implies the representation of a particular type of client. Once a lawyer narrows his practice, his mind becomes focused on the injustices the system visits on his particular type of client. Furthermore, since a lawyer is an advocate for a certain type of client, he becomes interested in changing the way courts work only to the extent that he can benefit his own clients as a class.

A lawyer's value, and hence his income, is directly related to what he can do for his clients. The more favorable the law is to his clients as a class, the more spectacular the results he can deliver and the less effort he must expend delivering those results. Bar associations divide themselves into sections corresponding to the specialties of the lawyers, and each section works on improving only one narrow area of the law. Frequently these sections' members represent interests hostile to one another in court. The administrative-law section of the American Bar Association, for example, has lawyers who represent the government, lawyers who represent businesses seeking favorable regulatory action, and lawyers who represent citizen protestors. Consequently, such improvements as these sections recommend will reflect political compromises among the representatives of the diverse client groups in the section.

Yet there will not have been any political compromises with interests *outside* the section, such as taxpayers and politicians. Furthermore, most active members of institutionalized "law reform" groups, particularly the bar associations, are lawyers who have devoted their lives to mastering the current system. This fact alone encourages all improvement to be predicated on making a bigger and better model of the current system.

The same phenomenon exists in slightly different form among law professors and lawyers working for foundations. Specialization permits academic lawyers to write journal articles that enhance their promotion within the academy, and specialization brings large outside consulting fees. Law, after all, is a profession that is usually chosen for its financial rewards. In the final analysis, thinking about reform of the total system is both financially and academically unrewarding.

The net result of specialization is a paucity of plans for overall court reform. In addition, although there are schemes to expand the existing system, very few of them have as their goal the development of a political consensus or take into consideration the purposeful political resistance to better courts.

At least once a year I receive a so-called comprehensive plan for improved courts prepared by a planning agency, such as the Governor's Committee on Crime and Delinquency. The preparation of such plans is funded with federal grants and political feasibility never enters into the planners' consideration. They assume that the only obstacle to a perfectly working court system is a lack of money, and the planners consider lack of money a legislative problem beyond their legitimate concern. The federal grant requirements are satisified if the plan is written. More to the point, the plan is not prepared for any politically active lobby that expects to predicate political rewards and punishments on whether elected officials adopt the plan.

Criticism of the total structure of the court system is usually left to lay, popular writers or else to lawyers who have never practiced but choose instead to be law-trained journalists. These critics are easily dismissed, particularly since most of the time they too are complaining about one narrow set of injustices. The most common injustice, of course, is the failure of the criminal law to catch, prosecute, and punish criminals. The basic problem with court-reform planning or criticism is that it does not proceed in the real political world. Professional planners are writing to satisfy government grant requirements; professional journalists are writing for magazine and newspaper readers who want to be entertained; and academic lawyers are writing for other academic lawyers in the hopes of securing university tenure.

No one is writing for an organized citizen lobby that makes campaign contributions, mails out newsletters about how elected officials perform on court-reform issues, and has representatives entering into the give and take of political bargaining in the committee rooms and corridors of real legislatures. Until there is such a real-life lobby around which not only political support but political opposition can coalesce, politically workable plans will not be generated, partially because until real proposals appear to have real political support, the opponents of court reform will not articulate their objections or settle for political compromises. Why should they? As it now stands they get everything they want.

The second conclusion, that responsible legislators have been diligently pursuing court reform for many years, is unfounded for the same reasons that no politically workable plans have been generated. Since there is no active citizen lobby for court reform and since, on the contrary, all of the day-to-day political rewards go to those who oppose court reform, the legislative branch is indifferent to the courts. In fact, I can't think of any subject of major social concern that intrudes itself less upon the imagination of the average legislator. Yet, as we have all observed, court reform, albeit in simplistic terms, is the frequent subject of campaign rhetoric, giving the illusion that politicians do have some continuing interest in the subject. Sadly, the courts are usually regarded in the same light as is the Federal Reserve Board—as an institution to be reviled and attacked but ultimately to be left unchanged.

When I use the word "illusion" to describe politicians' interest in court reform, I use the word advisedly but not necessarily judgmentally. The structure of American government is such that legislators frequently have no choice but to create illusions if they are to remain in office. When they create an illusion about something important, like good courts, they may be reprehensible, but the blame must be shared by all the good citizens who have no interest in politics, will not make political contributions, and frequently do not even bother to vote. While two wrongs do not make a right, they frequently reinforce one another.

Much of the rest of this chapter sketches the real world of elected politics, particularly in the legislative branch. Without some acquaintance with the mechanics of elected politics—the nature of machines, organized voting blocks, low voter turnouts, and the decisive effects of money and incumbency—it is impossible to comprehend where the courts fit on the political agenda. Furthermore, since the legislative branch's lackluster response to the public's demand for better courts directly reflects voter indifference, those actively interested in making the courts work must know what they are currently doing wrong and alternatively what they might do right.

The legislative branch of government, contrary to popular belief, is not in business to pass good laws. In fact, it is fair to say, ultimately without the least implication of derision, that a legislature is an institution designed to do nothing. In that characterization, the emphasis is not on "do nothing" but rather on "designed." American government is preeminently characterized by a measured straining in opposite directions. In this system a conservative force, a force straining toward inertia, is a legitimate component. In this sense the word "conservative" does not imply a reactionary movement of the propertied class but rather maintenance of the status quo, even if the status quo is at the moment hell-bent on the redistribution of the wealth. My ultimate conclusion

63

about the legislative branch, in which I once served, is close to Trollope's conclusion about Lady Carbury: "The woman was false from head to foot, but there was much good in her, false though she was."

In any given legislative session, either federal or state, the number of petitions for special-interest changes in the law are almost boundless. Labor unions want new rules permitting third-party boycotts in order to strengthen their bargaining position during strikes, while manufacturers want "right to work" laws that make union membership as a condition of employment illegal; bulk mailers want lower postal rates; natural-resource developers want greater access to public lands; environmental groups want more stringent pollution control; huge American companies like Boeing that need foreign sales to underwrite their fixed costs want a larger budget for the Export-Import Bank; lawyers want more money for the Legal Services Corporation; and state education associations and the American Federation of Teachers demand greater federal subsidies to state education.

Furthermore, all of these groups represent significant power centers that have legitimate demands on the political process. The question, therefore, becomes how to say no to the host of predatory vested interests without generating political opposition. It is at this point that the genius of the legislative design enters the picture. Since the machinery of a legislature is *designed* to do nothing, legislators can rest easily in the knowledge that almost all predatory legislation dies a natural death through the operation of the process itself. If the machinery works as it was intended, no one will ever be required to go on record as voting against a particular special-interest bill.

The structure of the bicameral federal and state legislatures didn't just spring from the minds of the Founding Fathers. The legislative branch is in no way "modern," nor is it even a modern reconstruction of a classical ideal; it is a copy of a feudal structure that evolved over six-hundred-odd years. In its original feudal form the English Parliament was an organization designed to do nothing in the strongest sense—it emerged from a deep-seated desire of English subjects to curtail, as far as possible, the king's ability to change certain accepted customs and usages of the realm. Most of the changes a king could make had little to do with improving life for subjects. The original medieval parliaments reflected the delicate balance of power between a central authority and local clergy and magnates of the realm. Any redistribution of power in favor of the central authority would allow those in control of central government to skim economic benefits off the top for themselves, their friends, and their kin, leaving less to be skimmed off by the powerful local folk.

In the Middle Ages taxation had little to do with redistribution of wealth from rich to poor; it was the other way around. Public works were limited, and in England enhanced military expenditures were almost always offensive rather than defensive. The king needed instant influxes of money to finance his grandiose foreign adventures or to underwrite his friends' and retainers' life-styles, and naturally the citizenry did not want to pay. Accordingly, resistance to the central government was essential to the preservation of a life worth living, and the notion of a "conservative" force in government had a strong attraction to almost all classes but royal retainers.

Parliaments, therefore, came into being not to initiate change but to prevent it. Parliaments were overwhelmingly concerned with the protection of the lives, property, and power of society's upper and middle classes. It is not by accident that the war cry of the magnates of the realm in Parliament during the thirteenth and fourteenth centuries was *nolumus leges anglicae mutare*—traditionally translated as "the laws of England shall never change." Here we have an express political commitment to the status quo in the strongest possible sense. Any student of the reign of Henry VIII in the second quarter of the sixteenth century when Parliament was temporarily in eclipse is aware of the rapacious taxation, wholesale land appropriation, and unbridled political tyranny that an unchecked power in the executive branch caused. While Henry may have gone down in history as a modernizing force who made succeeding generations much better off, during his reign the common man in England suffered a significant deterioration in his standard of living, largely because there was no conservative force.

Although democratic liturgy would have it otherwise, most people are at heart conservative and fear change in the legal or social structure that threaten the existing familiar and comfortable patterns of life. Obviously, everybody wants change that is in the "public interest," but people cannot agree on what the public interest is. Usually, the public interest is change for the other guy.

Tax reform is a case in point. Under "tax reform," someone else pays the taxes. Whenever one's own taxes go up, the words *rapacious*, *avaricious*, *squander*, *waste*, *needless*, and *unfair* leap instantly to mind— not the word *reform*.

I have a friend who owns a number of apartment complexes. They were built on the assumption that inflation would continue at the same average rate in the approaching ten years as it had over the past ten. Eventually he would make a profit on his investment, although he expected to lose money for the first three years because of vacancies and low rents. However, with annual rent increases of 6 percent, in only three years the complexes have become very good investments indeed. My friend calls this his yearly program of "rent reform." Reform is in the eye of the reformer, and whether something is or is not reform is largely dependent on whose ox is being gored.

When the words *reform* or *public-interest law* are used in a political context they usually connote some scheme that will redistribute the wealth from private hands to a public authority, either for further transfer payments (such as welfare) to a class of persons who appear to be in need or to construct public works for general enjoyment. However, trying to support the public interest is very much like trying to referee a hockey game in the public interest.

In a hockey game, what is the interest of the players? Probably it is the highest possible pay consistent with the lowest number of injuries to themselves. The players want the game played with the lowest risk to their continued ability to play. The fans, however, want blood! Nothing brings out the fans like the prospect of a major brawl on the rink. The dirtier the game, the more enjoyable it is for the average spectator. The club owners, on the other hand, want maximum revenue from a big gate and a minimum amount of property damage. While a little blood on the ice keeps the gate up, they do not want any free-for-all that might involve the spectators with all the attendant property damage, loss of concession revenues, and liability to lawsuits. There is no public interest for a hockey game, only a set of conflicting private interests (or class interests, if you will) that must be reconciled in a fashion that makes the game profitable for all concerned.

Since the maintenance of the status quo is, on balance, the most generally acceptable result that a legislature can yield, the entire machinery is designed to that end. First, it is necessary for any bill to be passed by both houses *in exactly the same form*. That constitutional requirement is hardly a device tending toward the rapid passage of progressive legislation. In England during the civil war of the 1640s there was a point at which the House of Commons took over all legislative functions, and its performance was so venal in terms of the passage of special-interest legislation that the House of Lords was gleefully restored to its former prominence at Charles II's accession. Even today in the face of its militantly egalitarian political philosophy, England retains a House of Lords with delaying powers so that there can be an appeal, as it were, from the people drunk to the people sober. After World War II Norway established a unicameral parliament, but the results were so perverse that the lower house voluntarily divided itself into two chambers and by internal rule required bills to be approved independently by both units before becoming law.

Although the abjectly venal and self-serving nature of central government has changed since the early parliaments, many other things have not changed at all. Of these, the most important is that when powerful interests come to the government seeking a change in the law, their intentions are almost always predatory. The difference between general-interest legislation and special-interest legislation is frequently very narrow indeed; most of the time, however, the bills that appear to be in the general interest are urged by individuals or institutions that have a special interest in their passage.[1] For example, most bills designed to further education are sponsored by teachers and administrators, not by parents and children. Improved education is obviously in the public interest, yet it is even more in the private interest of educators. Better education implies higher teacher salaries, smaller classes, better working conditions, larger travel budgets, and greater personal prestige for educators. The same observation about the enhancement of public-employee status can be made with regard to court reform proposals, particularly the ones predicated on bigger and better versions of what we already have.

When, as a young man, I went to the state legislature as a freshman

1. I can think of only one example of wholly general-interest legislation— the recent legislation in the states permitting a right turn on a red light: it had a negligible effect on the number of minor traffic accidents and thus made nobody worse off than he was; it cost no money to implement and contributed substantially to a more expeditious flow of traffic.

member, I was utterly confounded by the amount of time devoted to sorting out special-interest legislation versus the time devoted to general-interest legislation. The reason, of course, is obvious: special-interest constituencies are organized and can deliver publicity, votes, and campaign contributions. The most powerful lobby in West Virginia, for example, is the teachers' professional association. In any legislative session the most intensely considered piece of legislation is the package that includes the annual salary increase for teachers. Furthermore, this package frequently becomes the center around which other trades and bargains are struck, because in many areas the teachers can make or break a state legislator's career.

When teachers get a raise, that percentage increase sets a pattern for all other state employees and ultimately involves either increasing taxes or diverting money from other programs—usually ones like prisons, hospitals, and aid to the mentally retarded, where there is no militant constituency. Yet raises for teachers are not entirely special interest; it is a valid argument that higher salaries attract better personnel, which ultimately benefits public education as opposed to public educators. Most special-interest legislation has some at least arguable general-interest component. In 1981 when the Reagan administration reduced the maximum tax bracket for unearned income from 70 percent to 50 percent, the rationale was that lower taxes would stimulate the economy by encouraging those with money to make more speculative investments. How much of this package was general interest and how much was special interest? Many competent economists who had been in the liberal Democratic camp for years were sufficiently uncertain about the stimulative effect of supply-side economics to be willing to accept the Reagan plan as a good-faith experiment. Yet the general-interest effect of this change was entirely speculative, while the special-interest effect on the income of the upper class was remarkably concrete.

In the business of legislating, Congress has a substantial advantage over the state legislatures. The issues of local concern that Congress deals with usually permit an individual member to come out strongly for the folks back home. It is seldom indeed that a congressman represents local interests that are hostile to one another at the national level (although it happens frequently to senators). Congressmen come from either a farm district or from an industrial district; they come from either the Northeast, which is interested in continued social services, or from the Southwest, which hardly gives a damn about social services. At the national level a congressman can support a subsidized Amtrak line in his district without ever being brought up short by a taxpayers' lobby since there is no direct relationship between federal taxes and local train service.

The luxury of having a unity of interest among one's constituency rarely graces the life of a state legislator, however. There is a direct observable correlation between voting higher teachers' salaries and higher taxes, and one cannot vote for an environmental measure without incurring the ire of local industry's employees. The reason that legislatures tend to do nothing is that they faithfully reflect what a majority of their constituents really want: to be left in peace. The crucial point in understanding a legislature is that for every worthwhile bill introduced, there are ten predatory bills that would cause large groups in society either great expense or needless agony in return for very few benefits to society as a whole.

Badly functioning courts are a serious problem, but courts are only one of hundreds of problems a legislature must meet. The reason that Congress and the state legislatures do not attempt court reform is that the entire machinery of a legislative body is set up to be negative. The purpose of setting up this type of machinery is to ensure that only those bills that have broad-based political support, either by themselves or as part of an overall package, will be passed. It is not possible to evaluate the legislative branch's performance in the field of court reform without an understanding of the mechanics of the legislative process.

When I went to the legislature I was confounded by my total lack of power or influence. Not only was a new member a cipher in terms of getting anything positive accomplished, but the senior members rather enjoyed making life difficult for new members as a rite of passage. I discovered that I was nothing other than a high-class lobbyist and that my ability to deliver both legislation and appropriations depended entirely on the goodwill of the speaker, committee chairmen, and the select membership of the rules committee. Out of a hundred-member House of Delegates (the legislature's lower house), there were roughly eight people who controlled the committee chairmanships and the rules committee. With those jobs went unfettered control of the legislature's agenda and thus the passage of legislation.

The Congress or a state legislature contains all types of people. Some are smart and others stupid; some are well trained and others ignorant; some have had years of experience in legislating while others are serving their first few months; and finally, some are honorable and others are corrupt. The result of this mixture is that a legislative chamber must have some organization—leadership, as it were—to provide an orderly process that weights control of the machinery heavily in favor of the smart, experienced, and honest members. But that very system of organization imparts enormous power and influence to a very small number of members, all of whom have at least some parochial interests. No legislator is above using his power of leadership in the institution to further either the ends of his constituents or those of interest groups to which he is attracted either by philosophy or political alliance.

The power of the leadership of any given legislative chamber is exercised in a number of ways. The first, and most obvious, is control of the agenda. If members fail to go along with the leadership on leadership-sponsored legislation, the members' own bills will never emerge from committee. But there is a far more sinister side to leadership control—the allocation of office space, travel expenses, committee assignments, and countless other perquisites of office. Often, in fact, the leadership has access to sources of campaign funding that can mean the difference to some members between reelection and unemployment.

Since any small leadership group will ultimately trade for its own account, some system must be devised to prevent untoward control of a legislature by one political clique. The answer, obviously, is another chamber with its entirely different leadership. While the leadership of the lower house may have life-and-death power over the personal and political lives of ordinary members of the lower house, that leadership has absolutely no power over a member of the senate. And vice versa.

The power the leadership possesses is always voluntarily delegated to them for reasons that extend beyond the efficient organization of the legislature. Certainly, the organization does not *have* to be as it is; the

70

membership can at any point change the internal organization. The first vote I made in the house finance committee was to permit the chairman to organize the agenda. I did not know at the time all that entailed; however, I had been taught that to get along one must go along, so I just voted with the leadership, only to learn later that arguably I had voted away my own power. Yet people far more experienced than I consistently voted for this form of organization, so it was entirely deliberate. Its intention was to remove the control of controversial legislation from the hands of the members so that they would not need to take political responsibility for killing politically sensitive, but predatory, bills.

As I came to receive my real-life postgraduate course in government, I discovered that all legislative procedures are designed to permit the silent death of predatory legislation without anyone's being on record as opposing it. Thus a member can introduce a truly rapacious bill confident either that the speaker will assign it to a committee that meets infrequently and will never get around to considering it, or that the chairman of an important and diligent committee will never place the bill on the agenda, or that the rules committee will never allow the bill to come to the floor for a vote.

When predatory legislation has such well-organized support that total inactivity will cause outrage in the wrong places, more sophisticated techniques can be resorted to. Most legislative bodies are up against a time deadline. In West Virginia any legislation that has not been acted upon during any year's sixty-day session must be reintroduced at the next session. In Congress the deadline is every two years, when a new Congress is elected. One superb technique for limiting the amount of legislation passed is to devote most of the time allotted to legislation to the holding of exhaustive hearings so that the final work on most bills must all be compressed into a few weeks or a few days at the end of a session. A great deal of legislation can be put on the agenda for consideration by the entire membership with perfect confidence that the clock will run out before anyone has a chance to vote. When both houses are up against significant constituent pressure to pass certain legislation, they can each pass a different version of the bill and then let the clock run out while the conference committees of each house deadlock banging out a compromise. Every member can go back to his or her home district with a record of having voted for the pet legislation of powerful predators without ever having the legislation pass.

THE intentionally conservative organization of a legislature aids and abets the mediocre performance of the courts because court-reform legislation seldom if ever emerges from the Byzantine committee system for a floor vote. Crucial in this regard is the recognition that most court reform that is urged upon any given legislative body is itself predatory. The people who bring ideas for court reform to the legislature are usually uninterested in result-neutral changes. They are not reformers in the ideal sense; they are seeking a change in the way courts operate that will directly benefit themselves. The archetypal group in this regard is members of the trial bar, both on the plaintiffs' side and the defendant insurance companies' side. Since most personal-injury cases are taken by lawyers on the basis of a contingent fee, it makes a great deal of difference to the lawyers representing plaintiffs how the procedure of the courts is structured. Unless plaintiffs' lawyers win cases, they do not get paid.

In 1974 there was some interest in West Virginia in improving the settlements of claims in automobile accident cases. Personal injuries and property damage arising from automobile accidents are the most common tort claims in any court system, yet the legal system does not handle the majority of these claims particularly well. First, if there is property damage alone, retaining a lawyer and going to court will never recoup the total damage because the lawyer will take at least one-third of the award. Even if there are personal injuries, the subjective elements of damage—pain and suffering—are sufficiently open-ended that the award can be padded to pay the lawyer, but with all the legal technicalities involved in a major tort case, recovering at all is a chancy business.

The insurance companies were perfectly happy with the existing system for disposing of property damage since the costs of litigation and general delay almost guaranteed that claimants would settle for fifty cents on the dollar. Insurance companies were dissatisfied, however, with the jury-trial system in personal-injury cases because once the claimant overcame the legal technicalities and got to a jury, the awards were often enormous—a fact that the insurance companies had to consider in arriving at their own settlement offers.

The result of general consumer dissatisfaction was the introduction of a bill to establish no-fault automobile insurance, where in most cases it would be unnecessary for one party to prove another's negligence in order to recover. In fact, as in the workmen's compensation system, even the person primarily at fault could recover for his own property loss and injuries. The insurance companies were happy about the opportunity no-fault presented to reduce their personal-injury awards, but they were most unhappy about having to pay the real cost of property damage. The consumers' lobby was pleased with taking property damage out of litigation but wanted only the simplest personal injuries (those involving damages of under twenty-five thousand dollars) under no-fault. The trial lawyers, needless to say, wanted none of it because accident cases are the bread and butter of general practice.

In the end the trial lawyers won, but the way they did it was to turn the greed of the insurance companies against the whole scheme. In the legislative committee process the trial bar permitted the insurance lobby to amend the bill to the point where only major personal injuries were under no-fault while property damage and minor injuries were left to the full-blown litigation process. When the unions (AFL/CIO and Mineworkers) heard that the bill was coming out of committee in that form on the last night of the session, they rallied their troops and killed the whole bill on the floor with the bill's own initial supporters.

Many of these players in the no-fault game were still actively engaged outside of the legislature as trial lawyers, employees or agents of the insurance industry, or officers of organized labor. A state legislature is a very different animal from the federal Congress. United States senators and congressmen are full-time, professional legislators. State legislators, except in the most populous states, are part-time legislators who are still actively working somewhere else. Many state legislatures do not even provide a salary adequate to compensate legislators at the rate of minimum wage for their time and expense throughout the year. Most of the people in state legislatures are there for the purpose of furthering their own interests; they come as advocates for extreme positions and not as umpires.

More to the point, however, the people who send members to the legislature are not thinking about the public good but, rather, exclusively about their private good. Furthermore, notwithstanding our society's commitment to one man, one vote, everyone is not equal in the political process. A political campaign, like an army, runs on its stomach; the first ingredient of successful politics is money. Since money is not evenly distributed in society, it follows with elegant mathematical certainty that political power is not evenly distributed either. Money is used to buy television, radio, newspaper, and direct-mail advertising, and it's also used to make sure that all voters favorably disposed to a particular candidate get to the polls. This latter function is the *raison d'être* of a political machine, and political machines are oiled with money and jobs. Very few legislators have sufficient personal wealth to support a seriously contested election campaign without outside contributions.

In most places the decisive effect of money is compounded by low voter turnouts. In states, counties, or cities that have a predominant party that has been in power for decades, office is usually not won in a general election but in a primary. Typically, about 21 percent of the vote turns out for an off-year primary election, which heavily weights political power in favor of: (1) the organized vote; (2) the party faithful who are hired to be poll clerks; and (3) the bought vote. This last group may not be bought as crassly today as they once were, but one still hires heads of families to work the polls and to transport voters. It is implicit in this arrangement that the hired poll worker or driver will bring family and friends who will accommodate him or her by voting the machine slate. There is little of this in middle-class precincts, but in low socioeconomic precincts politics is personal, not ideological. Where hotly contested elections are decided by margins of 48 to 52 percent, the opposition of any significant part of the three groups will spell disaster. Consequently, most incumbent legislators devote a disproportionate amount of their time, effort, and political credit to satisfying those people who routinely make political contributions and those interest groups that can deliver the organized vote.

All interest groups have a legislative agenda as long as your arm of things that would help them; however, they are usually willing to settle for killing the legislative agendas of others who would hurt them. Since

74

a legislature is a consciously designed inertia machine, the commodity that any legislator has to trade in superabundance is inertia—the prevention of passage of hurtful legislation in return for active political support.

This strategy for winning support cannot always be implemented on high-visibility issues like rent control, unionization of public employees, or subsidies for public transportation. However, high-visibility issues comprise an infinitesimal portion of any session's legislative agenda, so legislators make their money on the low-visibility issues. In general there is no issue of lower visibility than court reform; not only are an overwhelming majority of nonlawyer legislators ignorant of the working of the courts, the citizenry in general is even more ignorant.

There is no active lobby *for* court reform, only lobbies *against* it. There are a number of respectable national organizations that work for court reform. These include the Institute of Judicial Administration, the National Center for State Courts, the American Judicature Society, the Federal Judicial Center, the Institute for Court Management, the National Judicial College, and many bar associations. However, they are not a lobby in the sense that they raise money, publicize their position, solicit organized support from individuals outside the judicial system, or otherwise behave like a well-funded, militant interest group. If all the lawyers at the trial bar, both those on the side of plaintiffs and those on the side of insurance companies, perceived the no-fault bill as a threat to their economic well-being, what advantage would there be to a legislator in making them angry? There was no organized lobby for no-fault, although the labor unions and consumer groups may have included the proposal in their general-interest legislative package. The unions certainly did not feel strongly enough about the subject to make it a condition of future political support of a legislator when there were other issues like workmen's compensation awards or unionization of public employees at hand.

In every county or city the lawyers are usually the mainstay of the political organizations. Since their occupation involves doing business with the government all the time, they are involved in politics professionally because they must have the goodwill of officeholders in order to get things done. They both contribute money and actively participate in party organization. When politically active lawyers indicate to their legislators that no-fault insurance or any other bill is a direct threat to them, they can count on a perfect do-nothing result.

The defeat of West Virginia's no-fault proposal was due to the orchestration of the committee process in such a way that the bill that ultimately reached the floor was so unacceptable to the bill's initial sponsors that they themselves ordered its murder. Everyone could be against the bill without incurring any political reprisal whatsoever.

While lawyers can get through to legislators on an individual basis to encourage opposition to a proposed reform, they usually lack the power to initiate any positive action. Although many people have trust in their own lawyer, lawyers as a class are largely distrusted and despised by both the citizenry and their elected, nonlawyer representatives. Everyone is aware that the legal profession represents a significant vested interest, and there is eternal vigilance in the legislature to limit the influence of lawyers, who are perceived as having a monopoly of the drafting, enforcement, and interpretation of all legislation.[2]

When I was a member of the legislature, the surest way to defeat a bill was to tag it as a "lawyers' bill"; if that sobriquet could be made to stick in debate, the majority in the house who were not lawyers and resented them would defeat the bill almost as a religious rite. This is

2. As a result of things I have written, I have received letters from people all over America with proposals for improving the workings of government. Concerned citizens are always looking for a sympathetic public official. Among twenty-five or so recent letters were included three proposals to limit the power of lawyers in government. One elderly writer from Florida proposed that no more than 50 percent of the national Congress be permitted to be lawyers. I wrote back that far fewer than 50 percent of congressmen were lawyers and that it had always been thus. What was important in his letter was not reality but the public's perception of reality. In general the most competent members of any state legislature are lawyers, and it is their competence that gives them rapid promotion in the internal power structure of a legislature. The problem is that lawyers, like doctors, appear to have disproportionate power over people's lives; and their power emanates from a monopoly of inaccessible information that often, as in the field of criminal law, appears to yield incompetent results. Alchemy, after all, was an inaccessible science that yielded such incompetent results that its practitioners went out of business. Many feel that the same fate should be reserved for lawyers.

why bills designed to increase the logistical support for the courts in terms of clerks, process servers, courtrooms, and even numbers of judges have been so universally unsuccessful.

Federal and state judges and administrators lobby for court reform, but they have no political power to back up their demands. Demands attract positive legislative attention when those doing the demanding can deliver money or votes. Schoolteachers have both, so an enormous proportion of legislative time is devoted to schools. Labor unions have both, so a high proportion of time is devoted to workmen's compensation and related subjects. Gamblers have both, so disproportionate time is devoted to dog racing, horse racing, off-track betting, and the legalization of other gambling. The court bureaucracy, bar associations (as opposed to individual lawyers), and consumer groups have neither money nor votes, so they are almost powerless.

Anyone can introduce a bill into the legislature. Yet passing a bill requires that some sizable group of legislators trade everything they have—goodwill, power over other members' bills, power over internal perquisites like congressional junkets or preferred office space—to get the bill to move. Legislators make trades of this order only when there are attendant concrete political rewards. In court reform there are no political rewards, concrete or otherwise.

Social issues like the quality of courts or the overall efficiency of law enforcement have a diffused, ill-informed general constituency. Economic issues, on the other hand, have a militant, organized, well-informed constituency. The social issue of the courts is difficult to understand—there is no consensus about how to improve law enforcement, and there is a reluctance to make the trades in the area of civil liberties, increased taxes, and government intrusion into everyday life that better law enforcement appears to imply. But with economic issues the questions are simple: teachers get raises or they don't; workmen's compensation awards go up or they don't; the capital-gains tax is decreased or it isn't; defense contractors get a big infusion of government money or they don't.

The reason, then, that social issues receive such scant attention is that the most important force in politics is indifference—if every person eligible to vote voted in every primary and general election for every office, the structure of government might be very different. While it is easy to condemn legislators for their indifference to social issues, they are at least in part forced into inactivity by the lack of effective allies who could mitigate the political penalties that activism in any area of concern naturally generates.

The political rules that apply to incumbents are different from the rules that apply to challengers. Incumbents predicate their political strategy on the strength of indifference because indifference is the reality with which they must deal on a daily basis. The incumbent, unlike the challenger, cannot be concerned with enlisting the passionate support of those involved with social issues; his primary concern must be with avoiding the animosity of any well-organized interests—interests that are primarily concerned with economic issues.

The power of incumbency is awesome. There is an old rule in politics that "you can't beat something with nothing." Every challenger has the uphill battle of establishing a recognizable identity. It takes money to convert a private citizen or a low-level officeholder into a viable candidate. A person must hire a press staff, must purchase television commercials, billboards, and newspaper advertisements; and must support an expensive direct-mail campaign. All of this is done automatically for the incumbent. Anytime an incumbent drops by a local radio or television station he will be interviewed. While an incumbent is not allowed to print or mail campaign literature at government expense, he may send a host of newsletters, information questionnaires, and personal correspondence free to constituents. In the state legislatures the districts are much smaller and the number of people who are known locally is larger, but even there the power of incumbency works its wonders.

Incumbents are interested in responding to their constituents primarily in two ways. First, they seek every opportunity to do personal favors. Getting a family's son into West Point places that family in the incumbent's camp forever. Attending funerals, extending the hospitality of the capitol to schoolchildren, and influencing employers to hire or retain certain workers all have similar positive benefits. At the local level, and this includes congressional districts, it must be emphasized again that politics is intensely personal and not issue-oriented. Personal accommodations require little effort, usually require the trading of no personal credit with other legislators, and embroil the legislator in no conflict where he is liable to incur hostility from other voters.

The other way the incumbent satisfies his constituents involves economic issues brought by organized groups. While here it is not always possible to support a particular supplication, it is critical not to appear hostile to the demand. The glorious organization of a legislative body is such that a person can actually sponsor a bill he is against with the absolute assurance that others will kill the bill, leaving him the credit for having been for it. He still has a clear conscience since the bill did not pass, and in the strange world of political morality that is a consummately ethical position.

Antagonizing organized groups can seriously disturb the element of indifference and dramatically counterbalance the force of incumbency. If, for example, the AFL/CIO decides to sponsor an unknown candidate to beat an incumbent, the incumbent is in big trouble. While ultimately the incumbent may win, as is still the likely case, the campaign will cost more money and effort than otherwise would have been required. Politicians hate to campaign not only because campaigning is arduous work, but also because a hotly contested campaign requires pleas for help that produce debts and obligations it is more convenient not to have.

The careful stroking of organized groups does something else of critical importance—it provides a quick and sure source of ready cash for a political campaign. Challengers who do not have the support of organized groups must either spend their own money or raise it in nickels and dimes from among hundreds of individual donors. Where individual donors must be relied on, the cost of raising money frequently comes close to the amount raised. The incumbent does business every day with lobbyists whose *quid* for the *quo* of cooperation from legislators is to put together clean, reportable political contributions. One or two such creatures can provide the financing for a state legislative race, and four or five can do the trick quite handily for a congressional race.

In any stable of interest groups an individual legislator must please, there are two types of horses: those whom he must not actively antagonize and who can be induced to support or at least be neutral about his candidacy, and those who actively help his election either by delivering voters or by delivering money that can be used to deliver voters.

In the service of the second group, the average legislator uses up all of his personal credit, political credit, and most of his creative energy and time. The intellectual, emotional, and physical demands on the average legislator are difficult to support. Correspondence must be answered, constituents must be entertained, committee meetings must be attended, staff must be organized and consulted so that other members' bills will be understood, speeches and other appearances must be made at home, and finally floor votes must be cast. It is not possible to initiate programs; the most we can expect is for legislators to react to programs.

In all the areas of economic confrontation, paid lobbyists on all sides bang out the compromises and refine legislation long before a legislator is required to take a position on it. The development of comprehensive, politically acceptable legislative packages requires scores of man-years of work, and no single legislator or even group of legislators has resources like that at their disposal. It is the business of paid lobbyists to bring to legislators proposed packages of legislation from which to work. While a proposed package will be amended, compromised, and possibly entirely restructured, the lobbyist's proposal is still the starting place.

When my court proposes changes to the legislature, we have a completed, polished bill already drafted and ready for introduction by members of each house. The same is true of every other organized interest group that is aggressively seeking positive legislative action. Not only do lobbyists draft bills and provide legislative packages, they follow the progress of the legislation as well, organizing support, informing supporters of impending obstacles, and structuring trades that will perhaps assure some compromised but on balance favorable action.

So-called court-reform bills are introduced all the time; however, as I have pointed out, they are not usually neutral "reform" bills but are rather efforts by one interest group or another to achieve a more favorable result in the courts. These bills, of course, create an equal but opposite reaction from interests that would be affected adversely, so they die a slow death at the hands of the legislative process. The bills introduced by the courts themselves make a more genuine effort at neutrality; yet, as I have pointed out, a well functioning court system is itself a disadvantage to numerous interest groups.[3] The courts don't have any votes or money to back their lobbying efforts, while those adversely affected by reform have at least one and often both.

Every time a change is made in the existing structure of the courts, some interest group suffers. Of course, some interest groups are strong and well organized while others are weak and disorganized. But the lawyers who represent these people *are* organized and will oppose any change in the court structure that makes it more difficult for them to represent their clients. This is the reason that a Justice Department-sponsored, revised federal criminal code failed to be adopted by the Congress in the late 1970s. After all, in the final analysis lawyers get paid for results. Notwithstanding the approach of the fashionable law schools, law is not an epistemological science. The truly experienced lawyer knows that a lot of very important law for specific clients is actually practiced in legislative halls and is entirely preventive in nature.

All of the political rewards are on the side of those legislators who oppose court reform, and none are on the side of those who favor it. No legislator will publicly oppose court reform, and, in fact, most make

3. It may appear silly to the average reader that the courts have bills introduced. Every state court system has some centralized administrative authority, even if it is only the state's highest court itself. In the federal system the Department of Justice has an entire bureau devoted to administering the federal judiciary, and while this bureau has no power to interfere with judicial decisions, it is responsible for deciding which cities will have federal courts, the level of funding for each court, numbers of personnel, and types of equipment. The Department of Justice also provides training for federal judicial employees and accomplishes other housekeeping functions. In many states the highest court has an administrative office that has even more power than the Justice Department has in the federal system. The state administrator assigns judges, authorizes travel, determines all logistical support, prepares the judicial budget, and undertakes myriad projects for improving the efficiency of the courts. It is through either the Justice Department or the state courts' administrative offices that the courts sponsor legislation as an organized, collective intelligence. In addition, of course, local judicial associations may concoct bills and urge their adoption; but these are usually concerned with improving pay, perquisites, working conditions, or systems of judge selection—basically private-interest bills.

law-and-order speeches that decry the courts' congested dockets and cumbersome procedures. Yet nothing ever gets done because those who oppose court reform want results and not rhetoric. Proponents of court reform (who are usually unsophisticated ordinary citizens) are placated if legislators introduce bills and publicly declaim against the courts; opponents are satisfied if the court-reform bills never pass. The opponents are sufficiently knowledgeable and cynical to maintain a low profile; they never let the world know where the opposition is coming from—like the Vietcong during our most recent war in Asia.

ENVIRONMENTAL and conservation issues used to be in the same position as court reform. Then in the early 1960s the whole question of pollution control and conservation of wilderness lands captured the imagination of the college-educated middle class. Suddenly, defense of the environment took on the aura of a religious crusade. Groups such as the Sierra Club and Common Cause organized on the national level, and in every state local groups developed and kept in communication with one another. By the 1972 election the environmentalists had resolved themselves into a substantial, active, single-issue constituency whose power rivaled that of major industry. Major industry could deliver money with which to buy votes, but the environmentalists delivered votes directly. They were particularly able to deliver votes *against* a candidate through their newsletters and public statements. As a result, environmental-protection legislation actually began to pass in Congress and the state legislatures, causing a dramatic improvement in the quality of American life.

One advantage ecology had over court reform was that it inspired passionate adherents. When I was in college in 1964 there were students whose primary interest was saving the environment. Many of those students went on to law school and then ran for office on an environmental platform. Their courtship of the ecology lobby had nothing cynical about it—they were part and parcel of the ecology lobby. The result was that by the middle 1970s a lot of people in public office were personally concerned with environmental issues. These officeholders were not at the mercy of lobbyists for information and ideas; they had their own expertise and their own ideas. The same is not true of court reform. There are no undergraduates out there today thinking about court reform as their life's work, and all law students understand that there is no money to be made worrying about the judicial system as a whole. The money is to be made making the judicial system work for their particular group of clients.

Occasionally the beginnings of a citizen lobby for better courts, or at least for better total law enforcement, can be perceived. In West Virginia in 1981 the relatives of persons killed by drunk drivers organized themselves to make the drunk driving penalties more severe. In general the enforcement of the drunk driving laws in the United States is a disgrace. The reason, probably, is that those who enforce these laws routinely drive while drunk themselves. Most judges and prosecutors I know are not beyond driving themselves home from a party having had one too many, and I suppose the same can be said for most members of local juries. A drunk driver with a skilled and energetic lawyer can usually manipulate the process in such a way that he avoids suspension of his license, although he usually gets stuck with a stiff fine and a large lawyer's fee.

The public outcry against drunk drivers was so loud that the West Virginia Legislature amended the law and made drunk driving a serious offense with a no-nonsense procedure for enforcement. Preeminently, the new statute takes the license suspension out of the hands of the courts and makes it an administrative determination by the commissioner of motor vehicles, thus avoiding the opportunities that the judicial system presents to frustrate that sanction. As later chapters discuss, the judicial system is engineered to provide a fair resolution of major controversies, and the procedures that have been designed are both expensive and time consuming. When the same procedures that are required to sentence a person to death or life imprisonment are required to suspend a person's driver's license or to exact a one-dollar parking fine, the judicial wiring gets overloaded and the machine shorts out.

Drunk driving is a serious problem; it is the cause of about half of all automobile traffic fatalities. Strict enforcement of drunk driving laws significantly reduces traffic fatalities; and, if the current court system cannot administer these sanctions efficiently, then alternatives must be found, since the alternatives are at least as fair as the current court system. West Virginia's decision to crack down on drunk driving was not unique; several other states amended their laws in 1981 with spectacular results.

Drunk driving differs from other criminal questions in that it is a comparatively easily understood problem and there is no active lobby defending drunk drivers. Even lawyers who represent drunk drivers are torn emotionally on the subject since they are also the parents of teenage children and users of the highways themselves. More important in the passage of the drunk driving laws, perhaps, was the lack of debate about how to reduce drunk driving. Everyone agreed that strict sanctions quickly applied would do the trick with the occasional drunk and that permanent revocation of a license would keep most of the habitual drunks off the road.

Because of the consensus about what would make the highways safer, the drunk driving laws have more in common with environmental issues than with court reform. I point to the revolution in environmental control as a hopeful example of what citizens can do in the legislative process, even in the face of well-financed, organized opposition. Environmental reform proves that the democratic process *can* work quite well. But the environmentalists had an advantage over court reformers: they knew exactly what they wanted—clean air, clean water, and preservation of wilderness areas. Furthermore, they also knew who the enemy was: industry that was belching smoke into the sky, dumping effluents into the streams, cutting trees, stripmining, drilling for oil, and constructing pipelines. Finally, the solution to the problem was comparatively simple—stop doing all these things. Court reformers, on the other hand, cannot agree on what they want, cannot agree on the enemy, and cannot agree on a solution (which in any case is far from simple).

The raging debate over the environmental laws concerned the timing of new pollution standards. Environmental controls cost money and frequently bankrupted old firms that had no money with which to comply with the new rules and no market for a more costly product. The trade-off was between jobs and a clean environment. Yet the level of background noise in the environmental debate was comparatively low. In the court-reform debate, on the other hand, almost all that can be heard is background noise. Civil-liberties advocates perceive the police as a greater menace than the criminals. The victims of crime have relatives who are criminals themselves. The advocates of a social welfare model of rehabilitation for criminals are at odds with those who believe in punishment. At least in the environmental revolution everyone, including the officers and employees of the largest polluters, agreed that pollution was bad and paid lip service to the goal of eliminating pollution.

When we look hopefully to the environmental movement, we must keep in mind that the elimination of pollution is a scientific question that can be answered by experts in chemistry and physics. We have always been more successful in solving scientific problems than in solving human ones. We could build an atomic bomb in four years, put a man on the moon in ten, but we could not fight a successful war on poverty. As the rest of this book indicates, the engineering in court reform is very complicated, and there are not nearly as many experts as there are in chemistry and physics. One factor militating in favor of pervasive conservatism in court reform is the plethora of proposals that would lead to a far less livable system than the one we currently enjoy. In this regard the authoritarian suggestions of the law-and-order lobby leap instantly to mind—the position of the television cop programs that although a person may beat the rap, he'll never beat the ride (in the police car).

When we get into more complicated areas of civil-court reform, such as how to handle petty controversies in small-claims courts, the potential for citizen activism becomes even more limited. Someone who knows something about courts must design a program before anything else can be done. Consequently, an activist citizen group must first decide that they want to do something about poorly functioning courts, then they must hire someone to design a program, and finally they must get behind the program. Again the difficulty is that people need to be careful whom they enlist to do the design, because in most areas of court reform there are far more wrong answers than there are right ones. The people who know the most about the design of courts are frequently not lawyers; they are systems analysts and administrators.

The reform of the civil law is an area where I have a low expectation for citizen activism, at least initially. The reform of criminal law, however, may be becoming ripe for the same type of crusade that the

85

environmentalists used. In both instances the amount of pollution has risen to a level that intrudes itself into the everyday lives of average, middle-class citizens.[4] In this regard it is important to differentiate between traditional law-and-order rhetoric and real criminal-law reform. Traditional law-and-order rhetoric addresses itself primarily to the decisions of the United States Supreme Court since *Miranda v. Arizona* in 1966, when the Supreme Court began the wholesale reform of the criminal law in order to further civil rights and civil liberties. A return to police brutality, official harassment of the lower socioeconomic class, and kangaroo-court summary convictions by forced guilty pleas is not my idea of criminal law reform. It is possible to have a perfectly well functioning system of criminal law enforcement without the violations of personal integrity inherent in the police state. But it would be expensive.

In urban areas, at least, where police go up, crime goes down. Where there are enough well-trained prosecutors and enough judges to conduct jury trials, convictions go up. Where prisons are well managed and not overcrowded, judges sentence people to jail. Where there are juvenile shelters and other social services for children and teenagers, the success rate of intervention at the first sign of trouble goes up. Where state hospitals for the criminally insane are not so overcrowded and understaffed that medical personnel seek any excuse to release dangerous sociopaths, most of the dangerous sociopaths can be kept under control. Finally it is necessary to recognize that an attack on the root causes of crime is not just a softheaded liberal cop-out.

4. I make a special point in remarking that the problem of street crime must touch the lives of the middle class before something meaningful is done. A conservative is a liberal who just got mugged. Most street crime is perpetrated upon the poor because they live where the criminals are. But as the energy shortage and other considerations, such as the rising cost of detached housing, draw more middle-class people back into urban areas, crime will touch their lives more forcefully. It is the middle class that has organizational and political skills, along with a spare hundred bucks to contribute to a political action group. It was essentially the middle class that accomplished the environmental revolution, partially because they were articulate.

A child who is born to a welfare mother on drugs in a household where a succession of boyfriends amuse themselves with child abuse hardly has a chance to avoid the criminal justice system. The young people who kill for kicks have usually been victims themselves for fifteen years before they become victimizers. That fact does not make them less dangerous, but this is not a world of total free will and personal moral responsibility. While middle-class children do indeed shoplift for kicks, most serious crime is directly related to poverty and drugs. Drugs make life bearable for those without hope, and drugs are expensive.

When I am confronted by the children of our slums and rural backwaters, it is an understatement to say that I am overwhelmed by grief. The point is not to be lightly dismissed that the very social and economic system that makes so many of us well off makes others very badly off. Our free-enterprise economy achieves wonders in the allocation of productive resources but has problems with the distribution of wealth. Other economies have the opposite problem, and on balance I believe that our system is preferable in the long run. Children, however, do not make a free-will choice of either their parents or their environment. The fact that some people can overcome a succession of handicaps to achieve greatness—the *Twelve Against the Gods* act—does not mean that ordinary human beings can do the same. Present efforts to improve the working of the criminal-justice system usually become impaled on the debate about enforcement versus elimination of the root causes of crime. That is because most of the people who think seriously about criminal-justice reform are professionals who are reminded every day how ludicrous the free-will model of life is, at least at the extremes of society. Getting at the root causes of crime implies a reordering of society of a magnitude that few are willing to undertake, not the least of whom are those caught in society's trap. Improving the conditions of slum dwellers probably requires spreading the current slum welfare population out over the rest of the country where they can be more easily absorbed into mainstream American life.

Yet if there is a diaspora of slum dwellers, what jobs and social support systems will await them? [5] Considerations like these are just the beginning—drugs, single-parent families, children having children, and congenital abnormalities such as retardation all play their part as well. Even with the will to spend money, we must all wonder whether we have the knowledge to engineer a solution that will not be worse than the problem.

The advantage of a citizen lobby seriously concerned with improving the criminal-justice system is that citizens want protection—they are content if the symptoms of the disease can be controlled, and that is probably the practical approach for the foreseeable future. The fact that there is neither the scientific knowledge nor the political will to eliminate the root causes of crime should not be accepted, as it is in some liberal quarters, as an excuse for failing to attempt the more possible task of attacking the symptoms. Such an attack need not be brutal, nor will it ultimately satisfy society to such an extent that no further efforts will be made to provide employment, decent housing, and a better family life.

5. I cannot resist mentioning my chagrin that when the capital-gains tax was reduced in the Economic Recovery Act of 1981 no attention was paid to the opportunity that this presented for dispersing the truly deprived throughout America. Had the tax been reduced not to 20 percent but rather much lower, and tied to the hiring of the hard-core unemployed, spectacular results might have been achieved. Under such a system—with certain exceptions relating to very small enterprises—any individual, partner, or corporation would be permitted to avail himself or itself of the new capital-gains tax rate only if a certain low percentage of the labor force were Department of Labor certified hard-core unemployed. The Department of Labor would issue a numbered card good for five years and an enterprise would be required to hire numbers, not individuals. That way when people did not shape up, they could be fired and others hired. Most unskilled and untrained people must lose three or four jobs before they develop the industrial discipline to be productive. Under this system, companies located in places without hard-core unemployed would have workers recruited in the slums. Shareholders would have forced management to qualify; the lower tax would have stimulated even greater investment; the tax revenue lost would not have been substantial; and the free-enterprise job market would ultimately have worked its wonders on today's minorities in the same way that it worked wonders with the Irish and Italians of yesteryear who migrated when America was a labor-scarce economy. Probably the problems of urban slums can be cured only if their inhabitants voluntarily choose to move elsewhere and disperse themselves throughout heartland America.

A good criminal-justice system that substantially reduces violent and petty crime could be established with far less political activism than was required for environmental reform. Furthermore, the costs would be dramatically less, although they would *all* be borne directly by the taxpayers instead of being paid through the inflation of consumer prices, as was the case with most environmental reforms. Cleaning up the environment cost a lot of jobs, higher utility bills, and more expensive automobiles. Criminal-law reform will cost higher taxes.

It is not necessary that everyone suddenly become interested in court reform. After all, only a small number of voters were actively dedicated to the ecology revolution. Extremely effective interest groups, like the National Rifle Association that opposes gun control, have comparatively few active members. It must be remembered that politicians are not concerned with influencing everyone who is eligible to vote, just the 21 to 65 percent, depending on the election, who actually come to the polls to vote. It is the militant and not the indifferent voter who must be satisfied first. Where contested elections are typically won by narrow margins, the single-issue group portends ominous prospects to an incumbent who fails to take it seriously.

Once groups are organized around the emotional issue of criminal justice reform, I have high hopes that they may continue in business long enough to deal with the reform of the civil courts. In that event much will depend on the understanding and originality of the experts from whom they solicit advice about the engineering of the new structure. If the new structure is merely a bigger and better model of the old structure, they will have wasted their time.

Politics being what it is, little can be expected of Congress or the state legislatures in the way of court reform until the issue becomes one with concrete political rewards and punishments. The first step is for members of the long-suffering citizen majority to get up, go to their windows, open them up, and yell, "I'm as mad as hell, and I'm not going to take it any more!" Then you have to borrow a school or a firehall and invite some neighbors to talk about criminal justice, but with the added requirement that some member of the group have a sensitive understanding of the subject. That is how we abated industrial pollution, and that is the only way we will ever abate crime pollution.

Square Pegs 4
in Round Holes

IF a person steals a five-hundred-dollar wristwatch from a jewelry store, he is guilty of grand larceny. In most places the penalty for grand larceny is between one and five years in the penitentiary. But if the person who committed the crime is a fourteen-year-old adolescent stealing for excitement, we take a different view than if our felon is an experienced adult thief. If the watch stealer is an ordinary worker who has recently lost his job because of a plant shutdown, has run out of his unemployment insurance, and needs money immediately to pay his child's medical bills, we take a different view of the matter than if the same unemployed person stole the watch to pay a gambling debt. Yet regardless of the reasons for the larceny, in the eyes of the law the crime is exactly the same. There is an artificial legal category—those guilty of grand larceny—and we are required somehow to abstract real life into that preconceived category.

Since real life does not abstract very well into preconceived categories, we have devised formal and informal subcategories to accommodate the subtleties of real life. For example, if our thief is a fourteen-year-old, he is not prosecuted for grand larceny but for juvenile delinquency, and unless he is an habitual offender, he is not sent to jail or reform school but is put under the supervision of some social service agency like the juvenile probation department. The habitual thief is sent off to prison, and his term may be extended because of prior criminal offenses. The person who steals to pay his child's medical bills will probably never be prosecuted. The authorities will assure themselves that the man will not do it again and then let him go. Why waste state money sending him to jail or supervising him on probation when the crime was justified by desperation and will never recur? Furthermore, a conviction would impair the man's continued earning power and thus make future criminal activity more, rather than less, likely. Far better to warn him and let him off. The first-time offender who steals to pay a gambling debt so that his legs won't get broken will probably be allowed to plead guilty to misdemeanor shoplifting and be let off with a few months' unsupervised probation.

In these hypothetical cases I assume a well-functioning court system that has made its decision about how to handle each defendant exclusively on the merits of the case and not because the system lacks the staff or resources to prosecute. The point is frequently made as a tribute to our society that ours is a government of laws and not of men. Yet the decisions regarding how to handle each of the hypothetical defendants were exclusively "men" decisions. With the exception of the juvenile who must be handled under the juvenile laws, the disposition of each case was entirely within the discretion of the prosecuting attorney in the first instance and the judge later on. The prosecutor could choose to indict the unemployed parent with the sick child for grand larceny, and the judge could send him to prison. The judge and prosecutor could let the habitual felon plead to misdemeanor shoplifting and suspend his sentence. The judge could even send the child to reform school for eight or nine months.

This is not a government of laws as opposed to men. Rather, it is a government of men whose understanding is instructed by the statutes passed by the legislature, and the body of precedent—the record of previous legal decisions—that we call common law. The preeminent rule of jurisprudence is that no rule determines its own application; only a living human being can determine how a rule applies to a given set of facts. When, for example, the Bible instructs us that "Thou shalt not kill," what does the commandment mean? Does it mean that one cannot kill an active aggressor? Most established churches do not interpret it that way; the Catholic Church even permits abortion when a woman has been raped, on the theory that the child is an "aggressor." Yet the Quakers do not countenance violence even in the face of aggression. Can a person fight in a "just war"? Again, most organized Western religions permit killing in a just war. There are mystics in the Orient, on the other hand, who take the commandment beyond its original application to human life and refuse to move lest they unconsciously destroy another sentient creature, an ant or a beetle.

The rule about killing as such, therefore, gives us very little guidance; everything depends on the exact factual context in which the rule is to be applied and on the predisposition of the people who are determining its application. An adolescent facing the prospect of his own imminent demise in the jungles of Southeast Asia may be predisposed to apply the rule one way, while a comfortable, middle-aged businessman sitting on a draft board may be predisposed to apply it another way. The mystic who gives the rule an absolutist application does so as part of a coherent passive philosophy, which in turn is the product of a deep-seated pessimism about the efficacy of action in this life.[1] Such pessimism follows from thousands of years of tragic history in that part of the world.

King Solomon is held up as the paradigm of the just judge because when two women were fighting over a child, Solomon ordered the child to be cut in half in the justified expectation that the real mother would abandon her claim rather than see the child murdered. Solomon's advantage over modern judges was that he could make law up as he went along. He was not circumscribed by either statutes or precedent—everything was equity.[2] His only concern was what was fair to the parties and society under each specific circumstance. Such a system has obvious

1. I have one judicial colleague who takes an entirely absolutist position with regard to all rules with which he agrees while at the same time displaying an unabashed willingness to "interpret" out of existence all rules with which he does not agree. He is in good company: Justice Hugo Black also took absolutist positions on those propositions that appealed to him and Justice Felix Frankfurter continually complained about it.

2. Our system of civil jurisprudence breaks down into two broad categories—law and equity. Law, incorporating as it does all the legislative statutes and an enormous body of common law precedent, is comparatively easy to

drawbacks, not the least of which is its lack of predictability. Further-more, what happens when a Solomon is succeeded by his idiot son?

If we were to try to list the law's most important qualities we would probably arrive at some variation of the following: fair general rules, predictability, and protection from the idiot judge who is to apply the general rules. Unfortunately, all of these qualities are at odds with one another. The fairer the law is, or the greater the extent to which the court system can take into consideration all of the real-life problems of the litigants, the less predictable it becomes. When a bank holds a mortgage on a piece of property and the mortgage is not paid, the bank expects its money. If the court can take into consideration that the person who owes the money is a widow with three children and that she and her children will be put on the street, the bank knows that it is an unusual court that will not always find in favor of the widow and against the bank.

Yet if banks cannot rely on the law to enforce debts regardless of the pitiable condition of the debtor, then they will not lend money to those who are likely to become pitiable. Business requires that the law be predictable, and in order for the law to be predictable, all of life must be abstracted into preconceived legal categories. If a person, even a widow, borrows money, she must pay it back or lose her property— it makes no difference whether she is a Rockefeller or the destitute widow Brown. All of her individual life circumstances must be ignored in favor of the abstract legal category of "debtor."

In a similar vein, the more we attempt to protect society from the vagaries of the idiot judge, the less discretion there is for the imaginative, creative, and intelligent judge. A leading example of this problem exists

understand, but equity defies succinct analysis. While there are thousands of English and American definitions of equity in the reported cases, I think that the best is still Aristotle's:

> When the law speaks universally . . . and a case arises . . . which is not covered by the universal statement, then it is right, where the legislator fails us and has erred by oversimplicity, to correct the omission [and] say what the legislator himself would have said had he been present and would have [wanted to] put into his law had he known [the particular circumstances of its enforce-ment]. . . . This is the nature of the equitable, a correction of law where it is defective owing to its universality. (*Ethics* [McKeon, ed.])

93

in the juvenile courts. Trial-court judges frequently complain to me that the elaborate procedural hurdles, such as detention hearings, exhaustive exploration of all "least restrictive alternatives" to incarceration, and severe limitations on what can be done to control "status" offenders (who are guilty of nothing that would be a crime if committed by an adult, i.e., truancy, sexual promiscuity, or ungovernability at home), are all set up to protect the children from the stupid or overly punitive judge. The complaint of our best juvenile judges, some of whom have devoted their entire careers to domestic relations and juvenile cases, is that the cumbersomeness of this procedural system makes it impossible for the good judge to act quickly and incisively at the first sign of trouble. They are quite correct; a few days in a detention facility for an eleven- or twelve-year-old—particularly where the child's problem is too much love and the absence of parents ever having said no—will frequently work wonders. However, the same technique will do nothing for the habitually abused slum child. Deciding the correct approach requires the enlightened use of discretion, but the existence of unenlightened judges makes the rules so protective that the good judge is almost powerless to do good.

I remember once asking a local policeman in a small rural town which of the town's two restaurants was the better. He reply was, "Son, they're both about the same—it doesn't make a bit of difference which one you go to, but whichever one it is you'll wish to hell you'd gone to the other." The same conclusion applies to the choice between judicial discretion versus predictability. No better example can be found than in the area of criminal sentencing.

It is a common criticism of criminal sentencing that one judge will be severe with a defendant while another judge will be lenient with an identical defendant under identical facts. Obviously, such a result is capricious—in the one case the defendant is outraged at the severity of a forty-year sentence for armed robbery while in the other case society is outraged at the leniency of only a ten-year sentence for a similar armed robbery. So what is the alternative? Simple. Every armed robber gets twenty years in prison and is eligible for parole after seven years. That's the one crime, one punishment position. But what happens to the adolescent who accompanies his father and uncle on an armed robbery? What about the person who has committed a series of armed robberies over a forty-year period being released from prison for one only to commit another? Shouldn't all of these factors be weighed in the sentencing formula? If they are, you're back to each trial judge being able to give a host of factors such weight as he deems relevant, and you get different sentences according to the philosophy of different judges under identical facts.

I rather like the middle ground that we have adopted in West Virginia. Under our system most crimes have a minimum and a maximum punishment—for example, grand larceny is from one to five years—and the actual amount of time a prisoner serves is determined by the parole board. The parole board is a three-person agency that has the advantage of being able to apply uniform objective and subjective standards, since the same three persons determine the length of sentence for everyone in the system. While the trial judges still make the initial choice between prison and probation, once the decision to send a person to prison is made, the length of the term for most crimes is beyond the discretion of the judge.

Under such a scheme it is inevitable that the parole board will apply some type of therapeutic model, that is, the board will look for evidence that the prisoner has reformed. What is this evidence? Well, first it is probably a willingness to go to prison school and get a high-school diploma or some technical training in a field like automobile mechanics where there is an active job market. If the prisoner has a prior record of alcoholism, joining Alcoholics Anonymous would also help, although drinking in prison is greatly circumscribed by the limited availability of liquor, so the success of any prison treatment for alcohol abuse is speculative at best. Being "saved" and finding Jesus can never be dismissed merely as a good ploy, particularly if there are guards or prison administrators who are born-again Christians. And since much criminal activity can be categorized as an affair of the heart rather than simply a response to economic circumstances, a true religious conversion often does work wonders. Finally, the parole board is very interested in the recommendation of the prison authorities, which means that going along on the inside goes a long way toward a hasty release. In short, there is a definite game, with a more or less understandable set of rules and a definite reward for being a good player.

Many convicts are not very good players. Inability to play the game on the inside usually indicates a low likelihood of being able to play the game on the outside, but not always. Sometimes the cultural background of the convict precludes his cooperation with the guards and administrators, and often an inmate's resistance to the institution's petty tyranny is more than justified. Those problems, however, are very hard to sort out.

Convicts do not like the indeterminate sentence system very much. In fact, in California the prisoners have unionized, and the prisoners' union actually fights any therapeutic model. The prisoners' argument is that therapy is an illusion because of insufficient scientific knowledge about rehabilitation. Convicts, they argue, may stop being criminals as a result of the prison experience itself, getting older, or having improved economic opportunities. But regardless of why they stop, the argument goes, it will not have been a result of any prison therapy. While this pessimistic conclusion is not universally held among sociologists and penologists, it has been grudgingly accepted in the better reasoned scholarly literature. The California prisoners argue, therefore, that the object of prison is punishment, short and sweet. Accordingly, they want every convict to know exactly how long he must serve when he enters the joint so that he will not need to play the Kafkaesque rehabilitation game. Among other things, such a structure makes relations with other inmates substantially easier because it leads to solidarity.

In West Virginia the prisoners want definite sentences on the low side of the parole board's current spectrum. If an indeterminate sentence is between one and five years, no prisoner seriously argues for a determinate sentence of five years—discretion is obviously better than that. Our court is constantly urged by inmates and their lawyers to set more and more definite standards for release on parole. Yet the more definite the standards, the more specific the rehabilitation game becomes. The person whose previous background would give any reasonable parole board fair notice that he is a dangerous sociopath can often still steel himself to playing the game for five or six years—long enough to ensure that on any objective checklist he is eligible for parole. If, however, we permit the parole board to take into consideration such factors as a person's previous record, unbridled discretion returns because the conclusion about the effect of a convict's prior record on his future behavior is largely subjective.

Law is not a science like physics or chemistry. In physics or chemistry there are principles like that of gravity or of gases that apply with exact regularity in every similar situation. The most important physical laws conform to simple mathematical functions. Typically, things behave according to the squares of other things or according to inverse ratios; the functions are graphed by straight lines, exponential curves, or logarithmic curves. While on the frontiers of science, such as the investigation of black holes, physics and metaphysics may have a certain mystical unity, in the operational world of flying airplanes, chugging steam engines, and petrochemical manufacture, everything goes more or less according to simple mathematical rules. The human condition—law's raw material—cannot be understood in terms of simple mathematical rules. The prediction of human behavior is largely art and not science. There are no experiments, no controlled conditions, and no factors that can be held constant. Any meaningful experiment requires a living, breathing, generation's worth of data. Then, ironically, the experiment's results can be applied only to a different generation under changed conditions.

The scientific method is based on inductive logic. We assemble a great deal of data, observe such patterns as the data appear to present, and then construct an explanative theory that can be tested under controlled conditions. In law the process is deductive. We look at the human condition through glasses tinted with religious, historical, and cultural experience and deduce operative rules that can never be scientifically tested. Economic, sociological, and philosophical principles can instruct our intuitive abilities only to the limit of the exactitude of those inexact and highly subjective disciplines. In the final analysis, reforming the law is rather like reforming religion. One tends to end up with an institutional structure exactly where one began in terms of a philosophical predisposition.

The way that the science of law recognizes the inherent limitations of concrete rules is not by having very few concrete rules and reposing great, explicit discretion in the judges who apply them. That would impair the element of predictability or, more important, the *appearance* of predictability. Such discretion would seem to repose too much power in the omnipresent bogeyman, the idiot judge. We achieve the desideratum of infinite flexibility, but without the appearance of unaccept-

97

able discretion, by having a plethora of rules, all of which can be selected and manipulated to achieve almost any result that the institutional hierarchy of judges chooses.

I use the phrase institutional hierarchy not from pomposity but for exactness, because the way we achieve some semblance of a government of laws rather than of men is to repose judicial decision making in an organized, collective intelligence that is expected to abide by certain historical, cultural, and economic traditions. While a trial-court judge could have the philosophy of a Communist or a neo-Nazi, it is unlikely that the multimember courts above him would tolerate the results that either philosophy implies. The ability of the Supreme Court to review the decision of all lower state and federal courts guarantees some judicial uniformity throughout the country—government of laws and not men, as it were. But five out of nine Supreme Court justices can change just about anything at will—segregation, abortion, state legislative apportionment, and private property rights are historical examples.

L AW involves three distinct elements: substantive rules, the concrete application of these rules, and the procedure through which the rules are applied and sanctions imposed. By substantive rules, I mean the general rules of conduct that determine a person's liability to the sanctions of the judicial process. Substantive rules are created legislatively or by court decisions. Historically the courts themselves have made the rules in many of the most important areas of our lives. One such body of court-made rules controls personal injuries. The amount of damages recoverable, the grounds for recovery (negligence, defective products, absolute liability for dangerous activities), and the acceptable defenses to an action (like contributory or comparative negligence) are all established by the courts. Occasionally a state legislature will modify a court-made rule, and in that event the statute will override the body of law made by the judges.

The application of the general rules to specific sets of facts is an exercise in abstraction. It is necessary to take a real-life situation and divide it into separate elements; each element then must correspond to elements of some preexisting legal category covered by a general rule.

Divorce is a good example of the difficulty of such an undertaking.

The general rule is that the party who is "at fault" in the dissolution of a marriage will have a divorce granted *against* him or her and as a result will either be required to pay alimony or will be barred from receiving any alimony. While, technically, women can be required to pay alimony to their former husbands, that seldom happens. But men are usually required to pay alimony to their ex-wives if the men are the ones at fault. Thus the whole history of a marriage—a complex web of human relationships involving children, parents, in-laws, and even neighbors—must be distilled and abstracted so that the court can make the only determination that counts in the law, the party "at fault."

The final element of law, and one that takes on inordinate prominence once a dispute actually goes to court, is the procedure used to get a decision. Which party, for example, has the burden of proof? In a criminal case the defendant is presumed innocent, and the state must prove him or her guilty beyond a reasonable doubt. Why beyond a reasonable doubt? Why not just by a preponderance of the evidence? Because we prefer to let the guilty go free rather than take the chance of convicting the innocent. This is a perfectly logical policy choice. Similarly, in a civil case the plaintiff must prove the liability of the defendant, and that makes recovery much more difficult than if the defendant were required to prove his or her freedom from liability.

In the whole process by which a case is "proven" there are numerous artificial rules of evidence. Everyone who reads mystery novels or watches television knows about "hearsay" evidence. In general, hearsay is testimony by one witness about what someone else, not present in court, told him or her. But there are myriad exceptions to the rule against admitting hearsay: business records entered by unknown clerks can be introduced into evidence with no proof other than that they are business records; declarations of dying crime victims to anyone can be introduced; admissions against penal interest, i.e., confessions to crimes, can be introduced by witnesses who only heard them; and, finally, utterances by participants or victims in accidents or crimes overheard by others can be introduced if the utterance occurred at the time of the accident or crime. There are so many exceptions to the hearsay rule that the exceptions almost obliterate the rule. As a result, for every rule of evidence excluding testimony there is a countervailing exception to the rule that lets the testimony in.

In order for a litigant to be successful in court, he must succeed in each of the three broad areas. He must find some general rule covering his situation that permits him to recover a judgment; he must characterize the facts of his case to demonstrate that his situation fits the general rule; and he must abstract the real-life facts so that they can be presented in a way that fits the procedural rules of the court. It is useless for him to be able to prove his case through mountains of unrefuted hearsay that any reasonable person would accept. If the artificial rules of evidence are not met, the litigant loses his case. There is often, therefore, a lack of harmony among the three integral parts of the law. A litigant can succeed in two of three parts yet fail in the third.

There is no better example of this than in day-to-day criminal law. A felon can be apprehended within minutes of an armed robbery with the fruits of the crime in his possession. Yet if his arrest was unlawful because there was no proper warrant, then the stolen goods must be excluded from evidence. If the robber was masked and there is no positive eyewitness identification but only circumstantial evidence—possession of the robbery loot—the robber goes free. If the arrest was illegal, then the search that disclosed the loot was illegal and the fruits of that illegal search cannot be introduced into evidence. The general rule requirement has been satisfied in that there is a statute prohibiting armed robbery; the facts fit the general rule—the defendant, using a weapon, took property against the will of the possessor of the property. But the procedural requirement—litigating the issue according to specific rules, one of which is that evidence obtained by illegal means cannot be introduced into court—has not been met. Therefore there cannot be a valid conviction.

Even more confounding than lack of harmony among the elements of law is lack of harmony within those elements. It is difficult enough to abstract real-life facts to the point where they fit one general rule, but usually the law provides several general rules, all of which contradict one another, and the same set of facts can frequently be abstracted by skilled lawyers so that those facts will fit any number of general rules.

As a hypothetical example, let us assume a twenty-four-year-old junior executive is seriously looking for a wife. He is smitten by a young professional woman of approximately his own age whom he encounters at work every morning in the elevator. On the fourth encounter he introduces himself and invites her to lunch, but she declines. After several subsequent short encounters he embarks upon a methodical program of conquest that initially involves the daily delivery of interesting floral arrangements. Since our young man has a sense of humor and substantial charm, he conducts himself in such a creative and interesting way that the young woman finally agrees to attend the opera with him one evening and then have dinner afterward. They set a date: he will meet her at the door to her apartment building at six o'clock on Friday evening, drinks at six-thirty, the opera at eight-fifteen, and dinner at eleven-thirty. Our young man purchases box seats at $55 apiece, buys a $350 dinner suit for the occasion, makes reservations at the most fashionable late-night restaurant, and proceeds with a large corsage to the lady's apartment building punctually at six on the day set.

When he arrives he discovers his Snow White dressed in jeans loading suitcases into an old Volkswagen in the company of a scruffy-looking male who could be a Hell's Angels reject. She politely informs our Prince Charming that her male companion just called and that she has decided to go off with him for a weekend in the mountains. Question: Can Prince Charming sue Snow White? Answer: Who knows?

Certainly there was a contract of sorts, and just as certainly Prince Charming suffered damages. Without Snow White's agreement to go out with him, he would never have bought a good dinner suit. He would not have invested $110 in opera tickets, neither one of which he can use since he hates opera. He has his taxi fares to and from Snow White's apartment, and don't forget his investment in all those flowers.

Futhermore, there was an offer and acceptance. He offered to invest time and money in all the arrangements for an extraordinary evening if Snow White would agree to go with him. She agreed; he relied on her agreement to his detriment; and now he is out about five hundred bucks and is mad as hell. Since he is a nice chap with honorable intentions who has conducted himself in the best traditions of courtly love, we, sitting as jurors, would conclude that Snow White did him dirt and that she ought to pay.

But now we must look at some of the rules that govern this seemingly simple human confrontation. First, was there a contract in the legal sense? Did the parties contemplate that the contract would be enforceable in court? Obviously not. Social rudeness, even rudeness that costs people money, is usually not a legal wrong actionable in a contract suit. Since people don't expect legal sanctions to be applied to breaches of social undertakings, the general rule is that those who make expenditures in reliance on the social commitments of others do so at their own risk.

Yet was Snow White's conduct so outrageous that for all intents and purposes she deliberately set Prince Charming up to spend a great deal of money so that she could enjoy his misery as she drove off into the sunset with someone else? If so, she inflicted intentional injury on Prince Charming and would have committed a tort by deliberately leading the prince into a trap.[3] But what is the evidence of an intentional tort rather than bare rudeness? Whatever the evidence, it is circumstantial. While in court the prince's lawyer can ask Snow White what she intended to accomplish by her course of conduct, her answer will obviously be that she intended no injury at all but just changed her mind.

Assuming that the prince can establish his tort theory—that Snow White unjustifiably and unreasonably trapped him into spending money—what is the measure of his damages? Certainly he should be entitled to the cost of her ticket to the opera, unless he could have gone to the theater and sold the ticket at market value or even at a discount (in a civil suit a plaintiff must mitigate his damages wherever it is reasonably possible). Is he entitled to the price of his own ticket? He could have used it himself, and the fact that he hates opera is subjective. Snow White's action forced him to lose only the value of her ticket unless the jury concludes that she reasonably could have foreseen that his ticket would also be valueless without her. What about the dinner suit? It will have other uses on black-tie occasions and should last Prince Charming until he is forty and starts getting middle-age spread. Did Snow White's action proximately cause (a lovely legal phrase) Prince Charming to lose $350, or would he have needed a dinner suit sometime in the future anyway, so that all he is actually out is the interest on his money from the time he bought the suit for the Snow White date until he would have needed to buy a good suit for another occasion?

3. It is almost impossible to define *tort* succinctly, and long-winded legal definitions are impenetrable even to lawyers. *The American Heritage Dictionary*'s definition is as good as any: "Any wrongful act, damage, or injury done willfully, negligently, or in circumstances involving strict liability, but not involving breach of contract, for which a civil suit can be brought."

There are numerous other issues that could be raised in the course of litigating the simple lawsuit of *Prince v. White*, but the point is sufficiently established that while there are general rules, there are so many of them that the judge can select the rule he wants, fit the facts into the rule, and achieve whatever result seems fair to him. If the judge decided that it is exclusively a question of contract law, Snow White wins. If the judge agrees that there is an intentional tort arising out of a "quasi-contract," then the prince will probably win because the case will get submitted to a jury. Any jury would probably conclude that Snow White is a turkey and would at least award the prince something.

Now let us return for a moment to what would probably be real life in the case of Prince Charming and Snow White, rather than the abstraction of real life into preexisting rules of law. What is it that Prince Charming really wants? He wants a wife, and more particularly he wants to explore whether he and Snow White might make it as a married couple. He doesn't really want money for his opera tickets or his suit or his taxi fares. Snow White can avoid the lawsuit—which by the way, will cost her lawyers' fees regardless of its outcome—by coming up with some lame apology, such as her friend was contemplating suicide and only her counsel over the weekend would save him, and then setting another date. The prince is happier than a pig in mud; Snow White saves the expense of a lawsuit and any monetary award; and, finally, Snow White can behave in such a way on the new date that Prince Charming will leave her alone thereafter. No court, however, can give that relief. Yet will Snow White be willing to render that relief herself without some plausible threat of a court sanction, a sanction that the plaintiff Prince does not even want?

If real-life common sense cannot resolve the human problem between Prince and White and it goes to court, the process of abstracting life to legal principles doesn't end at the trial-court level since an appeal is available to protect the litigants from the caprice of one trial judge. Most readers have seen a trial court, if only on television, with its lawyers, spectators, jurors, witnesses, and judge. Most, however, have never seen even a theatrical rendition of an appellate court, partially because appellate courts are so boring. If Prince recovers a judgment against Snow White and she appeals, the appeal will be based on the typed transcript of the proceedings conducted in the trial court. Lawyers for White, the losing party, will argue only points of law in the appellate court. They will describe the facts of the case and assert that under those facts no general rule of tort law fits and therefore the recovery was erroneous. The argument, if there is an oral argument, will be made before a three- or five-judge panel that will never have seen or heard of either Prince or White. Those judges will not have seen how sincere and decent Prince is nor how glib, self-centered, and inconsiderate White is. They will not have watched White pronounce bald-faced lies in open court, nor will they have observed the sorrow and disappointment in the eyes of Prince. To the appellate judges the whole case will boil down to whether, as a general rule, social situations should give rise to monetary recoveries through the courts.

The appellate court hears as many as three hundred appeals every four months. Their entire attention will be focused on the implications to the judicial machinery of permitting a new category of lawsuits—social torts as it were. Furthermore, since our case involves very little money, no loss of liberty, and no economic problems like a factory closing, it is unlikely that the judges themselves will be very interested. The case will be shunted off to "central staff," a group of kids right out of law school who will summarize the case so that reading or hearing about it will take the judges no more than five minutes. The irony of this process is that the issues about which the parties thought they were arguing in the lower court will probably not be the issues on which the appellate court and its law clerks ultimately decide the case. The parties believed they were arguing about whether White was unconscionably nasty to Prince. In the final analysis, however, the people who will decide the case are uninterested in either White or Prince and are equally uninterested in the "who struck John?" of their relationship. Appellate judges and their clerks will be interested only in the world of abstraction—legal principles as it were—because with four hundred cases on the docket, abstraction is all they have time for.

This leads us then to abandon Prince and White to their fates in the appellate courts and to inquire more generally why such a complex and uncertain system for administering law has been devised by people who should know better. Other societies don't necessarily have such complex judicial systems. In primitive societies the law is fairly clear because society is comparatively simple. People are not expected to kill, maim, rape, or rob one another, and when a crime occurs the community coalesces to apply a sanction through the village chief, village council, or even a local judge. The same single process exists in what we call civil law. In primitive societies most civil law involves land tenure and simple contracts that center in agricultural production. Violations of land agreements and breaches of contracts are condemned by the community—there is a consensus about how people should treat one another. Part of the reason for the consensus about what the law is and how it should be applied results from the relatively even distribution of wealth. Where people are more or less equal—where opportunities are dependent upon industry—a simple code of conduct is also a just code of conduct.

As society becomes more complex, political cleavages develop that must be accommodated in the legal structure. Usually at the heart of these political cleavages is the unequal distribution of wealth. In a society where people are more or less equal, it is generally considered fair that if a person borrows an ox for plowing, he should return the ox. These types of contracts are considered fair partially because they are voluntary. According to what we would call the criminal law, it is fair that a person who maims or kills another be punished. Again, an even distribution of wealth implies a higher level of free will and conscious moral choice; moral blame and the sanctions that moral blame implies appear justified. Once gross inequalities in the distribution of wealth enter the picture, consensus on the fairness of specific rules evaporates.

Court opinions frequently repeat the proposition that when a person goes into debt, he does so voluntarily. This is patently absurd, particularly with regard to poor people. Banks have money that other people need to survive. Banks are owned and controlled by the rich, who frequently use the power of their banks to further political and social ends unrelated to the profit-generating business of lending money.[4] Everyone knows this, and in a capitalist society where man is separated

---

4. Once when I was developing a housing project in a small West Virginia town, I approached a local bank with a sound proposal to borrow slightly under a million dollars. The bank, however, proposed ludicrous terms, and I quickly concluded that members of the bank's board owned rental property in that town that was grossly overpriced and that there was hostility to anyone else's entry

from his means of production by employer/employee relationships, poverty and unemployment do not necessarily imply moral deficiency.

While supposedly all contracts are entered into voluntarily, even contracts between the strong and the weak, in fact the terms are dictated by the strong, and the weak must go along. Both the strong and the weak have their partisans in the political process, which means, of course, that each group will have its partisans in the courts. The criminal law reflects the same cleavage; we keep grappling with the problem of economic determinism. Most violent crimes, except domestic crimes of passion, are committed by the poor. The schoolteacher who spends his weekends committing armed robberies, the bank officer who mugs old ladies after work, and the newspaper editor who doubles as a hit man for the Mafia are all remarkable oddities.

When a welfare client writes a bad check to the Kroger grocery store, the bank returns the check, the store goes to court, and a police officer serves the welfare client with a warrant to appear before a magistrate. When my wife writes a bad check to Kroger's, the president of my bank calls to "ask" whether I'd be kind enough to cover the check sometime soon. Although both the welfare client and my wife may be equally innocent or equally guilty of any intentional wrongdoing, since I can cover the check, nothing is thought of the problem in my wife's case. When, as usually occurs, the welfare client cannot cover the check, she becomes a crime statistic.

The existing distribution of wealth is only the most visible obstacle to achieving equity with the type of simple rules that exist in primitive societies. There are numerous other disparities that must be taken into account in the legal system, which is, after all, merely a reflection of the political system. The first is inequality in native intelligence. Some people are smarter than others. The problem of natural intelligence is aggravated by the effect of environment on "intelligence." In general I find that middle-class people living in middle-class neighborhoods get

into the housing market. The bank board used its power over local sources of money to forestall local competition with the board members' other businesses. Fortunately I was not limited in my contacts to that town, so two weeks later I closed the loan with a large savings and loan association in a neighboring city. The project benefited the town enormously, but it got built only in spite of the hierarchy of the town itself.

cheated less than the poor because they know how to protect themselves. In terms of natural injustice, perhaps the greatest source of injustice is the family itself. Unstable families permeated with brutality, drugs, and jungle ethics produce at best wards of the state and at worst sociopaths.

There are very few legal technicalities among primitive tribes. The citizens do not believe that the absence of elaborate procedure leads to arbitrary or capricious decisions. This can be verified by the reader from his or her experience in the home as a child and subsequently as a parent. A household usually has a set of rules that is imposed in an authoritarian way by the parents or is generally agreed to under a system approaching constitutional monarchy. Most of the time there is voluntary compliance, and when there is a transgression, the problem is not the procedure for enforcement but rather the power for enforcement. Young children can be disciplined easily, but teenagers and spouses present a real problem. The transgressing teenager can drop out, and the transgressing parent can quit the family. Both of these options establish the limits of the power for enforcement, but there is no question about whether a transgression has occurred. In a small, nonunionized company the same situation applies, more or less. Frequently one forbears from disciplining an employee who cannot be replaced, but again that goes to power and not procedure.

Since most people have experienced the "juridical" setting of both the family and the workplace (and if a person went to camp or boarding school, the "juridical" setting of the tribe) we ask why the state's legal process must be so rife with technicalities. The answer is that the technicalities are part and parcel of the overall "law" in that it is the technicalities that are used as the battleground for the political fights over equity in a society that is primarily characterized by natural and social inequity.

If the legal structure says that banks cannot collect debts owed to them by the poor, banks will stop lending money to the poor. If the legal system says that the lower strata of society must be excused from criminal responsibility because they are merely victims in a determinist world, the crime rate soars, and there ceases to be an incentive to the honest poor to stay honest. If a state legal system goes too far in enforcing greater equality in the distribution of wealth, the generators of wealth—the owners of capital—leave and seek more hospitable states.

107

Although it is true that different consequences follow from my wife's and a welfare client's writing of a bad check, it is not incidental that the bank pays Kroger's check in the case of my wife while Kroger gets stiffed in the case of the welfare client. If the *general* rule is something other than that Kroger can enforce its claim against the welfare client, then it will stop cashing checks for all but its gilt-edged clients.

Since it's not possible to tamper with the general rules, the general rules in America bear a striking resemblance to the general rules in a primitive society. Yet the response to the lack of fairness that Rhadamanthine application of the general rules implies is to nibble around the edges of the general rules with procedural rules or, occasionally, with alternate general rules (sometimes called "equity") that become operative under extraordinary circumstances. Even though the welfare client who issued the bad check will be served with a warrant, she will probably never be prosecuted because her court-appointed lawyers will place so many expensive procedural obstacles in the way of securing a conviction that everyone will give up. What is hoped is that welfare clients in general do not know this and will voluntarily pay their debts.

If I am an uninsured motorist and have an accident with an Exxon oil truck owing to the truck driver's negligence, I can collect more than a million dollars from Exxon for a serious injury. Similarly, if the accident is my fault and the truck driver is seriously injured, he can get a judgment against me for a million dollars. But he will never collect it. Why? Because I don't have a million dollars and there is no possibility of my acquiring such an amount over the course of the rest of my life. If I have some assets, like a house, that I want to protect, I can declare federal bankruptcy, give the trucker what is not exempt—which is damn little—and forget about the debt. Exxon, however, if their driver is negligent, must pay the whole judgment to me, with interest and costs, or my lawyers will sell Exxon's property until the proceeds are sufficient to satisfy the judgment.

The same general rules about liability apply to both Exxon and me—both of us are responsible for our careless acts—but I am excused because I cannot pay. Why shouldn't the Exxon trucker be able to put me in jail until I agree to give him 70 percent of my income for the rest of my life, and put me back in jail if I default? Why shouldn't the trucker be able to sell me into slavery? Why shouldn't the trucker be able to sell my whole family into slavery? The answer comes from a community sense of equity. Obviously it entails less human sacrifice for Exxon to pay a million dollars than for me to spend six months in slavery. But we haven't tampered with the general rules about responsibility; we have tempered the harsh effect of the general rules using *other* general rules about the enforceability of judgments.

As I have tried to make clear, judges are not machines. They are living, breathing, emotional, political, passionate human beings with definite ideas about the equity of any given lawsuit. In my experience, judges work backward from their intuitive grasp of the equities of a lawsuit to a manipulation of legal rules that will achieve what they consider an equitable result. Different trial judges will handle the same lawsuit in entirely different ways, producing contrary results. It is the job of the multimember appellate courts to achieve some uniformity and predictability in this mess, but many critical decisions of trial-court judges are beyond correction on appeal, if for no other reason than that appeals are expensive and time-consuming.

In some jurisdictions the trial courts are liberal in wealth-redistribution cases while the appellate court is conservative. Since the appellate court does not like the rendering of large judgments against industry and insurance companies, they will frequently reverse fair jury verdicts on minor procedural technicalities that have nothing to do with the integrity of the trial. On the other hand, liberal appellate courts may affirm all judgments for plaintiffs while judgments for defendants may often be reversed for minor technicalities.

The net result is that law is a chancy business at best. Going to court is like going into a chemistry laboratory and mixing a lot of strange chemicals at random. Only after mixing, shaking, boiling, reducing, and otherwise fiddling around, is it clear whether you have concocted a gooey mess or invented Saran Wrap. Obviously, some cases in the law are clearer than others. Yet more often cases appear to be clear until skilled lawyers begin to manipulate the panoply of half-hidden principles that lurk in a body of law eight hundred years old.

I once sat on a criminal case in which the defendant had stabbed the victim fifty-one times with a hunting knife, and the case was almost reversed on appeal because the trial court had failed to give the jury a very technical instruction on self-defense. To the layperson that case would have appeared open-and-shut, but the mass of precedent in law is so enormous that nothing is open-and-shut once it hits the courts.

WE usually envisage the courts as the battleground where right struggles against wrong. There are indeed many occasions when that characterization is accurate. However, the complexity of the legal system reflects the fact that much of the time one form of right is struggling against another form of right, and what we perceive as unadulterated wrong never enters the picture. In automobile accident cases judgments are frequently recovered against drivers who weren't negligent at all, merely because the victim has been seriously injured and the jury feels that the other driver's insurance company can bear the loss more easily than the victim and his family. The jury knows that the insurance company will pass the cost along to all policyholders as a class—a class that includes the jurors making the award.

The whole structure of accident law is artificial anyway. We are all negligent sometime or another; most of the time, however, no drastic consequences follow from our negligence. Overall, the victims of accidents are probably as negligent as those who cause accidents, yet when an accident occurs a victim must find someone else to accuse of negligence in order to dip into the pockets of insurance companies. When jurors know there is insurance it usually doesn't take much to convince them to permit reasonable pocket-dipping.

The very fact of jury caprice causes most people to insure against judges and juries, not against their own negligence. Companies, as well as individuals with property, insure against every conceivable lawsuit that can be brought against them for injury. If an apartment project puts up some swings, sliding boards, and seesaws for the children, there will be liability insurance to cover the owners from a lawsuit. These toys are not dangerous; they have been traditional amusement devices for centuries. Yet if a child gets hurt, a jury may very well conclude that it was negligence not to have a "playground supervisor," or negligence to permit a young child to climb a sliding board, or negligence to have a seesaw in which a child could mash his fingers. While none of these things is probably real negligence, unless we want to live in a world that is a cross between a hospital and a fort, the fact that the jury

110

may want to compensate an injured child forces us to purchace insurance. Since there is insurance, when a child is injured the insurance company will probably agree to some reasonable settlement that will ease the burden of medical bills and permanent disabilities without the need for a courtroom showdown.

The discussion so far leads to the question: Why does the law rely on an uncertain hodgepodge of general rules and counterrules instead of starting over and creating one predictable, integrated system? This has in fact been tried a number of times in narrow areas of the law like the criminal codes and the rules of procedure. Yet inevitably over the course of years, the original structure gets overlaid again with court-created rules and counterrules. In 1938 the federal courts adopted new procedural rules called the *Federal Rules of Civil Procedure* that were intended to simplify the old rules of common law pleading and achieve a simple and cheap system for getting issues before the courts on their merits. Today there are multivolume sets, such as *Moore's Federal Practice*, that catalog the thousands of cases that have interpreted these rules. Taken together, all these divergent cases make the new procedural system as complicated as the old common-law pleading that the new system was designed to replace.

The reason for the manipulation of all legal rules, no matter how well conceived initially, is that it is never possible to envisage all the real-life situations to which the general rules must eventually apply when drawing up the rules. And, on a very human, "legal realism" level, it is easier for a judge to do a little procedural sleight of hand to bring a case out equitably than it is to restructure general rules. I have always thought that bad law is the product of quick-witted but lazy appellate judges who work backward from the correct result in a given routine lawsuit to some tricky procedural reason that achieves that result, and then of successive generations of slow-witted judges who proceed to take them seriously.

As has often been remarked in defense of the terribly complicated federal tax structure, equity and complexity go hand in hand. Since more often than not the courts are asked to decide a battle between right and right, it is necessary to return for a moment to the proposition that all litigation in court is an abstraction from real life. Even with the host of rules and counterrules available to the courts, no real-life situation

111

is adequately reduced to preconceived general legal categories. All lawsuits involve the banging of square pegs into round holes.

This is not an attractive picture. Law, after all, if it is supposed to be anything, is supposed to be predictable and certain. The demand that law be predictable and certain, however, presupposes that all disputes will ultimately be disposed of in court when in fact almost no disputes are disposed of in court. To reiterate a point made earlier, courts are successful not for the cases they decide but because of the cases they do not decide. The very uncertainty of the judicial process allows enormous latitude for negotiation and settlement outside of court. It is uncertainty that permits the structuring of settlements that satisfy both parties and take into consideration the real-life problems of each.

When a person has a complaint against another person or company, the extent to which his complaint is taken seriously is largely dependent upon the wrongdoer's expectations about whether the complaint can go to court. For example, I have been a lawyer for sixteen years and have never sued anyone in my individual capacity. The reason is that everyone against whom I have a complaint knows that I can go to court for nothing, so he offers an attractive settlement if only to avoid his own litigation expenses. I, on the other hand, know just how difficult it is to prosecute a lawsuit to judgment, so I don't demand such unacceptable terms that I am forced to go to court. People who are not lawyers neither have ready access to the courts nor usually know enough about the law to understand what a reasonable settlement is.

A letter from a lawyer is the first sign that a person wants to talk seriously about his complaint. The second, and by far the clearer sign, is the filing of a complaint in court. Where companies are large and responsibility is diffuse, the filing of a complaint is often the only method of getting the attention of someone with authority to settle a claim.

In 1971 when I was practicing law, I was attempting to clear liens from a land title for a client and discovered that there was a lien in favor of the Standard Oil Company, which had recovered a judgment against the property owner of record years ago on a credit-card debt. I called all over America, from New York to Dallas, and could not find an officer of Standard Oil empowered to receive a $500 payment in satisfaction of this debt and sign a release on behalf of the corporation.

Finally I brought an action to quiet title in the circuit court and pled that my client was ready, willing, and able to pay the judgment; that Standard Oil was obviously operated by computers that could not sign releases; and that since none of Standard Oil's computers was licensed to practice law in Marion County, West Virginia, the company would be required to send a living human being capable of receiving the money and signing a release, or else suffer a default judgment.

The irony of the Standard Oil story is that a living representative of the company never did appear. The company's general counsel wrote to say that he could not conveniently produce an official capable of signing a release, but if we would send him a check for half the debt, he would not contest our action, and we could take a default judgment and clear the title. When I moved for my default judgment I brought the letter to the attention of the circuit judge, who honorably suggested that we send the company the $250, which we did.

The moral of the story is that it is often impossible when dealing with big companies or the government to find a responsible official. People who put in claims for Medicare and other health insurance, for example, find a nightmare of paperwork—computer printouts rejecting claims, mindless demands for documentation of claims already documented, and outright failure by employees to understand written English.

The one way to break the red tape is to file a court action, because in twenty days a lawyer must file an answer, and suddenly you have an educated, English-speaking, living human being who can answer questions and help you sort out the problem. The lawyer and the company don't want to go to court any more than the complainant, and often the problem has arisen exclusively because of a failure of communication and the gross indifference of today's office staffs to the inconvenience and suffering of others.

When we talk about the legal system, the forest consists of all the disputes that either get settled before lawyers become involved or get settled after a complaint has been filed with a court but before any proceedings are conducted before a judge. The trees of the legal system are the individual lawsuits that ultimately go to court and must be decided by judges and juries. While it is probably not a valid criticism of courts to say that the law is too complex given the direct relationship between equity and complexity, it is a fair criticism of the courts to say that they often miss the forest for the trees.

Appellate courts make almost all the law for this country, and even when Congress or the state legislatures enact statutes, the courts shape the way in which these statutes will be applied or enforced. Whenever courts make or interpret law, the central focus of their concern should be on rules that facilitate settlements out of court. Judges often conceive that their highest duty is to do justice to the individual parties before them. Certainly this is a very important responsibility, and in fact the judge who does injustice to the parties before him in order to tinker at general rules as an academic or political exercise behaves like a swine. But because judges have spent most of their adult lives before they became judges litigating individual lawsuits, and because they may never have focused their attention on an overall theory of conflict resolution, they frequently overlook their primary function. In their attempt to do perfect justice in a dispute that is already in court, they create more and more costly and elaborate layers of hearings and appeals that then have an overwhelming and inequitable effect on the structure of settlements in thousands of cases that are disposed of out of court.

To illuminate how legal rules can be designed to facilitate out-of-court settlements, let us focus on two West Virginia examples. The first comes from contract law and involves the use of arbitration clauses in all kinds of commercial contracts. The second example comes from divorce law and involves standards for awarding child custody. These two concrete examples weave together the separate threads that have appeared in my discussion of the difficulties encountered in any modern litigation system.

The enforcement of commercial contracts is among the things that courts do least well. Frequently the parties who enter into complex commercial contracts have been doing business with one another for many years and want to continue to do so. They bang out contract problems without the words *sue*, *court*, or *lawyer*, ever passing anyone's lips. On other occasions, however, very complicated commercial contracts are entered into by parties who are strangers and who intend to do business together only once. While there are many kinds of commercial contracts, one example will illustrate the problems shared by almost all of them. The example involves the construction of a shopping mall, and as is usual in these matters, the parties include the developer who has some personal money to invest, a bank that is lending about 80 percent of the construction price, and a contractor who has given a fixed price for the job and is bonded for his performance by a major bonding company.

These contracts typically will have arbitration clauses that provide that if a dispute arises over the interpretation of the contract, a panel of arbitrators will decide the dispute, usually in a very short time. While the contract price is usually fixed, there are eventualities for which the contractor assumes no risk, and in the event of one of these eventualities, the contractor expects additional compensation. Among the eventualities is the cost of excavating unexpected solid rock, which obviously will require expensive techniques. As often as not, the contractor will want to pad his bill a little for excavation when rock is discovered, and as frequently the developer has not figured this into his financing plans, which makes payment difficult.

Unless this dispute can be resolved quickly, everyone will be bankrupt. It usually takes more than three years to prosecute a contract dispute to final judgment in even an efficient court system. If the construction work is closed down during a lawsuit, everyone is a loser. The bank has money tied up on a half-completed project; the developer must pay construction interest on the part completed for years, if he is solvent, without the revenue that would be generated from a completed project; and the contractor has a large contingent liability if a court eventually holds against him, which will destroy both his profits and possibly his ability to secure future bonds.

What is needed is a quick decision far more than a just decision. The parties can probably live with any arbitration award, no matter how outrageous, better than a three-year job shutdown. The problem with arbitration, however, is that in most places it is difficult to enforce the award. Where an arbitration award is either not enforceable or enforceable only with great difficulty and after long delay, the whole arbitration process becomes meaningless whenever one party wants to frustrate it or use potential delay to exact concessions from his associates.

Why do most jurisdictions make it difficult to enforce arbitration awards? Once arbitration awards are made generally enforceable, they will be included in many contracts to which they are unsuited. Contracts between automobile dealers and car buyers, for example, might have a provision that any injury caused by a defect in the car will be arbitrated by a panel of automobile dealers. Consumer credit contracts might provide for a panel of bankers to determine whether money is owed, leading to an enforceable arbitration award. Artfully structured, an automatically enforceable arbitration clause offers endless opportunities for the strong to take advantage of the weak—insurance contracts, sales contracts, home-improvement contracts, and even employment contracts could be written to put the entire strength of the law on the side of what is already the strongest. Yet in commercial matters where thousands or millions of dollars are tied up in either goods in process or construction works in progress, arbitration is the best way to resolve disputes.

Although there are appropriate and inappropriate occasions for arbitration clauses, it does not follow that on an appropriate occasion the clause is binding while on an inappropriate occasion it is not binding. Traditionally it has been thought that courts must make a general rule about arbitration. Either all arbitration clauses are enforceable, regardless of the nature of the parties or the nature of the contract, or all arbitration clauses are susceptible to challenge. Certainly a general rule going either way is the easiest for judges to articulate, but neither general rule is serviceable in the real economic world. The better approach that we have adopted in West Virginia is to recognize the difference between contracts between commercial parties and contracts between a commercial party and a consumer. Commercial parties actually bargain about arbitration clauses while ignorant consumers usually have no understanding of these clauses or the rights they are bargaining away. Consequently, in West Virginia we give automatic enforcement to arbitration clauses in contracts between commercial parties, and we refuse to enforce those clauses in contracts involving consumers.

The result of West Virginia's more complicated yet more narrowly drawn rule has been that commercial matters are now settled quickly by arbitration. Since 1977 when we published the opinion authorizing binding arbitration in commercial contracts, we have had only three cases involving an arbitration clause, and two of them were merely to test whether we had been serious about our new rule. The question remains why such a system of speedy justice cannot be applied to other types of situations, such as debtor-creditor relations, landlord-tenant disputes, and even accident claims. There are good reasons, going again to the complexity of equity issues—political questions in a sense—and they are explored in Chapter 6. The point to be made here is that when there are not complex equity issues and what is called for is a quick decision (which, by the way, will probably be as fair as any decision reached in court), it is possible to structure the process to give quick, predictable, results.

The second example of how the legal process can be structured to facilitate settlements comes from child custody. Most of the time divorcing parents agree about who is to raise the child. In the overwhelming number of cases, both parties recognize that one parent will be the better primary caretaker. If the mother is leaving the marriage because she feels frustrated and wants to pursue a career, she may voluntarily relinquish custody to the husband. But more often than not, the mother expects to assume responsibility for children, and a visitation agreement with the father is accomplished amicably. The overwhelming proportion of consensual arrangements is obscured, however, by the few vicious custody fights. Where both parents are attached to their children and want them with them, it is sometimes impossible to work out a mutually satisfactory adjustment. This is particularly the case where only the wife wants the divorce and the husband wishes to deprive her of the children as punishment. As our social mores have moved toward viewing divorce as a no-fault problem in a human relationship, the courts' focus has shifted from the rights of the divorcing parents to the best interests of the children.

How does a court figure out what are the best interests of the children? How does a judge determine who is the better parent? There are all kinds of psychological experts ranging from expensive psychiatrists to cheap school social workers who can testify in a custody hearing, but I usually find their testimony to be based on only a fleeting acquaintance with the parents, children, and other family members involved. In short, their expert opinion is usually garbage—particularly since professional experts are not hired unless they are prepared to testify for the side employing them. In extreme cases, expert opinion may be useful if it is supported by a detailed presentation of the reasoning behind it, but in the ordinary American family setting no expert can figure out very much about relative degrees of fitness between two good parents. Among other things, much depends on the values of the expert. Frequently, for example, a father will have a superior education and will place higher value on formal learning than the mother, while the mother is the warmer and more emotionally supportive parent. Which quality is more important?

In a divorce case litigation about custody of the children per se has a dramatic effect on all the other issues. Even in this era of liberated women, it is still the mother who is usually closest to the children by virtue of her role as primary caretaker during infancy. Where that is the case, a husband can terrify his wife into accepting a pittance for alimony and child support by threatening to take the children. Thus, even when men have no interest in custody of the children, lawyers will still routinely tell them to demand the children anyway because such a demand is a throwaway chip in the overall bargaining process.

The one thing that is certainly not in the interests of children is protracted litigation about their custody, with all of the uncertainty and instability that litigation entails. Divorce is a traumatic experience for children anyway, and litigation that demands that children be pawns in the fight between their parents is destructive. Very young children *feel* the tension and uncertainty that surround litigation about their custody. Older children *understand* what is going on and do not want to be forced to choose between their parents. Child-custody litigation can take years, during which parents are tempted to bribe their children to secure favorable testimony. Such bribery usually takes the form of relaxing discipline, but it can take other forms as well, such as unreasonably generous allowances or parental indulgence in childish whims. Obviously this bribery is not in a child's best interest.

From a theoretical point of view, because both parents have equal claim to the companionship of their children, and the children have a right to be placed with the parent who will best care for them, it should be the judge's job to listen to all the evidence and render a tailored, individualized judgment. And in most jurisdictions this is the adjudication model that is followed. It all sounds wonderfully fair; everyone gets a complete hearing and a chance to act out—particularly a chance to show some third party what a truly rotten person the other marriage partner is.

What this model misses, however, is the emotional and financial cost of litigation per se, as well as the effect that *potential* litigation about child custody has on settlements about alimony and child support. In this regard a word is in order about the economics of working-class life.

Heartland America is very different from New York's Upper East Side, Wellesley, Massachusetts, or Washington, D.C. Where the majority of the population work with their hands, either on farms, in coal mines, or in automobile plants, there is not the potential for wage equality between men and women that exists where the economy supports administrative, middle-class jobs. For example, a coal miner makes almost twice the salary of a schoolteacher or a registered nurse. The reason has nothing to do with education but rather with physical strength and danger.

While there are families where the husband and wife earn comparable incomes, that is still the exception rather than the rule. Consequently, in the real world of working Americans—rather than in a hypothetical world created from wishful thinking about sex equality— a husband must make a financial contribution to the support and upbringing of his children if they are to enjoy the same standard of living after a divorce as they did before. The 1980 U.S. Government Census demonstrates in overwhelming detail that women as a group are very poor relative to men. Divorce may liberate women in some ways, but it also makes them poor, even if they secure acceptable work. Alimony and child support are extremely important, and where the threat of a child-custody fight causes an unreasonably low settlement, the children suffer from a childhood of penury.[5]

With the coming of some form of no-fault divorce almost every-

5. Women often have unrealistic expectations before a divorce concerning their potential earning power. For example, according to the 1980 census, among married couples where the husband was employed (thus excluding unemployed men or the retired) 35.9 percent of the wives did not work at all; another 36.2 percent had part-time jobs or worked for only part of the year. While 64.1 percent of the wives worked, only 43.6 percent of them did so on a steady

where, the courts increasingly have handled divorces as administrative matters like parking tickets. Most divorces are uncontested, and usually the parties agree about alimony, child support, and custody. When this occurs, trial judges generally sign the order jointly submitted by both counsel and agreed to by both parties. Under these bargains the mothers get the children without a fight, and the fathers get to keep their money.

The important point is not who wins or loses a real custody battle but rather the enormous impact the *possibility* of a custody battle has on the terms of child support and alimony settlements. While most trial judges tend to give children of tender years to their mothers, most mothers are unwilling to take even a 10 percent chance that they will get the aberrant, woman-hating judge, or come off badly in a hearing before a competent judge and lose their children.

An equally important consideration is that courts are not equipped to determine which of two loving, competent parents will be the better for the children. Every practicing lawyer has a stable of experts who he knows will manipulate every principle and strain every observation to arrive at a conclusion favorable to the side hiring him. In the natural sciences, where experts are talking about the laws of chemistry and physics, they can bend their testimony only so far, but in the open-ended, inexact field of psychology, the opportunities for scientific bunkum are limitless.

basis. This implies a fairly low level of work experience and marketable skills among married women.

Furthermore, for all working wives, median earnings amounted to $6,336 in 1979, and their contribution to total family income came to 26.9 percent. In those cases where a wife and her husband were both year-round, full-time workers, the wife's earnings were $10,199, which contributed 34.7 percent to the family's earnings. We can reasonably infer that if women could do significantly better after divorce, they would have done so before. Finally, among all working wives, with or without children, only 9.1 percent earned more than $15,000 in 1979. Most important for our purposes here, the census reveals that in 1979 the median income for mothers raising two children alone was $8,314, while the median income for couples with two children was $23,000. Even if we allow for the expenses of a second adult, children in two-parent homes can count on having twice as much spent on them than if they are raised by their mothers alone.

120

And now to the solution to these problems. In West Virginia we have a rule that we believe works better than any other, although we have frequently admitted in our reported opinions that it does not work perfectly. In an area as complicated as child custody, all that can be done is to trade in a rule that does not work very well for a rule that works marginally better. Our marginally better rule is an absolute presumption about the award of the custody of children of tender years. The custody of very young children is awarded automatically to the "primary caretaker parent" if he or she is a "fit" parent.

Children of tender years are children who are too immature to formulate a reasoned opinion about their own custody. Once a child is able to formulate an opinion, but before he or she is fourteen years old, the trial court can take into consideration the child's preference and give that preference as much weight as the judge thinks is appropriate. After a child reaches fourteen, he or she can live with either parent of his or her choice if the parent is fit. Thus under our law the children themselves become the primary expert witnesses if they are old enough to understand what is going on and the judge believes they can testify without substantial emotional damage to them.

Now that sex roles are rapidly changing, we can no longer say that the mother always has the more binding relationship with the child, but we can say that the primary caretaker parent, of whatever sex, probably has the strongest ties. Therefore in West Virginia we look to see who had primary responsibility for most of the chores of child raising before the divorce was initiated. Who fixed the meals and fed the child; who took the child to the doctor; who changed the diapers and gave the baths; who interacted with the school personnel? Where it can be shown that child-raising duties were equally shared, there is no choice but to hold a full-blown hearing about relative degrees of competence, but that is a rare occasion.

Furthermore we require that the primary caretaker parent be fit, an objective standard that can be established by lay testimony. Does the parent keep the child clean, provide supervision and nourishing meals, protect the child from danger, avoid child abuse and protect the child from abuse by other adults?

The result of our simple, ironclad rule (which any lawyer can easily

121

explain to his clients) is that in West Virginia there is almost no custody litigation. The rules are so clear that the specter of a custody fight does not intimidate mothers since all the issues involved in child custody, assuming the mother is a fit caretaker, can be disposed of in fifteen minutes. Furthermore, except in those cases where children are between about seven and fourteen, the children are not required to testify or be involved in the emotional strain of litigation. Even where arguably the child can testify and have his or her opinion accorded weight, the trial court can refuse to hear such testimony if the judge thinks that undue pressure is being placed on the child and that his testimony will be valueless or damaging to him.

Rules about when and how people go to court are made by the appellate judges I have described, who come from the ranks of practicing lawyers. The normal perception of these men and women is that the litigating process should be consummately fair, regardless of the time or expense required to render a result with perfect justice. The point that most judges and lawyers miss is that the whole litigation process is inexact—perfect justice under ideal conditions is illusory. To ask perfect justice of a court system is like asking a skilled surgeon to perform brain surgery with a meat ax. He might be able to do it 5 percent of the time if he is really skilled, but the smart money does not bet on it.

Into any litigation process go the skill of counsel; the intelligence, experience, and integrity of the judge; the passions of the jury; the credibility and attractiveness of the witnesses; the demeanor of the litigants; and the cost of the process. After trial there is the appeal, and the final result then depends on the attentiveness of the judges; the quality of their supporting staff; the backlog of the court; and such intangible considerations as whether the appellate court wants to use the case as a vehicle for molding the law, in which case the opinion will be long in coming, and a perfectly fair trial may be overturned to permit the higher court to make a point that interests the judges.

Courts miss the point when they think of making the litigation process per se more perfect in its justice. Far more perfect justice is achieved by designing rules that expedite settlements and encourage

122

people to sort out their own problems on some reasonable basis. We have now had eight hundred years of experience trying to make the court system produce perfect justice, but we have just as many dissatisfied litigants today as ever before. We should always keep in mind that the cases that are actually in court are but an infinitesimal percentage of all the conflicts that the threat of going to court have settled.

An objection to my emphasis on settlement is that sometimes the parties don't want to compromise since each believes that he or she is in the right, and in those cases the parties are entitled to a quick, just, all-or-nothing decision by a neutral court. Furthermore, in many cases the lack of a neutral court that is quick and just forces people who are in the right into unjust compromises. In extreme cases both these objections are justified, but as Chapter 6 demonstrates I cannot envisage any real-world structure that will obviate this problem without creating far more intractable problems elsewhere. In the majority of cases the system is designed more or less consciously to compensate for its own structural deficiencies at one point with counterbalancing structural deficiences at another point.

A scale can be in balance when it is empty or when it has two three-hundred-pound weights, one on each side. The scales of justice involve a weighted balance rather than an empty balance. The threat of outrageous jury awards in personal-injury cases balances the delay in getting to trial, and the potential prodefendant emotional bias of one judge is balanced by the potential proplaintiff emotional bias of another judge.

When we think in terms of court reform, we must think of designing systems that will keep people out of court rather than giving them a better result once they are in court. Of course I do not mean that people should be kept out of court and unjustly treated at the same time; I mean that first and foremost all procedures concerning litigation should always take into consideration how in-court procedures can lead to equitable out-of-court settlements. This principle applies, by the way, to the criminal law as well. Most criminal cases are disposed of by plea bargains, and those "settlements" differ very little from settlements involving commercial contracts or domestic relations.

We need a system that at every point is designed not to process litigation but to reduce the need for litigation at all. If every time an appellate court wrote an opinion all the judges devoted fifteen minutes to asking themselves how the new ruling could be molded to make settlements easier, within about ten years the system would be dramatically improved. It would not be perfect, because it cannot be perfect.

The Political
Accommodations
of the Criminal Law

5

THERE is a world shared by people who write books like this one
and people who read them. And then there is another world—the
world of the street, which most of us will never understand. It is a rich
world where savagery coexists with love, loyalty, struggle, desperation,
and ambition. The world of the street extends from urban slums to small
towns and the rural hinterland. We can see it and work with it all day
and still never understand it. Yet it is life, the only life of millions;
those of us who flatter ourselves that we organize society do not organize
the street. Like the Lady of Shalott in her tower, we see but a reflection
of the street through a poorly made mirror. The pulse of the street,
however, resonates in a thousand different ways into our world. Most
important, the street makes itself felt in the emotive rather than the
rational side of politics.

Criminal law today is largely about neither criminals nor the law.
It is about civil rights, civil liberties, overcrowded dockets, inadequate
judicial personnel and, particularly when we deal with teenage criminals, it is about social services and education. It is also about the
messages that are being transmitted by the street. These messages concern the resistance of street culture to the imposition of a majority culture

125

that is alien and oppressive. The culture of the street engages in a guerrilla campaign around the flanks of the majority culture's criminal law. The old criminal law was about criminals and law; it was primarily concerned with questions of guilt or innocence in a social system in which the majority had the political power. Today's criminal law reflects a lack of consensus about both moral standards and the distribution of wealth because the street now has a voice in political affairs. Some of the messages the street is sending are just and good, and some are corrupt and evil. All the messages, however, are political.

England and the United States have always been proud of the accused's presumption of innocence and right to a jury trial. For two hundred years our law has been more concerned with protecting the innocent than with convicting the guilty, a predisposition that has never been seriously questioned even by law-and-order enthusiasts. It is worth pointing out that an American jury is a wonder to behold. Ordinary citizens who serve on juries are careful that they do not convict an innocent person. Nine-tenths of the time the same barber who regales you in his shop with a neo-Fascist general philosophy of law enforcement becomes a different animal when he is serving on a jury and has the fate of a real human being in his hands.

I take citizen demands for greater law and order extremely seriously. People who remain in their houses for fear of violent attack, or who are constantly terrorized by adolescents, or who return from work each day in dread that their houses or apartments will have been ransacked all have a legitimate and, indeed, urgent complaint. It is, after all, the highest calling of organized society to provide freedom from fear.

Yet those who demand freedom from fear do not urge any tampering with either the jury system or the presumption of innocence. There is no groundswell of support for convicting the innocent. Everyone is aware that it is possible to be "framed" or to be the victim of incriminating circumstantial evidence. Therefore, when we talk about the criminal law, we must distinguish the traditional judicial function of determining guilt or innocence from all the other things that go on in the criminal courts that have nothing whatsoever to do with whether people did or did not commit the crimes with which they are charged.

Once a suspect has been apprehended, the criminal-justice system can be divided into three distinct stages. The first stage is the preliminary process where, among other things, it is determined whether there is probable cause to believe that the suspect is guilty so that he can be held for trial, bond is set, and at a slightly later time, the procedure by which the suspect was apprehended or the evidence against him was gathered is scrutinized. The second stage involves either a guilty plea pursuant to a three-way bargain among the defendant, the prosecutor, and the court or a not-guilty plea with a full-blown jury trial. Finally, the third stage involves the determination and administration of the appropriate sentence—prison, probation, juvenile detention, or hospitalization. Of the three stages of this process, the one that receives by far the least criticism is the second stage where the courts do a good job of separating the guilty from the innocent. Although in general the courts err on the side of freeing the guilty in close cases, this is perceived as preferable to convicting the innocent.

Yet the second stage is not wholly untainted by the systemic failures of the other two stages. Where, for example, there is arguably some defect in the procedure by which a suspect was apprehended or a procedural irregularity in the seizure of evidence, it is likely that a plea bargain will be struck where the defendant is allowed to plead guilty to a less serious offense. The accused pleads to a reduced charge to avoid the chance of the court's ruling against him on the procedural irregularity, and the prosecutor permits the plea to avoid the chance that the defendant will get off scot-free.

Furthermore, the nature of the facilities available to receive convicted criminals has a substantial effect on the second stage. Judges and prosecutors are aware of the lack of prisons, hospitals, and juvenile facilities. Particularly in the populous urban states, it is not possible to send all convicted felons to prison or all dangerous adolescents to a residential juvenile facility. Accordingly, since the prosecutor knows that the court is likely to place certain categories of defendants on probation because there are no facilities fit to receive them, a plea bargain involving probation is often entered that assures the defendant of the favorable result he wants while saving the prosecutor the time and expense of a trial.

Except to the extent that stage two reflects problems that are primarily attributable to either stage one or stage three, there is general consumer satisfaction with the court's truth-finding function. If there is any dissatisfaction at all, it emanates from the incentive that expensive and time-consuming jury trials give prosecutors to reduce charges significantly in the plea bargain process. In a jurisdiction like New York City there were 91,531 felony arrests in 1981 but only 2,393 felony jury trials; there is little alternative to the plea bargain. We are reasonably satisfied so long as the plea bargains reflect only a "fair discount" for pleading guilty.

Scholars, both here and in England, seem to agree that a 20 percent reduction in penalty is a fair return for foregoing a jury trial. Where the prosecution has the goods on a defendant and there are no stage one or stage three problems, 20 percent is about the going rate. Given that American statutory penalties are the longest of any Western industrial country, there is a good bit of fat in our penalty budget. The plea-bargain system does not work perfectly, but the alternative of trying every felony to a jury is an inefficient use of scarce resources that could better be used elsewhere in the law enforcement system—for example, hiring police or building juvenile rehabilitation facilities. In the real world the efficient allocation of money matters a great deal.

The fifty state jurisdictions, the District of Columbia, and the federal system all have separate criminal courts. There are numerous miscarriages of justice in the criminal courts. They can result from one of two causes: a systemic breakdown in the structure of the courts or an incompetent handling of a particular case by the personnel involved—judges, lawyers, prosecutors, jurors, and police. The group of botched criminal cases must be written off for our purposes here because discussing unrealistic schemes to exact higher performance from judicial personnel than from doctors, teachers, plumbers, or automobile dealers is futile. The purpose of this chapter is to explore a representative sample of the systemic problems of the criminal courts, which in turn exacerbate normal personnel incompetence. I have selected problems that give a fair idea of the magnitude of the task that an active, single-issue political lobby would face in any serious effort at crime control and law-enforcement reform.

Since stage one and stage three of the criminal process give the system its greatest trouble from the perspective of the consumer of government protection services, we must now address ourselves to each in turn. The preliminary proceeding stage of a criminal prosecution is the place where criminal law is least about criminals or law. In fact, we have chosen the preliminary stage as the vehicle for regulating official government conduct and enforcing American society's vision of civil rights and liberties. This is a comparatively new phenomenon reflecting the revolutionary change in the status of the common man that has occurred during the thirty-five years since World War II.

One initial observation is in order. America is unique among Western industrialized nations in terms of the ethnic, racial, linguistic, and cultural diversity of its population. It also has the most mobile population. Much of this mobility since World War II has involved the migration of impoverished rural people, particularly black and Hispanic, to the urban centers in search of employment. Migration, of course, was not limited to the poor or to racial minorities, but it was the poor and the racial minorities who were most likely to run afoul of arbitrary and oppressive official power when they moved in search of economic opportunities.

In the early 1960s the Supreme Court, under the leadership of Earl Warren, began a wholesale crusade for civil rights and civil liberties using the procedural aspects of the criminal law as the primary vehicle. The object was to create and enforce a balance of power in a system that was dominated by a majority racial and ethnic population and that majority's engine of authority, the police. Itinerant, poor, and politically powerless people had no protection and very little remedy from even outrageous abuses of official power. The Court's achievements in redressing this imbalance of power cannot be lightly dismissed.

Except for older readers, it is probably difficult to conceive what the criminal-law system looked like twenty years ago, before the Supreme Court began its reforms. For the college-educated middle class there are a few years—college and military years—when there is a greater than normal likelihood of experiencing official harassment or police brutality. However, once a person has a family, a job with a respected company, friends with money and connections, and access to lawyers, the likelihood of being on the receiving end of official repression fades dramatically. Criminal law is in practice largely an exercise in protecting the "haves" from the "have-nots." Once a person becomes a respectable have, his or her interaction with law-enforcement officers becomes limited to traffic offenses, official complaints as a

129

victim, or intercession on behalf of others, usually children or employees, who have been arrested.

Thus to understand the Supreme Court's achievement we must wander back through the years to circa 1950 when the criminal-justice system treated the have-nots as if they were meat on the way to dressing and processing. A few jurisdictions already had public-defender systems, but throughout most of America there was no right to a court-appointed, competent lawyer at government expense. Usually in state courts serious crimes like murder and armed robbery warranted a court request to a local practicing lawyer that he defend the accused for free, and lawyers did so as part of their public responsibilities. Whether a skillful lawyer or a hack was chosen was within the discretion of the judge. More to the point, in ordinary prosecutions for assault, grand larceny, daytime breaking and entering, or receiving stolen goods, no lawyer was usually appointed. Without a lawyer to argue for bail and without friends to put up a property bond or pay a bondsman, a suspect remained in the local jail until the court system got around to disposing of his case—often for as long as a year. This was the case even when the person was innocent.

That was only the beginning of the gallery of horrors to which the ordinary under-class member was subjected. Police interrogation was not circumscribed; the scenes from 1930's movies showing the bright light burning in the suspect's face while two cops take turns administering the third degree are accurate. Most interrogation was accompanied by substantial slapping around, denial of access to toilet facilities, and frequently deprivation of food and liquid. Once a signed confession was obtained, nobody looked very carefully into how it was obtained. Even the decent members of local juries tended to believe the best about the police, and when the police lied under oath—as they frequently did—they made convincing witnesses. In those days, by the way, jurors were usually selected from among property owners; a have-not was rarely judged by a jury of his peers.

When a crime was committed, the police would often put out a dragnet and bring in anyone in their bailiwick who had ever been involved in that sort of crime. Such a roundup ignored the need of the "suspects" to be at their jobs, their children's bedsides, or just home getting a night's sleep. Once a person had been convicted of a felony and released from prison, he was still likely to pass a substantial part of the rest of his life sitting on hard benches in crummy police stations, waiting to be grilled by the local constabulary.

Where the police suspected that some criminal activity was going on in a person's house or that the fruits of a crime were located there, they just came and kicked in the door. They turned out drawers, ripped open pillows, and tore out wall panels. If they had been mistaken, what was the remedy? Why, a lawsuit, of course, with its attendant legal fees and the additional obstacle of jury sympathy for police efforts to prevent crime and apprehend criminals.[1]

There were no standards for what constituted probable cause for arrest. Often, being a stranger in town without any job or association with the locals justified an arrest for "vagrancy." Sometimes there was actually a local conviction with a term in jail or the county prison farm, but more frequently an agreement to get out of town by sunset was the informal disposition.

The conclusion that the old system produced "good law enforcement" is misplaced. In general there was little official concern about murders, robberies, and assaults in the slum community. I remember when I was a child police and newspaper indifference to crimes perpetrated by blacks on other blacks. Occasionally the police went through the motions, and if apprehension and investigation were easy, they even prosecuted. In general, however, one's chances of police protection corresponded closely to one's position in the geography of political power. The same is true in New York City today. More time is devoted to investigating a barroom murder at Second Avenue and Sixty-third Street than to a comparable incident in the South Bronx.

Back in the good old days, an innocent suspect who was arrested because he was the victim of incriminating circumstances was likely to plead guilty. In the first place, he had no lawyer to protect him from the police, who routinely threatened dire consequences if he failed to confess. A person in a cell, cut off from outside information, is likely to believe anything he is told about the strictness of the

1. Juries may not convict innocent defendants, but they rarely convict guilty cops.

judge or the viciousness of the prosecutor. Even a confirmed skeptic could have little doubt as to the probable judicial irritation his un-cooperative attitude would engender. When such a person—frequently a person of limited intelligence, experience, and education—was told to plead guilty to grand larceny and take his two years in prison or he would be prosecuted for robbery and get at least ten years, that offer was hard to refuse. Members of the under-class knew full well that the system was set up to get them and that either way they were dead meat.

What about the persons who administered this system? Were they monsters? Probably not, but they were comparatively insensitive to the plight of a group of people with whom they did not identify. Also, the majority of the people who ran afoul of this system were, in the case of serious felonies, probably guilty. Police, prosecutors, and judges quickly became cynical about the value of a lot of "due process" when it cost them money and time. In this regard, let us look for a moment at the police-prosecutor-judge structure of the typical small American city at that time.

First of all, the judges, the prosecutors, and either the mayor or local sheriff were probably elected officials. Furthermore, since in most places one political party was usually in long-term control, these officials probably came from the same party, and the same faction of that party to boot. While sometimes there are divisive power struggles among local incumbent officeholders, the intelligent approach is cooperation and friendship. The police, prosecutor, and even the judge had a com-munity of interest stretching from the organization of the polls on elec-tion day right down to the division of the county budget and the allocation of office space in the county courthouse.

They also, of course, shared in the broad American community of interest in work avoidance, and due process of law has never been easy. It takes time and effort to investigate crimes and prove them in court without using confessions. It takes time and effort to hold jury trials and accord convicted defendants exhaustive hearings on the length of sentence and possible probation. Police officers, prosecutors, and judges were no more enamored of work than the average elevator operator or posthole digger; there was every incentive to secure quick convictions by a combination of confessions and guilty pleas. Defense lawyers merely complicated this otherwise expeditious process.[2]

At the local level there was a sufficient community of interest among all the political officials who had some element of control over police procedures that no one was going to change the traditional way of doing business. In many places, the police themselves—either city police or deputy sheriffs—were the strongest *local* political force. Since judges and prosecutors were and still are elected, no one was available to restrain police abuses. In a system where the judge, prosecutor, and sheriff had lunch together most days (occasionally at the jail where the food came from the inmate kitchen), it was hardly to be expected that the judge would be an active crusader for civil rights and civil liberties against his friend the sheriff. Thus the under-class of politically powerless defendants was left to its remedies in the political process, and that amounted, in most places, to no remedy at all.

In the big cities, with their slums, ethnic divisions, and race- or class-oriented political organization, there was occasional political furor over police brutality. Also, in major cities there was not just one judge or several judges but scores of judges, and the community of interest among judges, prosecutors, and police was less clear-cut. But any potential advantage to such a structure because of the plural nature of the political machinery was offset by the sheer volume of crime and a pervasive demand for law and order.

It was in response to these types of problems that the Supreme Court began to revise criminal procedure. Since the political process was unwilling to concern itself with the civil rights of the under-class, the only government agency capable of correcting the existing abuses was the federal judiciary. The federal courts were outside the control of the

2. One supervising force was outside of the local political community: the appellate courts. The constituency of the appellate court was either statewide or, in the more populous states, districtwide. Consequently, once a defendant got to a jury trial, he usually received a comparatively fair trial—everything was a matter of record and appellate courts would reverse convictions based on insufficient evidence or irregular procedures. The problem was that most defendants never saw a jury trial, and when they did they frequently had no lawyer to prosecute an appeal.

state political machines—federal judges had life tenure, applied federal law, and had federal power to back them up. However, they did not have any money, so they could not build a new system. The only remedy at their disposal was to release defendants whenever the procedure by which they had been arrested or convicted offended the court's sense of fairness. This sense of fairness was tied to comparatively vague clauses in the Constitution, so the institutional reform that the Supreme Court achieved flew under the colors of according citizens "constitutional rights."

The biggest reform involved the right to counsel. The Supreme Court held that in the prosecution of any felony, even where the defendant wanted to plead guilty and did not ask for a lawyer, the accused had to have competent representation at government expense. Furthermore, since the right to counsel is meaningless if the police exact incriminating statements or written confessions before the accused's counsel arrives, no person could be interrogated until his counsel arrived unless he intelligently waived his right to counsel. All suspects were entitled to a warning that they had a right to counsel; that if they could not afford counsel, counsel would be appointed for them at government expense; and that unless they specifically waived their right to have counsel present, the police would not interrogate them in the absence of counsel.

This simple expedient alone did not eliminate all coerced confessions or involuntary guilty pleas, but it went a long way. Incidentally, it was not sufficient just to require that counsel be appointed, since any hack lawyer who otherwise could not make a living practicing law would fill the bill, so the Supreme Court required "competent" counsel. Any confession taken without counsel being present, unless there had been a voluntary waiver, was excluded from evidence. This is one facet of the famous "exclusionary rule," which often resulted in the release of guilty defendants because frequently the only evidence the police had was the defendant's own improperly obtained confession.

There remained the whole area of unreasonable searches and unlawful detention to be dealt with. The Constitution had always required a warrant to search a person's home, but since the only sanction in most states against illegal search was an action for damages, the rule was never closely followed. Furthermore, there were certain exceptions that are recognized even today—for example, when the police have

134

reasonable grounds to believe that criminal activity is in progress inside a person's home and do not have time to procure a warrant. To eliminate warrantless searches that were not within any recognized exception to warrant requirements, the Supreme Court applied the exclusionary rule to evidence acquired by illegal searches—the fruits of that search could not be introduced into evidence in court.

The same rule was applied to unlawful arrests and detention. Under the Constitution no arrest could be made except upon a warrant issued by a magistrate. There are a few exceptions covering extraordinary circumstances, but they are comparatively narrow, involving either fleeing felons or crimes in progress at the time the police arrive. In the days of the dragnet, the police could bring in anyone who merely *might have* been involved in a particular crime for interrogation and intimidation. Now when this occurs, even if the defendant has knowingly and intelligently waived his right to counsel and confessed, the confession is the fruit of illegal arrest and hence inadmissible.

The initial effect of the new rules on the police was nil—they could not believe that the Supreme Court was serious. So in the middle 1960s the Supreme Court accepted hundreds of petty appeals from state courts, and, since the Supreme Court could not even then review all the cases of official abuse, it gave the lower federal courts expanded habeas corpus power to review decisions of state courts. In those jurisdictions where the state courts were reluctant to follow the Supreme Court's new guidelines, state convictions were taken to federal district court on a wholesale basis where the federal judges essentially heard appeals from the state's highest court. Eventually both police and prosecutors came to understand that the federal courts were serious. At that point the system started to change.

Before the nationwide adoption of exclusionary rules, there had been little political pressure to improve police methods. It is difficult for nonlawyers to understand the "exclusionary rule." Actually the exclusionary rule about which there is so much complaint involves two separate elements. First, in the early 1960s the Supreme Court began to supervise state criminal prosecutions and devised rules about how those prosecutions should be conducted. Some of those rules had previously been applied in federal courts, and some had also been used in a few state courts. What was new in the 1960s was that the Supreme

Court, by interpreting the U.S. Constitution, required a uniform system of criminal procedure in state courts that enforced certain rights. Theoretically many of these rights had existed before, but usually they had not been enforced. Among them were the right to counsel, the right to be free from unreasonable warrantless searches, and the right to be free from unreasonable warrantless arrest and detention.

The second element is the remedy that the Supreme Court applied when its new rules were not followed. The Court required that confessions or evidence obtained in violation of these rules be "excluded" from jury consideration in the trial of any criminal case. Thus even if a person was guilty and had confessed, if his confession had been taken before he was advised of his right to counsel, the confession could not be used at trial. Consequently, when we discuss the exclusionary rule we must be clear whether we mean the rules the Supreme Court has made or the remedy of exclusion designed to enforce those rules or both.

The new procedural rules changed political pressure to get convictions into political pressure for proper convictions that could be sustained. Police officers began to be trained to understand and observe constitutional rights. Police department budgets went up, modern equipment was purchased, and most important, training programs were inaugurated. Twenty years ago local sheriffs' deputies and small-town cops were country boys who had strapped on a gun and pinned on a badge—such training as they received they got on the job. While many old-time police exercised substantial common sense and had good community rapport, in the main they were bumpkins and rubes, frequently of the most malevolent sort.

Suddenly police were expected to attend some sort of police academy. The larger cities had always had academies, and in most states city and county police were allowed to attend the state police academy if the local authority paid the freight, which was an infrequent occurrence. Training is now mandatory for all but the constabularies of small villages. In recognition of the difficulty of getting more money out of the states and cities to fund local police departments adequately, the federal government created the Law Enforcement Assistance Administration, which provided money for everything from training to police radio equipment. (This agency finally went out of business in April 1982.)

With the federal courts looking over the shoulders of the state judges and issuing mandates, it was no longer possible for members of the old-boy political network to wink at each other's transgressions. Where the police and prosecutors erred, the local judge had little choice but to release defendants unless he wanted to appear an unprofessional buffoon in front of his own bar. By 1976 when the Supreme Court began to withdraw from case-by-case supervision of state-court criminal convictions, lawyers who had been in school when the criminal law revolution began were themselves becoming judges. They knew no other system, and they enthusiastically enforced the new system.

THE average citizen confronted by daily street crime asks, "Why?" Every time some felon's constitutional rights are vindicated, he is back on the street committing more crimes. It would appear at first blush that the Supreme Court has a screw loose. Certainly the object of the whole exercise was not to release the guilty or to protect the criminal class at the expense of everyone else. Rather, the object was to effect a change in the way all the enforcement institutions of government operated. But the only tool available to the federal courts, however, was their power to require evidence to be excluded.[3] Another instance, if you will, of trying to do brain surgery with a meat ax.

3. Most objections to actions of the criminal courts go to the new rules about arrests, searches, and the inadmissibility of confessions. Frequently, however, when convictions are overturned it is not for any pretrial police error but because there was insufficient evidence to convict, or because prejudicial material like a former criminal record was introduced before the jury. Unlike procedural errors, these latter problems go directly to the truth-finding function of the court—the question of whether the defendant is guilty. Eyewitness identification, for example, has always been a problem; the traditional eyewitness frequently makes a wrong identification. Cross-racial identifications are particularly suspect since "they all look alike," so where there is no evidence *except* an eyewitness, the witness's testimony must be received and scrutinized with caution. Part of the criminal-law reform was to eliminate police procedures that suggested certain suspects to the eyewitness as likely candidates.

137

While the last twenty years have seen a substantially higher crime rate, the reforms themselves were probably not responsible for most of the increase. In the same twenty years we have witnessed the departure of mothers from the home to enter the labor force, more single-parent families, a general decline of community, church, and school discipline, and geographical mobility that tends to undermine the social and community ties that have an ameliorating effect upon deviant behavior. While criminal-law reform has had some marginal effect on the number of dangerous felons abroad, because no one can gainsay that procedural requirements do result in robbers and murderers being released, an overall evaluation of the costs and benefits of the Supreme Court's policies requires a careful dissection of the numerous related factors that have combined to increase crime.

One of the finest studies on criminal motivation was done by the Department of Labor and published in 1978. The Labor Department tested the effect of money income on criminals in Baltimore and determined that an income of about $125 a week drastically reduced the incentive to commit crime among recently released felons, but that when the money ran out, the felons began to commit crimes again.[4] The study tends to support my own conclusion that a 2 percent reduction in unemployment for unskilled labor would have a greater effect on the overall crime rate than the abolition of every procedural rule that the Supreme Court has initiated in the last twenty-five years.

Furthermore, crime comes in all shapes and sizes. The increase in the juvenile crime rate is associated more closely with the breakdown of the family than with the exclusionary rule and related obstacles to prosecution. Increase in the use of "recreational" drugs since the 1950s has spawned a whole new criminal industry, and the cost of drugs along with their pervasive use by the poor is an incentive to crime. While it cannot be disputed that the exclusionary rule and related procedural changes in the criminal law have had some effect on the level of crime,

---

4. "Unlocking the Second Gate" by Kenneth J. Lenihan was a contract research report funded by the Department of Labor Employment and Training Administration and undertaken by the Bureau of Social Science Research, Inc., of Washington, D.C., a private agency. The study showed a 27 percent lower rearrest rate and a 15 percent higher employment rate among the group receiving financial aid than among the control group.

their effect is usually blown out of proportion because the exclusionary rule sticks out so obviously in a system that is otherwise often mysterious. Criminals who escape conviction because of some procedural irregularity cast a very long shadow.

The Supreme Court succeeded in changing basic ground rules for interaction between the average citizen and the law-enforcement industry. The entire institution of law enforcement was dramatically improved: police departments expanded, training became thorough, legal representation was systematized, random police harassment was discouraged, and the judiciary itself was upgraded. Since the Supreme Court expected procedural regularity at all stages, the tobacco-chewing, one-gallused, part-time justice of the peace of yesteryear was replaced in most states by a full-time magistrate who was either a lawyer already or had undergone some kind of formal training.

Yet even from this perspective it must be admitted that the exclusionary rule carried significant social costs. The strict enforcement of the warrant requirement before stops and searches can be made interferes, for example, with the intelligent use of the police officer's sixth sense. The ordinary beat cop does have a "feeling" for which people in the neighborhood are up to no good. People driving vans in residential neighborhoods late at night; men carrying tool boxes down back alleys for no apparent reason; and prosperous looking men in Cadillacs parked near high schools at the same time every day all put an experienced officer on notice of possible criminal activity.

Frequently the police take a fairly practical course; while they do not have sufficient information to get a warrant or to justify an arrest without a warrant, they stop a suspect anyway. Where their suspicions are justified and they go ahead and make an arrest, they will probably not be able to get a conviction. It is at this point that arguably legitimate police activity is frustrated by the courts. Since the most important job for the police is the prevention of crime rather than convictions after the fact, it is most important that the police have authority to investigate suspicious behavior.

Another and even uglier side to the last twenty years is that almost all the costs of reform have been borne by the lower socioeconomic class. The Supreme Court has never said that the release of felons when their rights have been violated is required by the Constitution. The

Supreme Court has merely said that release will be the remedy until Congress or the states provide another sufficiently punitive remedy that will achieve the same protection of civil rights. Obviously, any other remedy would involve some sort of a civil fine on the offending officers or, more realistically, their government departments. The reason that the political establishment has never sought another remedy that would be acceptable to the Supreme Court is that such a remedy would be expensive. (In terms of tax revenues, the release of dangerous felons is very cheap. The cost of the sanction then is shifted from the government treasury to the lower socioeconomic class because that is the class that disproportionately bears the brunt of crime.)

This may appear a shocking proposition, but it is indisputable. The likelihood of a woman in a family that makes under $3,000 a year being raped is almost four times as great as that of a woman in a family that makes $25,000 or more. The same applies to all other violent crimes involving jeopardy to the person. Property crimes, most of which are covered by insurance, are the crimes that the upper middle class suffers most regularly. Furthermore, there is a higher statistical incidence of violent crime being perpetrated on racial minorities than others, even when income factors are held constant. This is because minority members have a higher likelihood of living in or near poor neighborhoods than whites of comparable incomes.[5] Gas stations, fast-food stores, and all-night markets are the most frequent targets of armed robbery. Inner city schools look like armed camps, and the weak child often finds just going to the bathroom terrifying. The districts in which the elderly poor live are also the districts where the criminal element find lodging, so the streets are never safe. In working-class neighborhoods the immediacy of the threat of crime dictates high-visibility police procedures, which to the very sensitive might appear as harassing.

As I have observed before, the Supreme Court has tried to effect a

5. Exhaustive statistical material proving the perfect negative correlation between violent crime and income is found in M. Hindelang, M. Gottredson, and J. Carofalo, *Victims of Personal Crime: an Empirical Foundation for a Theory of Personal Victimization* (Cambridge, Mass.: Ballinger, 1978) and *Criminal Victimization Surveys: A National Crime Survey Report*, U.S. Department of Justice, Law Enforcement Assistance Administration, National Criminal Justice Information and Statistics Service (Washington, D.C., 1977).

dramatic social revolution, an upgrading of all state and federal government enforcement—but in doing so they have used extremely primitive tools. Since the general civility of the police and prosecutors, and the professionalism of the courts themselves, are nebulous social issues that inspire only yawns from the political process, no agency but the country's highest court can have a nationwide impact. Because the Supreme Court has established an acceptable remedy that is financially cheap, there is little incentive for the legislative or executive branches to engage in a dialogue with the Court over alternative means to the same end.

It is difficult to convey a *feeling* for the two sides of the criminal-law reform debate because personal conclusions about the proper balance between the police and the criminals are grounded in personal experience. For example, in my entire life I have never had an unpleasant encounter with the police. Yet I know that the police can be bullies, and other judges as well as readers have seen them at their worst. Some people radiate a challenge to authority that embroils them in a constant battle of ego with police officers. In small towns the police are often agents of one dominant political faction and single out certain individuals or families for routine harassment. Therefore, if some readers wonder why I am as tolerant of the new procedures as I am, or other readers wonder why I am willing to manipulate exclusionary rules to permit the police to follow their sixth sense, the answer is that I have tried to see both sides.

In the final analysis the whole exercise in civil-rights/civil-liberties reform effected through criminal procedure is another attempt to bang square pegs into round holes. We are using legal rules to achieve cultural reform. Every serious student of the exclusionary rule, regardless of his or her position on civil liberties, agrees that the exclusionary rule is a limited deterrent to the most persistent forms of police bullying. A political position that abandons any effort at cultural reform by returning criminal procedure to the system of yesteryear will never be accepted by all the law-abiding citizens who have been on the receiving end of police bullying. Yet a serious effort to eliminate bullying at all levels, particularly where it occurs without a criminal prosecution to which the exclusionary rules can be applied as a sanction, would meet with popular willingness to compromise on such issues as the scope of permissible

141

stops and frisks, as well as the application of the exclusionary rule to the unintentional violation of very technical rules by police acting in good faith.

The reason that alternative approaches to protecting civil rights and civil liberties must be considered is that twenty years of court decisions on search and seizure, the warrant requirement for certain types of arrests, and police interrogation have spawned an entirely artificial system of procedural rules that even lawyers find difficult to master. When a five-judge state supreme court after three months' deliberation splits three to two on whether a particular search was within the narrow exceptions to the warrant requirement, how can the average police officer be expected to decide the issue correctly in the approximately fifteen seconds allotted to him out on the street?

Furthermore, from the point of view of institutional performance, it makes a great deal of difference whether a particular violation of a person's individual rights was intentional or merely negligent. Given the artificiality of the rules, their violation is inevitable. For example, as of this writing, the Supreme Court has said that where there is a lawful arrest of a motorist, the police can search the entire passenger compartment of the vehicle without a warrant, including suitcases, paper pokes, glove compartments, etc. However, the police cannot open the trunk. But what about a station wagon? To any reasonable person, everything in a station wagon is within reach of the passenger compartment, so the entire vehicle can be searched. Now, however, what if there is a locked steamer trunk in the luggage compartment of the station wagon. Is that more like the trunk of a car or more like a suitcase in a passenger compartment? Who the hell knows? Or for that matter, who the hell cares? The important rule concerns whether a person has a right to be free from searches of his or her vehicle. There is no reason to do medieval scholastic exercises about the different privacy expectations between a poke on the front seat and a trunk in the back of a station wagon. While even the stupidest police officer can understand a rule that says "never search a vehicle without a warrant," not even the smartest can understand post-doctoral-level legal gymnastics about privacy expectations and so will blow it almost every time.

Many of the rules regarding search and seizure were developed during a particularly revolutionary period in American social and economic history. Twenty years ago the police were almost entirely white, while the criminal class was disproportionately black or Hispanic. All over America communities fought migration of economically disadvantaged people. Zoning ordinances forbidding low-cost housing, residency requirements for public assistance, and vagrancy laws were all part of an effort to "keep the neighborhood up." Private discrimination in housing, employment, and public accommodations did its share as well. Court decisions striking down residency requirements, declaring vagrancy laws unconstitutional, and limiting certain types of zoning combined with the Civil Rights Act of 1964 to further mobility. Part of this package, but only part, also involved restricting the level of police harassment that had been used to inspire a quick moving-on of outsiders.

Also, for whatever it is worth, during the 1960s and 1970s many of the important cases on search and seizure involved possession of marijuana by teenagers and college students under a highly punitive system of local laws where simple possession could land a person in prison for twenty years. These laws were obviously obsolete from the perspective of the contemporary morals of the majority, but they were slow to change. The Supreme Court could not hold the laws against drugs themselves unconstitutional, but the Court could nibble away around the edges by making it difficult to enforce those laws. Here we have a perfect example of how the pulse beat of the street resonates into the political judicial process.

In West Virginia when I first came to the bar, the penalty for smoking marijuana was five years in prison. Smoking marijuana and taking other drugs, particularly hallucinogens like LSD, were, at least in the middle class, part of a political movement that gathered around civil rights, the war in Vietnam, and general opposition to the "establishment." The one thing that very strict search-and-seizure warrant requirements did was almost guarantee that people who used marijuana in their own homes could not be prosecuted, and that people who had it on their person but otherwise were violating no law could not be arrested or searched. While neither judicial sympathy for drug users nor the peculiar demands of a society in the throes of social, economic, and racial

143

integration entirely explain the imposition of the exclusionary rule on state courts, both phenomena played their parts.[6]

It is time to catalog the successes and failures of the new criminal procedure and begin to tinker at the rules to reduce the failures and increase the successes. At the moment we are at a dead end. As I read today's criminal cases from the Supreme Court, all I see are rewrites of yesterday's news. In order to make any dramatic improvement from this point on, we must focus on the doughnut and not on the hole. In this case, the doughnut is the institutional structure of police departments, prosecutors, and courts, and the hole consists of all the artificial rules designed to influence the behavior of these institutions. This set of artificial rules is like some ancient steam engine that loses about 90 percent of its power from the boiler to the driving wheel.[7]

Legal scholars and sociologists have done numerous empirical studies to determine whether the exclusionary rule actually deters unacceptable police conduct. The studies are inconclusive, although some of the more thorough studies were conducted in the late 1960s and early 1970s, before the institutions affected had had an opportunity to adjust fully to the new rules.[8] Civil libertarians object that the exclusionary rule punishes the police only when a person is guilty and a trial is contemplated. The rule does not protect innocent victims of police harassment. Thus if the police break down your door, turn out your drawers, and bust open your walls with fire axes only to find nothing incriminating, the exclusionary rule will not pay to have your house

6. The federal courts had been excluding illegally obtained evidence since 1914 and many state courts had followed suit long before they were required to do so in the 1960s.

7. The exclusionary rule for searches and seizures tends to benefit selected classes of criminals disproportionately. While any criminal can be in a circumstance where the exclusionary rule will be beneficial, the rule primarily benefits drug pushers, those who carry dangerous weapons, and violators of the vice laws. Interestingly, it is with regard both to drug use and vice prosecution that there is least agreement in this society about the legitimacy of the substantive law.

8. Part of this adjustment is generational; younger police officers and administrators have never known any other system and accept warrant requirements and the exclusionary rule as the way the system *ought* to operate.

put back together. The innocent victim of police intrusion is left to the cumbersome, expensive, and long-delayed damage suit.

The empirical studies lead to the conclusion that the deterrent effect of the exclusionary rule depends entirely on the level of police training, the political climate of the jurisdiction, and the commitment of senior officials to obeying the law.[9] The effect of training is obvious when we observe the difference between the success rate of federal as opposed to local police. The FBI and other federal agents are highly paid; they have extensive training in their own professional schools; and they have adequate logistical support. Furthermore, the supervisory personnel require that agents obey the law both for political reasons and for high conviction rates. As a result federal agents seldom run afoul of the exclusionary rules—they are careful to do everything by the book. Of course, they are not in the business of controlling street crime, so their officers seldom have to make the split-second decisions a foot patrolman must make. Nonetheless, the difference is so remarkable that it must be attributed at least in part to better training.

The first question to be asked is whether the substantive rules about search and seizure are really what we want. After all, the exclusionary rule is merely a method for enforcing the requirement that a search be conducted only after some judge is convinced that the person or place to be searched probably has some incriminating evidence. Yet we do not require a warrant to search a person and/or his baggage at an airport. The theory is that if a person wants to use a plane, he must be willing to submit to a search. Nowadays the search is usually conducted with X-rays and hand-held metal detectors, but ten years ago the searches were done by hand, particularly at small airports, and some stranger went methodically through one's carry-on luggage. The thing that makes an airport search so acceptable to most of us is that it's done politely and doesn't discriminate among races, social classes, sexes, or ages. And it's expected—if you want to take your Swiss Army knife on a trip, you know that you must check your baggage. Airport security was designed to accomplish one thing—reduce the number of hijackings.

9. A good summary of the empirical studies is Bradley Canon, "The exclusionary rule: have critics proven that it doesn't deter police?" *Judicature* 62 (March 1979): 398.

The Fourth Amendment generally protects against unreasonable searches of persons, papers, and houses; however, its interpretation is artificial from the outset. In constitutional law interpretation is everything, since the text is usually sparse and vague. The Fourth Amendment literally requires a warrant for all searches, yet we have never required literal compliance. Once the words are not to be taken literally, all interpretations are just that—interpretations.

Why can we search the passenger compartment of a car when there is a lawful arrest for speeding but not the trunk? Why can we frisk a suspect incident to a lawful arrest *and* open a closed briefcase? Why does the exclusionary rule apply when your financial papers are illegally searched on your own premises but not when the same papers are illegally searched in your accountant's office? These examples merely illustrate that the Fourth Amendment is not a talisman with a charm all its own that can never be tampered with lest the whole structure of civil rights and liberties fall to pieces. The Fourth Amendment is already a jerry-built structure that can be improved substantially from both law-enforcement and civil-liberties perspectives. The level of training, commitment to civil rights and civil liberties, and general civility of the police are inextricably intertwined with the scope of the warrant requirements.

I suspect that the overwhelming majority of Americans would be willing to tolerate increased *polite* police intrusion into their daily lives if it would lower the crime rate. Furthermore, there is an important distinction between the search of a person's home or office—with all the attendant property damage—and the search of one's person or automobile. Possibly this is the difference between a destructive and a casual search, and a warrant should still be required to tear open the seats of a car or to do a cavity search of the body. However, the exclusionary rule per se, which is only a remedy, is not at issue as much as the substantive rules about both the extent and the cultural conditions—politeness—of searches and seizures. This approach would permit the police to capitalize on the use of their sixth sense while at the same time scrutinizing the procedures used to make on-the-spot searches. If we follow this analysis very far, ultimately we come face to face with the need for a significant upgrading of culture in a very direct sort of way.

When a so-called conservative suggests greater latitude for the police to prevent crime by prophylactic searches, the objection is often made that this will lead to a "police state." This immediately introduces an emotion-laden term into the discussion, conjuring up the image of totalitarian countries. However, the real police state involves far more than just authority to search individuals on the street or in their cars; it involves incommunicado incarceration; unjustified arrests; denial, as in South Africa, of any appeal to the courts; and a host of other unpleasant police powers. When much of America can fairly be characterized as a "criminal state," at least for the poor, thinking people should be wary of the use of the term "police state."

The exclusionary rule of course applies to a host of situations unrelated to unlawful search and seizure. Confessions, for example, obtained without an intelligent waiver of rights or after counsel has been requested but not supplied are excluded, as is evidence uncovered as a result of an unlawful detention where there were no grounds for arrest. In these instances there is little criticism of the substantive law but rather criticism of the application of an exclusionary rule that excludes the most trustworthy evidence of a crime. Defenders of the exclusionary rule maintain in these circumstances that the rule is required to sustain the moral integrity of the courts; we cannot permit the courts to condone illegal prosecutorial conduct by permitting the state to secure convictions through illegal means.

The correct position is somewhere between the two extremes. We cannot assert on the one hand that citizens have certain rights and then on the other hand permit the police to violate these rights to secure convictions. However, it makes a great deal of difference whether a particular violation was intentional or merely negligent, and this is especially true when police are working with a highly artificial structure in the complex area of criminal procedure. Of course the idea of permitting negligent intrusions is dangerous too, since conceivably it sets a premium on ignorance of the law.

In the real political world where civil rights and civil liberties are extremely important to a significant political constituency, no change in the current structure will be acceptable unless it enhances civil rights and civil liberties at the same time that it tinkers at the exclusionary rule to eliminate dismissals when the only violation has been unintentional or technical. For all these reasons, a dramatic improvement in

147

enforcement must involve two distinct aspects: forthright modification of the rules governing stops, personal searches for weapons, and searches of automobiles on the public streets; and alternative sanctions for violations of constitutional rights. These sanctions should, unlike the exclusionary rule, operate regardless of whether the person whose rights have been violated is ultimately prosecuted in court.

The police should be allowed to stop and search people in a polite manner under circumstances that would arouse suspicion in a reasonable, well-trained police officer. Thus the black Cadillac parked in front of the local high school could be searched, as could the two furtive figures loitering at a late-night grocery store around closing time. The *quid pro quo* for such a modification is that where the police are either rough or impolite or are using their power to harass unpopular people or their own personal enemies, draconian sanctions be applied very quickly. As I indicated earlier, one of the attractions of the exclusionary rule is that it is cheap—state and local budgets are not required to respond in damages to the thousands of rights violations that result in discovery of no incriminating evidence.

If, however, the police are to be given wider prophylactic powers, then the abuse of these powers must be discouraged by a quick payment of substantial money damages to those abused. This almost inevitably implies petition to a court sitting without a jury. While the amount of damage awards need be no more than five hundred dollars plus attorney fees and any actual property damage, such an amount multiplied hundreds or thousands of times during any given year will have sufficient impact on local budgets to deter police abuse, and there is no reason to believe that the courts will enforce this sanction with less integrity than they currently enforce the exclusionary rule.

Since in other areas of individual rights, such as the right to counsel and the right to be free from unjustified arrests, the exclusionary rule is designed to improve law-enforcement institutions, our threshold questions should focus directly on those institutions. How much money has been appropriated for training? What educational levels are expected of new recruits? What is the standard operating procedure of the department? To what extent does the command structure expect and demand strict compliance with existing law? What sanctions does the department itself impose on officers who are abusive?

The answers to these questions will tell us what the commitment of any institution is to protecting personal rights. If the answers indicate an inadequate institutional commitment to protecting personal rights, then there is no alternative to the exclusionary rule since the violation is objectively intentional. But if the answers demonstrate an institutional commitment to doing the job right every time, then the next question must be whether in a given instance the law-enforcement officer intended to violate someone's rights to secure a conviction or was merely negligent. Again, if the intrusion was intentional, there is probably no alternative to the exclusionary rule.

If there is a mistaken conception about the exclusionary rule as a general deterrent to police abuse, it is the assumption that the police and prosecutors care desperately about whether they secure convictions. In my own experience that is just not true. Both police and prosecutors are salaried employees who are no more interested in doing extra work than anyone else in society. Certainly they care about certain convictions—murder or rape—but in the run-of-the-mine breaking and entering, grand larceny, or simple assault they couldn't care less. What they do care about is their departmental budget, and if we begin systematically penalizing illegal official conduct even when there is nothing to exclude from evidence, the effect will be far more dramatic than anything contemplated by the exclusionary rule. This too requires some system for imposing the sanction that avoids an expensive and time-consuming jury trial.

The defenders of the exclusionary rule have grave doubts about whether such a system would work. They fear that the focus on institutional qualities is so subjective that over time protection of individual rights will be eroded by courts' casting a blind eye to local policies. Furthermore, they immediately question whether local fiscal bodies will appropriate the money necessary to pay the damages in all the instances of rights violations not currently covered by the exclusionary rule. Unfortunately, these problems will never be sorted out until we begin experimenting with alternative systems. Since the Supreme Court has never required the exclusionary rule per se but only some meaningful sanction against illegal police conduct, the state legislatures are free to experiment. Why haven't they experimented? Because any new system will cost money, and currently all of their available money goes to satisfy organized constituencies in other areas.

The public at large doesn't know enough about the alternatives to the exclusionary rule to demand that money be spent on an alternative. I doubt, for example, that if the West Virginia Supreme Court of Appeals were to articulate an alternative to the exclusionary rule that would be acceptable to us, and which then passed the Supreme Court of the United States' constitutionality test, the West Virginia Legislature would enact such a program if it cost money.

In the final analysis, discussion of the exclusionary rule merely returns us to the discussion of Chapter 3 concerning the need for an active, militant, citizen lobby. One reason that no serious attack on the exclusionary rule has been made is that no effort has been forthcoming to reconcile the conflicting political goals that are involved in the exclusionary rule. Opponents of the exclusionary rule talk about "good faith exceptions" or other modifications, but the gist of their proposals is that we substantially reduce the barriers to illegal police intrusions. An active citizen lobby would quickly understand the dimensions of the problem through its representatives' interaction with civil-rights and civil-liberties activists—in other words, with another single-issue lobby— and that would inevitably lead to real-world political compromises and real-world political progress. As it currently stands, organizations like the American Civil Liberties Union have a near-monopoly of the political arena, and since there is no organized opposition to their efforts, the civil liberties forces feel no compulsion to compromise, and no progress is made.

ONE conclusion that recurs in scholarly analysis of the exclusionary rule is that some police departments deliberately enforce the drug and vice laws in such a way as to make all prosecutions vulnerable to challenge for constitutional rights violations. Thus it can still appear that drug and vice laws are being enforced, while at the same time guaranteeing no convictions. I find this a believable analysis based on my experience in politics, and it is worth exploring this phenomenon in greater depth with regard to corruption in general.

Local mayors, prosecutors, and judges are usually elected, or they are appointed by officals who are elected. Winning elections requires money and the support of organized political blocs. The people who are most intensely interested in politics are those who have something to gain from favorable political decisions or something to lose from unfavorable ones. As I explained in Chapter 3, the highest level of political involvement comes from organized economic constituencies that have concrete, selfish interests in political decisions. And no one is more interested in local politics than the organized denizens of the underworld. While rapists, murderers, armed robbers, and muggers usually have limited political entrée, the more criminal activity resembles organized business—drugs, prostitution, gambling, theft and resale of automobiles—the more criminals defend themselves politically, just like any other business. The personal rewards to police and prosecutors from selective enforcement are almost beyond description.

The police, prosecutors, and criminals are members of a community in which personal relationships abound. At the most innocuous level, the purveyors of vice can always be counted on to contribute money (often through their lawyers) to local political campaigns. In addition, their prostitutes, policy runners, barbershop or dry cleaner fronts, and other miscellaneous employees have families and friends who all vote in poorly attended local primary elections. While a local sheriff is unlikely to look the other way where murder or rape is involved, vice appears both so harmless and so pervasive that lax enforcement in return for political support is accepted as a fact of life, since active political support is unlikely to come either from the churchgoers or the Women's Christian Temperance Union.

Although sheriffs, local prosecutors, and mayors receive political benefits, their minions may receive direct payoffs. Often they are disguised—a police officer with a sick child suddenly finds that all the medical expenses have been paid by an anonymous good Samaritan. Public officials in personal trouble find that competent lawyers volunteer to represent them for nothing; good business opportunities appear; or good buys are available on houses or automobiles. This is not to say that the paper poke of long green does not still change hands, but the crass payoff involves unnecessary risks that are obviated by more subtle forms of indirect graft.

The old adage that people get the government they deserve is well illustrated by a current example. For years there was a disagreeable, in many ways mediocre, yet basically honest county prosecutor. This prosecutor's personality caused strained relations with the members of the bar, but he did strictly enforce the vice laws along with all the other laws. Obviously he was unpopular with the underworld element, and numerous serious efforts were made to beat him in primaries. Finally an attractive young lawyer was found who I suspect was funded by the underworld, and he narrowly defeated the old prosecutor. The result was that the county was immediately opened up to gambling and other vice by a conspicuous policy of nonenforcement of the vice laws.

Over the years the old prosecutor made many enemies but no friends. Ordinary citizens considered prosecuting to be merely his job and thus were ungrateful, while the families and friends of those he prosecuted came to hate him. The young scoundrel who replaced him is now opening the county up to an element that was previously discouraged, but that fact is generally lost on the average middle-class voter. Vice rarely touches the average voter's life directly. The indirect results— greater drug use among children, higher incidence of venereal disease, stealing to buy drugs or to pay gambling debts—cause a deterioration of the social fabric, however, which these voters eventually will notice.

It must always be remembered that both the passage and the enforcement of laws are political and that the political element is an intentional feature of our government structure. The Constitution's guarantee of a trial by jury, for instance, has a purely political dimension. It reserves to local communities the power to nullify oppressive laws by refusing to convict. The process is set up to protect certain important political rights, such as freedom of speech and freedom from oppressive laws that may be passed when one narrow interest group momentarily captures the government. This is politics in the highest sense—jury trials, elected judges, elected prosecutors, and the power of executive clemency all unite to mitigate the opportunities for tyranny.[10]

Yet the proposition is repeated endlessly that "the courts should not

---

10. For example, the reluctance of elected state judges to grant injunctions in labor disputes is notorious. The Clayton Act of 1914, which specifically denies the power to federal judges to enjoin strikes, was intended to forestall the opportunity for employers to go to life-tenured, nonelected judges to get

be political.'' More often than not what is really meant is that the courts should not vindicate a political position different from that of the speaker. Sometimes, however, all that is meant is that the courts and their supporting agencies should not be corrupt. Obviously everyone concurs that neither judges, prosecutors, nor police should accept money, gifts, or other things of value in return for official action. But if a person wants to be a judge or prosecutor, with the prestige and salary that those jobs provide, what is the difference among outright bribes, campaign contributions, and machine support on election day? In a functional sense, very little indeed. The whole political process is potentially a grand exercise in corruption.

The exercise of popular, majoritarian politics has two distinct dimensions: the number of people who favor a particular political position, and the intensity with which they favor it. In the final analysis, it is intensity and not bare numbers that translates into effective political power. In the politics that touch the court system, numbers and intensity are usually at odds. And as in warfare, sports, and even religion, a sufficient level of intensity will offset numerical disadvantages. In politics intensity is a product of financial commitment, organization, and a single-minded purpose.

Any analysis of politics leads inevitably to the question, Why do we not appoint all local judges, prosecutors, and sheriffs? Federal judges and prosecutors are appointed, and public satisfaction with their performance appears to be at least as high as or higher than that of state and local officials. Yet the opposite charge is made against federal judges to the charge leveled against state judges—that many of the most important political decisions in America are being made by nonelected, life-tenured judges who are accountable to no one. While appointment tends to reduce corruption by eliminating opportunities to exchange decisions for political support, it also reduces the degree of legitimate political control. The proof of the pudding is probably in the eating: in those states where judges are appointed by the governor or elected by the legislature, there doesn't appear to be any higher citizen satisfaction with court perform-

labor injunctions. Thus the labor lobby placed an important economic question in the hands of state judges who would be overwhelmed by the number of voters rather than ties of social class.

ance than in the states where judges are elected by the people. Similarly, counties that are policed by elected local sheriffs don't appear to have any more corruption than big cities that have appointed police commissioners and chiefs of police. Appointed officials still depend on elected officials for reappointment, departmental budgets, promotion, and a host of other important things, so the difference is probably a wash.

When we scrutinize the politics that surround the subversion of the criminal-law process, either by undermining enforcement, influencing prosecutors not to prosecute, or convincing a court to be lenient after conviction, a pattern emerges that is similar to warfare. In war the defending army must maintain security along a perimeter of many miles. An attacking army can concentrate its forces at one small point on the perimeter, outnumbering and outgunning the defenders at that one point.

Organized criminals think of nothing but subverting the criminal-law process as it applies to the conduct of their business. They don't attack the entire perimeter. When a criminal is caught, he can mobilize all of his friends, lawyers, family, and political influence to mitigate the effects of prosecution and conviction. Police, prosecutors, and judges can be overwhelmed with social and political pressure at one point in their perimmeter defense, and a surrender or collapse of that point will be unnoticed. This is particularly true because the defending army is really a phantom army—there are no organized groups actively defending the perimeter. Except in circumstances where the problem has reached outrageous proportions, nobody monitors the progress of criminal cases to detect abuses of prosecutorial discretion; nobody raises money to support political campaigns of candidates who will eliminate police corruption; nobody watches the sentencing patterns of judges and is vigilent to catch political favoritism.

SO far I have dwelt on stage one of the criminal-justice process—enforcement, constitutional rights of suspects, and police conduct. Since stage two, the jury trial that determines guilt or innocence, presents few systemic problems other than the plea bargains that are struck because of the expense of jury trials, stage two is beyond the scope of this book. The appropriateness of the insanity defense and related issues concerning criminal responsibility are important, but they go to basic value judgments about moral accountability about which I have no greater insight than the reader's next door neighbor. The third stage, where convicted defendants are punished, does present some opportunities for improvement and economy.

By far the most expensive part of the criminal-justice system is the treatment of offenders. New prisons cost hundreds of millions of dollars, depending on the price of land and local construction costs. In 1982 the federal government offered to make its federal prison for women at Alderson, West Virginia, available for state prisoners, and the contract price was $41 a day per inmate. That yearly cost of $14,977 is greater than the median annual wage and applies to incarceration in an old medium-security facility where the price offered does not reflect today's costs of construction. Prison is very expensive, and the higher the requirements for security and the closer the prison is to an urban area, the more expensive it becomes.

Long-term imprisonment for crime is a comparatively recent punishment. It was invented in the last century because Americans believed that in a free society the greatest deprivation is loss of individual liberty. In England corporal punishment, capital punishment, and transportation beyond the seas were used. A form of enslavement was a traditional punishment, but simple locking-up is modern and reflects Western society's abhorrence of capital punishment, corporal punishment, and even temporary slavery. (Southern prisons, until recently, often employed a modified slavery model, but they were considered barbaric by the rest of the country.)

The typical state or federal prisoner is not only expensive to house and feed, but he or she is a dead loss to society in terms of productive work. The southern chain gang of yesteryear shocks our conscience because of the way it was administered, but the proposition that prisoners should be doing useful work under humane conditions meets with almost universal approval. The problem appears to be that it costs more to administer prisoners doing useful work than to keep them in idleness, and often useful work implies taking jobs away from working people who would otherwise receive a salary. Here again we run up against a political problem of significant dimensions.

Prisoners are frequently qualified only for unskilled work, and it is among unskilled labor that unemployment runs highest. State and local employees doing routine maintenance and janitorial jobs will violently object to prisoners taking these jobs. Even if the prisoners are used only to supplement current employees, there is a clear reduction in status associated with working with prisoners. Certainly highway contractors, who by the way are notorious for making large political contributions, do not want competition from prison road gangs.

The horror of most prisons serves as an enormous disincentive to judges to sentence nonviolent offenders to confinement. If the choice is between prison and probation, the court often concludes that the physical danger of prison is so disproportionate a punishment for the crime that probation is far better; but probation gives little satisfaction to the community as a whole because it is not enough punishment.

The greatest punishment for those in prison is not loss of liberty; it is association with other prisoners. (A substantial majority of the American male population over forty has experienced a loss of liberty almost as drastic as that of prison—the armed services. The difference was the quality of one's companions and the command structure.) Today's prisoner is concerned with surviving among violent, even savage, people. Thus most experienced prisoners prefer a maximum-security prison to a minimum-security one. Maximum security provides individual cells, constant monitoring by guards, structured showertaking and recreation, and generally more protection from other inmates. The most dangerous prisons are minimum-security facilities where inmates are housed in dormitories and may freely mingle with one another beyond the watchful eye of protective guards.

There is of course a class of felons who must be locked away in maximum-security prisons. These are the sociopaths—the dangerous people who will take every opportunity to escape and who will be an immediate danger to society if they succeed. But minor, nonviolent, criminals—forgers, Watergate conspirators, confidence men, embezzlers, and bad-check passers—are all good prospects for structured community punishment centers. In general these convicts will not run, and they are adequately punished if they are required to live in a restricted barracks, follow strict rules, and work for nothing at public-service jobs. Only upon failing to follow such a regimen should they be sent to prison.

The advantage of a community-service system is that it is cheaper than constructing and maintaining new prisons. No pretense is made concerning strict security; any old hotel or army barracks is suitable. Instead of guards there are supervisors who resemble something between probation officers and social workers. In fact, this is the basic structure of the work-release centers that most states have as halfway houses between prison and parole. Prisoners could be required to work for the department of highways, the sanitation department, local hospitals, or nursing homes.

Such a system has great problems, which is why it has not been tried more extensively. Prisoners are difficult to work with—since they are not being paid and are involuntary laborers, they malinger. They require supervision, and they also require some sanctions in the event they fail to take the whole enterprise seriously. Once we abandon the classic punishment of putting prisoners within a walled area; feeding, clothing, and housing them for the duration of their sentence; and depriving them of their liberty, we encounter enormous legal problems. These problems, many of which have been created by courts, have discouraged innovation in the area of punishment.

When the courts started to exert some supervision of prisons and prisoners through the Eighth Amendment "cruel and unusual punishment" and the Fourteenth Amendment due process provisions of the Constitution, they "legalized" inmate rights in order to protect the prisoners. For example, a prisoner cannot be transferred to a more restrictive setting in the prison without notice and a hearing at which the inmate's misconduct warranting the transfer must be proven. If we abandon the central punishment location and begin placing prisoners in the community to work on roads, in hospitals, or in nursing homes, the problem of "legalization" of inmate rights becomes a significant obstacle to efficient management.

The legalization problem can be illustrated by imagining a creative governor who decides to do something dramatic in prison reform. Initially, our governor understands that there is insufficient money in the state road account to upgrade the rural roads that are not main highways. Yet he perceives that if he could get prison labor, national-guard camping equipment—tents, mobile mess kitchens, and portable toilet and shower facilities—he could enhance by four times the return to his rural road building dollar. The governor is not interested in a coercive chain-gang system but wants instead enthusiastic prisoner cooperation (like

157

the British prisoners in *The Bridge on the River Kwai*). He has his warden cull the records to find prisoners convicted of nonviolent crimes and those convicted of violent crimes who could be involved in such a program without danger to the community.

The governor gets all of these acceptable prisoners together and offers a deal: (1) through the executive clemency power, prisoners who work hard on the project receive double credit against their sentence (in addition to regular "good time"); (2) prisoners participating will have liberal visitation privileges with their families; (3) prisoners will receive enough pay so that when the amount is multiplied over a two-year period or more, it will be a significant stake at the time of release; and (4) during that part of the year when road work is impossible, prisoners will be housed in state facilities and employed in painting hospitals or doing similar work, not returned to the mainline prison population.

This would all work well if the prisoners did indeed conduct themselves like the British prisoners in the movie; however, that will never happen. Many prisoners, even a majority, will be grateful and at least initially will work with some enthusiasm. Yet this very enthusiasm is predicated on the remarkable difference between doing road work and being in the mainline prison population within the four walls. Once prisoners get used to the road gang as the "standard" punishment, they will begin to make trouble, malinger, sabotage, and fight with one another. Oddly enough, escape is not a problem; these prisoners will have been free on bond pending trial and will have made their court appearances notwithstanding that they knew they would be convicted. A far more serious problem is the occasional unauthorized furlough where the prisoner slips into town to find a woman or get some liquor or drugs and then gets into trouble. Alcohol and drug abuse figure prominently in the lives of most petty criminals, and their social milieu is frequently the tavern. If prisoners have any freedom whatsoever, it is likely that many of them will return to the tavern whence came many of their original problems.

The governor who has started all this in good faith will find it difficult to enforce discipline in any setting less restrictive than the chain gang. If a prisoner misbehaves and the on-the-spot supervisor decides to send him back to prison, the inmate will immediately go to court alleging lack of procedural due process. He will demand a minitrial to determine whether his transgressions were sufficient to warrant being sent back to prison. The court will be sympathetic because there is a strong possibility that the supervisor of any such operation will be a petty tyrant. This minitrial presents a two-fold problem: the effectiveness of the on-the-spot decisions necessary to maintain discipline is diluted, and the administration bogs down having to defend its decisions.

And what about the murderers, rapists, armed robbers, and arsonists who are left in the standard prison? Will they not file writs of habeas corpus asserting unequal treatment because they were not permitted to participate in the program? The nineteen-year-old kid who accompanied his father on an armed robbery is probably a good prospect for a program like the road gang, but the forty-year-old habitual armed robber is not. While an acceptable legal line might be drawn between first offenders and habitual offenders, that is not a satisfactory distinction from a practical perspective because some habitual offenders would do better in the program than many sociopathic first offenders.[11] Legalization is like the bed of Procrustes; it protects the weak from the most outrageous tyrannies of petty administrators, but at the same time it circumscribes the capacity of well-meaning administrators to experiment with creative programs. If, for example, the governor through his agents attempted

11. I once had a criminal client who was accused of breaking and entering a store. He was a three-time loser, and I offered to plead him guilty in return for the state's not filing a recidivist information against him, which would have resulted in a life sentence. The local prosecutor agreed, but since the statute gave the prison warden authority to file the recidivist information, I had to get a similar agreement from the warden. When I called the penitentiary the warden was all smiles; he agreed with alacrity not to file the information if I would get the man to the prison quickly. Apparently my client was the prison expert on the ancient steam heating system, and winter was approaching. The warden promised me my client could have his old cell back and would immediately be awarded trustee status if he would just make the heaters work. I informed my client who allowed that he liked the warden and enjoyed his job as chief of the prison heating system. He was genuinely worried about the condition of his steam pipes, and he pointed out with some pride that nobody else could keep the plant in operation. This man was happy in his work; habitual offender or not, he would enjoy building roads and would work fifteen hours a day all summer to make sure that a school bus had a safe passage up a hollow during the winter. He just could not survive without the structure of an institution, and he cheerfully admitted it.

to reward outstanding work through the liberal use of his clemency authority, the malingerers would go to court demanding set rules and regulations governing awards.

When alternatives to prisons are suggested, they always appear so logical that an intelligent outsider wonders why someone on the inside doesn't implement them. Yet it is important to understand that alternatives to prison elicit the enthusiastic participation of prisoners only so long as they are *alternatives*; without an ever-present fear of confinement in a traditional penitentiary, alternative punishment that requires prisoner cooperation in the form of labor and adherence to strict rules of conduct will receive nothing but the prisoners' passive resistance.

Even with all of the potential problems—not the least of which is the *appearance* that convicted felons are not receiving enough punishment—we should be experimenting with alternatives to prison. Since for the large majority of prisoners escape is not a serious problem, at least we will be transferring resources away from bricks and mortar to salaries of corrections officers, work supervisors, and even counselors whose watchful eyes will constitute the basic security. Even if, as I expect to be the case, the prisoners' labor only equals the amount spent on supervision, there will still be a net economic gain because in the current system all the expense of a prison is a dead loss. And if the community-punishment-center approach slightly "underpunishes" many of those currently being sent to prison, the same system gives more severe punishment to those currently placed on probation as first offenders or for other reasons.[12]

12. Perhaps the most aggressive pursuit of the "alternative sentencing" ideal has been in Iowa. In 1977 the Iowa Legislature passed a bill creating a "community-based correctional program." Under the program each judicial district runs four correctional services: (1) a pretrial release program featuring both supervised and unsupervised arrangements with accused persons; (2) a presentence release program; (3) a street probation program; and (4) residential treatment facilities. Currently Iowa treats 81 percent of its offenders in its community programs. The remaining 19 percent are treated in institutions. Iowa calculates that street probation costs the state $1.30 per probationer per day. The residential treatment facilities that provide a structured living setting, employment in the community, training programs and education as needed cost

It is generally accepted that there are three goals of punishment—deterrence of others, preventing recurrence in the offender, and vengeance for society.[13] Certainly alternative punishment will not significantly reduce the deterrent effect of criminal law. Who wants to be separated from family and friends for several years, living under strict rules and in a state of poverty? As for recurrence, it is possible that the alternative sentencing scheme will have a better rehabilitation component than today's prisons; certainly it is capable of teaching job skills and work discipline. Only vengeance is inadequately served, and in the current system vengeance is too expensive. I can think of a lot better things to do with $120 million than build a new prison.

$42.00 per resident per day. While the residential treatment facilities are about as expensive on a daily basis as prisons, great savings are realized because the average length of stay in a residential treatment facility is four and a half months compared to fourteen months at a prison. So far the program has been fairly successful. Sixty-five percent of the people sent to residential treatment facilities successfully complete the program and are released to street probation. Communities and employers have been receptive to the treatment facilites. Apparently employers find that the individuals from a treatment facility are more likely to show up for work regularly than are individuals from the labor force at large.

13. The systemic difficulties in the problem of punishment are not only administrative but go to the problem's conceptual basis. Deterrence and retribution are perhaps the two most important goals of punishment. The retributive theory looks to what the crime was "worth" and assesses a punishment of corresponding weight. In its more sophisticated forms it is predicated on the theory that the very right of a society to punish is limited by the weight of the crime. A fair retributive punishment will, however, be insufficient from the point of view of deterrence, since a prospective criminal will discount the penalty by his chances of getting caught and being successfully prosecuted. In addition, the contemplation of a crime, even in America today, is likely to be an event characterized by foolish optimism if the plan is to go forward.

The converse of this proposition is demonstrated by the apocryphal story of a Chinese potentate who, fed up with the unruly traffic in his province, ordered traffic violators to be immediately hanged at the spot of their violations. The deterrent effects were salutary—traffic violations were eliminated. From a retributive point of view, however, the elimination of the violators was drastic overpunishment.

I have attempted only to highlight a few examples in order to present the case that criminal law is in every regard political. It is generally assumed that the management of the courts is a technical matter like the management of city water systems, federal flood-control projects, or state parks. Where any of these latter functions is done poorly, it can correctly be assumed that the problem is either incompetent management or lack of money. In fact, most government agencies provide benefits that everyone thinks desirable. The court system with all of its supporting agencies definitely does not fit in this mold. Courts provide a service that a substantial element of society resents, which means that fixing the criminal-court system requires a high level of political sophistication combined with a sufficiently intense level of commitment so that a lobby *for* effective courts can match the intensity of the lobby *against* effective courts.

For example, the day a state legislature enacts a comprehensive scheme for compensating all citizens with reasonable money damages for *all* unconstitutional police intrusions and then prohibits the use of the exclusionary rule in the courts of that state, the Supreme Court will be required to rethink its exclusionary rule. In fact, in 1981 in one case pending before the Supreme Court the Court asked for briefs on possible "good faith" exceptions to the exclusionary rule. The Court itself is struggling with the competing goals of the criminal law, and just one good, comprehensive state statute would, in my opinion, knock the Supreme Court off dead center. Obviously such a statute would initially entail a significant additional state expense, but if it properly allocated the cost of damages to the budgets of the departments responsible for rights violations, financial incentives would quickly force a higher conformity to constitutional standards than the exclusionary rule ever provided. In a similar vein states could experiment with statutory guidelines on searches and seizures outside of private houses and offices in an effort to convince the Supreme Court that individual and automobile searches under suspicious circumstances can be conducted with the same minimal intrusion into individual privacy as airport searches.

Finally, it is generally observed that the level of corruption on the part of federal officials is remarkably lower than it is at the state and local levels. While this can be attributed in part to the lower involvement of federal officials in local communities (usually federal agents do not work in the state in which they were born), much of it is also attributable to high salaries that attract good people, excellent training, and professional organization. Where local police are paid less than cashiers at the grocery store and little is expected of them in terms of training or professional performance, corruption is almost inevitable. Furthermore, where better pay and professionalism will enhance the performance of officers, active political support will enhance the performance of elected officials. The intelligent citizen lobby that solicits broad-based political contributions can also, through its paid staff, monitor the performance of prosecutors, sheriffs, police commissioners, and judges. When they are incompetent or corrupt, a good citizen lobby can recruit attractive candidates and beat corrupt officials at the polls every time.

Courts and the Tragedy of the Common

6

IT is now time to look at some of the characteristics of the current civil-court system that make it function so poorly. Court resolution of contested cases is a highly skilled, labor-intensive industry that has few if any economies of scale. All work is custom produced, but our strong egalitarian tradition precludes any arrangement for self-financing. Because the courts are available free of charge, they are overused, and the result is justice-defying delays.

The courts are used unequally by different taxpayers. There are groups in society that use the civil courts all the time and groups that never use them. The government, large corporations, local landlords, and retail businesses all use the courts extensively; lawyers call them "specialized" users. Most of the taxpayers who pay for the courts, however, are at best only occasional users of this terribly expensive machinery. Ordinary taxpayers or their representatives understand that bigger and better models of expensive court machinery will not eliminate the problems of delay that confront the occasional user. Specialized users will consume more additional court services, while the delays for the occasional user will remain the same.

Our egalitarian tradition forbids any explicit price system to ration court services; however, since demand for free court services exceeds supply, rationing must occur, and it is accomplished by standing in line. Unfortunately, the people who can afford to stand in line the longest are not necessarily the people who have the most urgent need to litigate, yet the egalitarian tradition prohibits the sale of one's place in line to someone with a more pressing need for court services.

Since a place in line cannot be sold or exchanged, all litigants must pay essentially the same price for use—a price that bears no relationship to the urgency of individual needs or the importance to the public of certain issues like highway or power plant construction. The currency in which the price of access to courts is paid is what economists call a "dead weight loss," currency that is of no value to anyone else.

In the civil courts customers come in competitive pairs. They are involved in a zero-sum game where the alternatives available to at least one of the pair are significantly less attractive than the product that can be obtained free from a court. Often the attractive products that the court delivers free are delay itself or a forum that provides the stronger litigant with an opportunity to wear out or outgun the opposition. There is no ceiling on competitive expenditures—with regard to lawyers' fees, expert witnesses, discovery and investigation expenses, the sky is the limit. The nature of the adversary system leads then to the irrational and needless consumption of private resources in an effort to gain a competitive advantage. Whenever opposing sides can match expenditures, enormous amounts of money are spent that secure no improvement at all in the basic product. When one side cannot match his opponent's expenditures, the financial power of the stronger side will usually determine the result.[1]

It is axiomatic in political science and law-school courses that civil courts are in business to resolve disputes. Consequently, the machinery of the courts is predicated almost entirely on the postulate that any time a competitive pair of litigants appear in court there is a full-blown dispute to be resolved. Of all routine cases, the ones that come closest to the

---

1. I am indebted to Professor Thomas Schelling of Harvard's John F. Kennedy School for many of these observations and others throughout this chapter, which he presented in a brilliant, but unfortunately unpublished, lecture.

model of the full-blown dispute are the contested domestic relations cases. There, both parties sincerely believe themselves in the right, and in my experience both parties do have some "right" on their side. Yet in the universe of all the routine cases that go to court, most of the time one party will be flat wrong, and he or she will know that from the beginning. The motorist who collides with the rear of another's parked car is obviously wrong, and if there is a dispute it is only about damages. The person who owes money on an account to a store is wrong, as is the tenant who does not pay his or her rent. The egalitarian bias that demands free access to court services is predicated on the assumption, however, that both litigants in all lawsuits have a good-faith dispute. Empirically this is an entirely unfounded assumption.

Courts are not primarily in the dispute resolution business; they are really in the business of making the side in the wrong pay up. Enforcement, not conflict resolution, is what courts largely accomplish—but because most ironclad claims still can be disputed one way or another, no matter how frivolously, the court must go through the sham of resolving a so-called dispute before it can make an enforceable award. Since parties who are in the wrong do not want to pay money or be enjoined to do something, disputes are concocted so that the court will get bogged down and delayed in extracting payment.

There are certain classes of cases on the frontiers of the law where there are real disputes, but these are political disputes between interest groups where the battleground is a lawsuit. For example, workers who are injured on the job are constantly going to court in efforts to get the courts to erode the statutory immunity from an ordinary lawsuit that an employer who subscribes to a state workmen's compensation fund enjoys.[2] In many industrial states the courts are nibbling away at immunity in serious accident cases where the employer has failed to follow prescribed safety standards or has ordered workers to do things that are abnormally dangerous. The workers who brought these lawsuits knew that under prior court interpretations of the immunity statutes they could

2. The academic literature prefers the sex neutral "workers' compensation"; however, the statutes in most states still use "workmen's compensation," and so I use this term to avoid any confusion.

166

not recover. They went to court to get new interpretations of these old statutes, and often they were successful. Efforts to change existing laws can be characterized as "disputes," but they are political disputes rather than the factual disputes that courts are theoretically in business to resolve.

The current machinery of the courts contemplates parties quarreling over who is right and who is wrong under a disputed set of facts governed by predictable and accepted legal principles. Oddly enough, in today's society, characterized as it is by fast-paced changes in the legal landscape, the legitimate disputes in court do not concern what the parties did or did not do but rather what the law governing their action should be. Thus we have cases deciding whether punitive damages can be recovered against the operators of nuclear reactors for diseases caused by radioactive material, and other cases determining the extent to which private employers can discharge employees without "good cause," and what "good cause" means in a private employment context.

Twenty years ago it was assumed that private employees, in the absence of a contract, worked at the sufferance of the employer. That is still generally the law, but the nibbling process has begun—a decision for the employee here and another decision for the employee there where the actions of the employers were particularly outrageous. Eventually all of these *ad hoc* decisions will begin to form an intelligible pattern, and at that point the rules on job security will have changed, or change will have been definitively rejected.

The fabric of the law is woven in the courts, one strand at a time, through the adjudication of individual cases. The legislatures pass laws, but the interpretation of those laws is left to the courts, which frequently give statutes an interpretation entirely different from what the legislature intended. Furthermore, over time, legislative enactments become obsolete, but the legislative inertia explained in Chapter 3 prevents legislative change. In such circumstances the courts often update the law through creative interpretation. Even in this age of statutes, the old common-law processes are at work to update the law notwithstanding legislative inertia. One statute is held unconstitutional, another statute is given a dramatically new and different interpretation, and in

167

another place a statute is ignored entirely in favor of a parallel common-law doctrine that has been permitted to evolve independently of the statute.[3]

Most cases that go to court are not on the frontiers of the law. They go to a low-level, minor court variously called, depending on the state, traffic court, magistrate court, justice of the peace court, or small-claims court. These minor courts are neither dignified, deliberative, nor professional. For example, in 1981 in West Virginia there were 316,342 cases filed in magistrate courts but only 65,224 filed in the major circuit courts. Actions to evict tenants, collect on store accounts, or recover for a bad check do not usually involve disputes, which is probably why magistrate and small-claims courts have such an ugly reputation for farcical justice, lack of due process, and plain, inconsiderate meanness.

Almost all traffic violations, for example, involve no dispute. Many people feel unjustly treated because they are given a ticket when thousands of others get away with it, but almost always the person given the ticket violated the law. It may be stupid to have to come to a full stop at a country intersection, but that is the law with regard to stop signs. Courts can become so callous when clear-cut cases are converted into "disputes" that when a real dispute comes along the machine just processes it callously like all the phoney disputes.

There are endless examples of nondisputes that are in major courts as well, but two examples should suffice. The first concerns the insurance company that makes the policyholder sue to recover property damage. It can be a nightmare for a policyholder to recover for the contents of his house destroyed by fire when the company wants "proof" of the fair market value of the house's contents. Actually, the company wants to wear out the policyholder. How do you prove the fair market value (or even replacement value) of an old suit? I wear suits for fifteen years; other people wear suits for two years. Unless a company has reason to suspect fraud, there is no reason not to pay the face amount of the policy. Yet the companies require the filling out of elaborate forms, and then they argue, delay, and attempt to intimidate the policy-

3. For an elaborate discussion of this process, see Guido Calabresi, *A Common Law for the Age of Statutes* (Cambridge, Mass.: Harvard University Press, 1982).

holder with the specter of going to court so that the policyholder will accept less than full value in return for not going to court.

The same problem often arises in automobile accident cases where the policyholder's company refuses to pay the full cost of repair because the cost of repair exceeds the market value of the car, and then the company fails to provide sufficient money to purchase an adequate replacement car. The policyholder believes that he or she is insured against loss—if the car is serviceable it should be replaced with another serviceable car of comparable quality—yet the company argues and fights. The only reason that such a charade is conceived as a "dispute" is because the insurance company can demand that a dispute be settled in court. It is indeed a charade because the insurance company knows that in court the jury will find for the policyholder every time.

The second example of frivolous disputes concerns landlord-and-tenant cases. Landlords are regarded by adults as the Sheriff of Nottingham is regarded by children. Yet in the majority of landlord and tenant cases where the only issue is the payment of back rent, the landlord is right and the tenant is wrong. Many landlords, and slum landlords in cities in particular, have treated their tenants so outrageously that landlord-and-tenant law has become extremely pro-tenant in the last fifteen years. It used to be that when a tenant rented premises he took them as they were, and the landlord had no obligation to keep the building in repair. This was obviously ludicrous, since tenants rented not only square footage but a bundle of services like elevators, heat, air conditioning, water, and clean hallways as well. The courts developed law that required landlords to keep the premises in a "habitable" state of repair as a condition of the tenant's obligation to pay rent.

The majority of landlords, particularly those renting premises outside of the slums, are in a competitive market and are as interested as their tenants in keeping the premises in a decent state of repair. Tenants complain about everything, with and without justification, but most of the time landlords and tenants treat each other reasonably. However, tenants don't like to pay rent, and frequently they are unable to pay rent. In general, renters are the least stable people in the economy (except in big cities where all classes rent). Renters are mobile; one reason they rent is to avoid the impediment of owning property. Renters are young and have the lowest expectation of continued employment because of less seniority, less experience, and their own willingness to change jobs to improve themselves. Renters lose their jobs frequently, and they fail to pay the rent just as frequently. When they fail to pay the rent they must be evicted to make room for tenants who will pay the rent; otherwise the landlord will go bankrupt since he must still pay his mortgage, maintenance, and taxes.

Yet getting a deadbeat tenant out of an apartment is like pulling teeth if the tenant goes to a legal-aid lawyer and decides to turn the simple proposition that you can't have something you don't pay for into a legal "dispute." If the tenant answers the landlord's eviction complaint and asserts that the tenant refuses to pay rent because the premises are in disrepair, then this comparatively simple issue must be scheduled for trial, and eviction may take as long as a year, during which time the landlord receives no rent but continues to incur expenses. In some places a tenant can stay in possession when there is a contest of this type only if he pays his rent into court pending final adjudication. But this is a cumbersome process, and when the rent is not paid into court, the landlord must invoke new, expensive procedures to get a final eviction.

Sometimes, of course, property owners make outrageous claims against insurance companies—it is not reasonable that when a person's eight-year-old Cadillac is destroyed the company should be required to buy a new Cadillac. And landlords live up to their abysmal reputation with sufficient frequency that tenants must be permitted to refuse rent payments in order to exact decent treatment. The problem becomes how to sort out the real disputes that require serious court attention from all of the abuses of the court processes by people who have no higher purpose than to use court delay as an oppressive tactical weapon.

Discussion of techniques to encourage real dispute litigation and discourage nondispute litigation brings us inevitably to the "tragedy of the common." For courts are very much like a traditional common in an agricultural community where everyone has the right to graze livestock on the pasturage held in common. Any rational farmer will graze all his sheep or cattle on the common, notwithstanding that if everyone does the same thing the common will degenerate, and everyone's livestock will suffer from malnutrition.

Any time a good or service is provided free of charge, it is in everyone's interest to get as much of it as possible since we cannot expect our own forbearance to be followed by everyone else's. That is why in such circumstances explicit regulation is required, like the fish and game laws that every state enforces to assure that wildlife will not be hunted to extinction.

Throughout a free economy the price system is usually the mechanism chosen to regulate the allocation of goods and services. Where a good or service is in high demand but short supply, the price goes up and the users with the least urgent need or the least money drop out of the market. Price-system rationing, however, presents a significant equity problem: those with the most money get the most goods and services. Consequently, when necessities of life are in short supply, like food during World War II or medicine during an epidemic, there is broad social resistance to allowing price-system rationing.

Yet every time demand for a good or service exceeds supply, some rationing system, either price or nonprice, will go into effect. In the case of the unregulated and thus overused common, the quality of the pasturage degenerates to such an extent that the weaker livestock die and leave enough for those who are strong enough to survive. It is merely luck whether a farmer has a strong or weak cow; if farmers keep replenishing the livestock that die so that more of them continue to die, then the farmers who are the last to run out of money to buy livestock ultimately get the benefit of the whole common. That is not a very intelligent system of rationing, but it is *a* system of rationing nonetheless.

In the Communist world, particularly Russia, rationing is accomplished by the political authorities. The "bidding up of prices" is not done in the monetary currency but rather in the political currency. Those with influence and official position can shop in special stores that have stocks of desirable goods. The price of these goods in the regular stores is the same as the price in the special stores, except the regular stores never have any goods to sell at the regular price or, for that matter, at any other price. Where there is reluctance to let either the price system or the political system ration or to adopt any other form of explicit rationing, like the World War II ration card, then goods and services are rationed by other natural mechanisms. The most common mechanism is standing in line.

Courts are available to all potential litigants in almost the same way that the common is available to all farmers. Just as the villagers must be able to afford livestock before using the common, American litigants must be able to afford a lawyer before they can go to court. Once, however, this precondition to usage is met, litigants can take as much of a court's goods and services as they want when their turn comes up. In most places, of course, their turn doesn't come up very often because of the length of the queue.[4]

Where the cost of a commodity goes up, the use of that commodity goes down. In an apartment house where all utilities are included in the rent, tenants use more lights and hot water than in an apartment house where each tenant pays for his or her own electricity and gas. People would probably litigate less if they bore a share of the cost commensurate with their actual court use. There are, of course, two components to the costs of the courts: the cost of the courts themselves—rent for the buildings, salary for judges and supporting staff, books, typewriters, etc. and the cost to both parties of trying a particular case. The second category includes lawyers' fees for both sides, witness fees, and the loss in terms of employee time and expenses in getting ready for trial.

The public nature of the costs of the courts themselves is easily accepted. Courts are like fire departments or schools—a necessary part of civilization that anyone may need at any time. Requiring litigants to pay on a user basis for the courts themselves would be as discriminatory as requiring schoolchildren to pay for public education on a user basis.[5]

4. In New York it still takes over four years to get to a jury trial in a simple automobile accident case, and that is a great improvement over the delay experienced several years ago.

5. There have actually been attempts to set up a private system of courts to which litigants can go for more rapid, and theoretically more competent, dispute resolution. Such a scheme is largely for specialized users like large corporations litigating complex, multi-party commercial matters where there are real disputes that cannot be settled and all litigants want a prompt and competent resolution of issues. Private commercial arbitration also falls into this model—a prompt, competent method of resolving real disputes without the expense and delay of going to court. Private courts, however, are very much like private schools. Except for religious schools that

At least theoretically it is possible to tinker at some user-based allocations of litigation costs without being so radical as to challenge the courts' fundamentally public nature. Every time a person who is right must go to court against a person who is wrong, the person who is right sustains substantial private expenses. Obviously the person who is wrong also sustains private expenses, but usually in such circumstances the benefits of litigation per se outweigh those expenses. The most frequent benefit to a wrongdoer is the use of money for as long as six years while a meritorious case proceeds laboriously through the trial and appellate courts. As I pointed out earlier, just the time and inconvenience of going to court often lead to unfair settlements that are favorable to the wrongdoing party, so that a willingness to litigate for years and sustain high litigation expenses is often profitable to a wrongdoer in a case where there is a large potential liability.

But the value of litigation is even greater in cases where there is a small potential liability. The general rule is that a party who has been damaged, unless the injury is intentional, is entitled only to actual damages, not legal fees. Suppose the damage is only three hundred dollars. Who can afford to hire a lawyer to go to court for three hundred dollars? When a skilled lawyer for some reason takes a case that involves a small real-damage claim, he or she always attempts to inflate the damage claim to inspire settlement. Where, for example, a person's car is damaged to the tune of three hundred dollars, a lawyer will sue not only for the repairs but for the cost of renting a car while the repairs are being made and for aggravation and inconvenience. In West Virginia we have authorized jury awards for aggravation and inconvenience in

are subsidized by the churches in order to make the tuition affordable, the use of private schools in the United States is comparatively rare. While parents who place a high value on education can elect not to use public education, while still paying local school taxes, and buy at their own expense a system of superior schools, private schools as the standard model are not an alternative to public schools exactly because we know that if individual choices were required between education and other types of consumption, too many people would choose other types of consumption. Litigation, like education, serves a public function, and that function cannot be impaired by relegating it to the private sector where it cannot attract sufficiently broad-based financial support to ensure its continued availability.

small property-damage cases so that these claims will be settled promptly rather than litigated. Unless a jury has authority to award damages in excess of the actual damages the injured party incurred, the injured party cannot afford to hire a lawyer and go to court.

Yet the general rule in litigation is that the winning party cannot recover attorneys' fees and other litigation expenses from the losing party. The rule is so strict that in many places even when two contracting parties agree in their contract that if a dispute arises that must go to court, the losing party will pay the litigation expenses of the winning party, the courts refuse to enforce that agreement because it is contrary to the public policy of allowing unimpeded access to the courts. As a result it is very difficult to litigate commercial cases arising from a contract or a property-damage case.

In contract or property-damage cases where there is enough at stake to justify hiring a lawyer, the net return to the damaged party may be reduced by as much as 50 percent because of the litigation expenses. In personal-injury cases, however, there is less of a problem in this regard because the jury can take into consideration the subjective element of pain and suffering. Usually the award for pain and suffering is sufficient to pay the plaintiff's lawyer. In fact, plaintiffs' lawyers usually have a contingent fee agreement to the effect that the lawyer will receive about one-third of the final award if the case goes to trial and about a quarter if the case is settled. At least one of twelve jurors will be aware of how these things work, so he or she will explain it to the other jurors, and they will figure into their award enough money to pay the lawyer.

Probably the most persistent frustration with the civil courts is that average citizens cannot afford to litigate small grievances. It is a nightmare, for example, to attempt to get alimony and child support from a former husband who will not pay voluntarily.[6] When the average citizen

6. Domestic-relations matters present an exception to the rule about payment of attorneys' fees—a husband must pay his own and his wife's fees. Usually, however, he doesn't have the money, and the wife's lawyer knows that. Most lawyers require that the wronged wife advance the fee, and if the husband pays, the wife gets the fee back.

But the wife is broke too—that's why she's suing. She cannot advance the attorney's fee. The most efficient technique is to wait until the husband is in

has a run-in with a store, a plumber, or an aluminum-siding salesman, seldom does the amount in controversy justify the time and expense of a lawsuit. Small-claims courts have been set up to permit individuals to go to courts without lawyers. As long as individuals are suing other individuals, or businesses are suing individuals, small-claims courts work fairly well. But as soon as an individual tries to take a business to one of these courts, the business' lawyers appeal to a regular, general-jurisdiction court where the complicated procedures require a lawyer. This is especially true in state systems where the appeal to a regular court is actually a new trial, and the whole procedure that was done in the laymen's court must be duplicated.

IT IS surprising that no systematic effort has been made to eliminate or reduce the litigation of nondisputes. However, it is heretical to suggest such a proposition, and among even respectable lawyers and jurists, a person who advocates a scheme to penalize nondisputes can quickly attract intense, vociferous, personal animosity.

A new system of allocating attorneys' fees and other litigation expenses is not a panacea for all frustration with the courts. However,

arrears for about a year, since it costs her no more to sue for thousands of dollars than for hundreds, and bring suit then. The problem with this scheme is that if the husband is an ordinary working stiff, he will have spent the money, and the judgment will be impossible to collect. The husband's wages can be attached if he continues to work at the same job, but if he changes jobs or moves out of state, the lawyer's fees in executing the judgment exceed the value of the judgment.

I mention all this to point out that systems for allocating costs are not necessarily panaceas for some of the greatest frustrations with the current system. The problem in alimony cases is really that working people can't afford to support two families. There is not enough money to pay even the alimony, much less the transactional expenses of squeezing it out of reluctant husbands. The solution is a system similar to the one used in Pittsburgh—a public official is charged with enforcing alimony awards, and all alimony is paid directly to an agent of the court who can keep track of who has paid and who has not, bringing appropriate contempt actions at public expense against those who don't pay, charging a small percentage of the money collected for all users of the service.

175

the specter of wrongdoers escaping liability by outgunning just claimants in the attorneys' fees showdown should persuade us that our current rule that attorneys' fees can seldom be awarded is highly questionable and should be revised.

In all societies there are subjects that involve such emotionally charged issues that the only discussion permitted is a recitation of the accepted liturgy. When Galileo pointed out that the earth is not the center of the universe, he was not just making an interesting scientific observation. He turned the religious and secular world upside down and delivered a devastating blow to Christian eschatology. Since the social, religious, and political structure of the Western world depended in the sixteenth century on the Christian assumption of a personal God who had created the universe around his creature, man, and his habitat, Earth, Galileo's discovery could not be accepted with equanimity. Had he not recanted he would have been murdered.

The way today's lawyers, businesspeople, and political community do business is predicated on a court system that permits *anyone* who alleges a dispute to go to court. Anyone who suggests the alternative— that those who abuse the process be punished—threatens to turn the world of lawyers and their clients upside down. But the status quo of free access has much more going for it than just self-interest. If penalizing nondispute litigation threatened only the interests of lawyers, businesspeople, and politicians, a lot of radical lawyers would have taken up the cause. What in fact the whole concept of penalizing frivolous litigation does is threaten the existing distribution of wealth—it threatens all the rules and counterrules that have grown up in an attempt to create a weighted balance not for law but, in the grandest sense of the word, for justice.

It is at this point that the structure of political accommodation comes into the picture. It would appear at first blush that the rule regarding attorneys' fees is a creation of business-oriented, upper-class judges who want to protect professional defendants like insurance companies, manufacturers, and merchants. In fact, the opposite is the case, which is why any discussion of allocating the costs of litigation to the losing party is considered heresy in respectable legal circles.[7]

7. I argued the thesis of this chapter, that we should be tinkering at the allocation of private costs when nondisputes are litigated, at the May 1982 meeting of the National Council on the Roles of Courts. This organization is

While it is true that the average citizen is confronted several times a year by occasions when he wishes he could sue some wrongdoer, most of the cases filed in small claims courts are by businesses against individuals. The majority of civil cases filed in the West Virginia magistrate court are either eviction proceedings against tenants, suits on credit accounts, or actions to recover for bad checks. Furthermore, insurance companies are not always defendants. What happens if a neighbor's child is playing with matches and burns down my house? The insurance company pays, but it can still sue the child to recover a judgment against him (and possibly his parents if they were negligent in their supervision) and can collect the judgment against the child when he starts to work.

The average wage earner is constantly up against financial pressure. Creditors know that most wage earners have very little money and few assets available. While large stores and collection agencies do sue wage earners, their efforts to collect judgments are lackluster at best. The reason is simple: while it is easy to get a judgment against a debtor if the debtor defaults and doesn't answer the complaint in court (as is usually the case), the collection of a judgment requires some arduous work by a knowledgeable lawyer. I own two large apartment complexes, and of the hundreds of tenants who over the years have left me high and dry during the winter months in disregard of their lease agreements, I have allowed my managers to sue two—both of whom were doctors.

I do not run businesses for eleemosynary reasons; if a tenant has lost his or her job or fallen on hard times, I am usually willing to forgive the rent based on simple, neighborly West Virginia principles. But where the tenant has no good reason, I would like to sue him. I do not sue because I know enough about the system to recognize that getting and

funded by federal government and Ford Foundation grants, and its members (of whom I am not one) include the most prominent lawyers, professors, and judges in the United States. My suggestions about tinkering at the allocation of private litigation costs were received by this august group with the same enthusiasm as the bastard son at the reading of the will. While my colleagues understood perfectly the abuses to which I alluded, they were convinced that overall better results are achieved under the current system of unlimited access because, they apparently believe, any cost allocation scheme would ultimately be abused more than the current system is abused. This is an intelligent position, but I disagree.

collecting a judgment costs more than it brings in. If I could recover attorneys' fees as well as my damages, the economics of this collection process would change dramatically. There are hundreds of young, unemployed lawyers available to do legal work if they can be paid by the hour. If attorneys' fees were awarded, it would make little difference how long it takes to track down an absconding tenant or how difficult it is to inventory his personal property, list his exemptions, and sell his nonexempt property to satisfy a judgment. The lawyers' meter would be running all the time. Once the tenant found work, the lawyer would attach his wages to satisfy the judgment plus all attorneys' fees, which would exceed the actual damages by several times.

In fact, if the rules about attorneys' fees were changed, the structure of law firms would also change. Groups of young and hungry lawyers would organize into firms that specialized in collections, and they would refine and computerize excellent techniques for sucking almost all the blood out of any poor working American who had ever defaulted on his debts. These firms would join forces with one another throughout America so that a debtor could no longer run, and each time more lawyer and computer tracking work was required, the cost would be added to the debtor's bill.

When I was in private practice I represented a credit jeweler in Fairmont, West Virginia, who had numerous delinquent accounts. Frequently a threatening letter on my letterhead would prompt some effort to pay off a debt, but if the debtor still did not pay, the store went to magistrate's court through one of its own employees to get a judgment that was seldom executed. The store could not afford to hire me to sue people for five hundred dollars and to collect the judgment. The result was that judgments were occasionaly paid when the debtor had a steady job and wages could be attached; otherwise, the debtor got off scot-free, at least until he decided to sell real estate he owned (since an uncollected judgment is a lien on property). Those without property never paid.

In suits between landlords and tenants or stores and debtors, the rich are the plaintiffs and the poor are the defendants. These types of suits accord with my initial observation that in most litigation there is no real dispute. Debtors who buy merchandise on credit owe the money as do tenants who either move before the expiration of their leases or refuse to pay rent. Stores are generally accused of trapping the customer into buying more than he or she can afford through advertising, easy credit, and high-pressure salesmanship; and landlords are always thought of as bloodsuckers. The way this perception of both institutions is reflected in the law is not by rules that say stores and landlords always lose, but by the cumbersomeness and expense of the techniques required to enforce a judgment.

If we move away from the classic suit of rich versus poor to the classic case of poor versus rich, we find another good political reason for not allowing recovery of litigation expense. The classic case of poor versus rich involves a suit for personal injuries where the real defendant is an insurance company. In a suit of this type we have already taken care of the legal expenses of the "poor" plaintiff. Since typically in these cases substantial money is involved, the plaintiff's lawyer will take the case on contingency; if the plaintiff loses, the lawyer gets nothing; but if the plaintiff wins, the lawyer makes more than he would have made if he charged by the hour. This Las Vegas parameter assures lawyers who specialize in plaintiffs' work a very handsome income—so handsome that good plaintiffs' firms underwrite all the costs of working up a case for trial.

These expenses can include expert witness fees, transportation costs, and film dramatization, where appropriate, of a "day in the life" of the plaintiff who may be suffering the pain and inconvenience of permanent injuries. Where the plaintiff prevails, all these expenses will be paid for by the "pain and suffering" award from the jury, and in the statistics of such things, the prevailing plaintiffs in a few cases will pay, in effect, for all the cases where plaintiffs as a class lose. But what would happen if the loser had to pay for the winner's attorneys' fees and the winner were the insurance company?

Lawyers for defendants typically charge two hundred dollars an hour, and they are masters at busywork. They love depositions, pretrial motions, interrogatories, expert testimony, and, where possible, appeals of every adverse ruling. If an ordinary losing plaintiff had to pay the attorneys' fees of the insurance company, he would go bankrupt. Certainly he would lose all the equity in his house as well as his life's savings if he had any. Or, alternatively, he would spend the rest of his life working to pay off that one debt. The result of such a rule, of course, would be greatly discouraged access to the courts in personal-injury cases. In addition, test cases attempting to redefine the contours of the law would be discouraged because the plaintiff's potential liability for the defendant's attorneys' fees would be so enormous in terms of the plaintiff's personal resources that the plaintiff could not take a chance. It would be like offering the average person a bet where the minimum stake is one hundred thousand dollars, the terms are double or nothing, and the chances of winning are nine to one. The average person cannot take advantage of the favorable odds because in the not entirely unlikely event he loses, he will be wiped out.

It should now be apparent why anyone who suggests tampering with cost allocation to ameliorate the tragedy of the common is received as a heretic. While there are instances where the average individual must suffer small-change abuse he cannot afford to redress in court because he can't afford to go to court, by far the greatest beneficiaries of our current system are the poor and the middle class. In effect, the trade is that while the poor and middle class cannot prosecute their minor grievances, they can fully prosecute their major ones. More to the point from the perspective of the distribution of the wealth, no one can afford to prosecute a minor grievance *against* the poor or even the middle class.

Lawyers and judges do not like explicit discussions of rules that have different effects on different income classes; thus political accommodations that go to the heart of the distribution of wealth are generally left undiscussed in court opinions. While the legal structure reflects certain political conclusions about how much we want to enforce legal rules against certain classes, we are not a society that is comfortable talking in class terms. We are far more comfortable leaving these considerations in the background while the foreground is dominated by general rules that are often idiotic on their face. As I pointed out in Chapter 4, the law is comfortable only when talking in general rules.

Nonetheless, the general rule we have devised about never permitting litigation expenses to be recovered by a winner works poorly since it continues to encourage the litigation of nondisputes. Hidebound liberals who have concluded that a rule that forbids any allocation of costs has a salutary wealth-distribution effect have in effect removed that issue from the court-reform agenda and relegated it to the land of liturgy. I agree that the rule works better than any other *general* rule, but the fiction of a general rule is no longer necessary. In effect, the rule works quite well in consumer-debt, landlord-and-tenant, and personal-injury cases. But it works very badly in contract disputes, litigation over property damage, and litigation over some substantial inconvenience such as being bumped from an airline flight. Of course, many cases like will contests or boundary-line disputes fall outside the extremes, and some intermediate rule must apply to those intermediate cases.

The theory behind tinkering at costs is not really the allocation of actual expenses but rather the establishment of further incentives to settle cases rather than to abuse the common. The oft-repeated proposition that everyone is entitled to his day in court is almost as ridiculous as the proposition that everyone is entitled to a welfare check regardless of income. Everyone who has an honest, good-faith dispute that requires decision by an impartial arbiter is entitled to his day in court, but greedy bloodsuckers who abuse the legal process to oppress others should be punished just as the welfare cheat is punished.

There is, for example, a great deal of difference between an ordinary individual's apartment lease and a business's commercial lease. Where a business rents a store in a shopping mall and defaults on its rent so that the landlord must sue, then the landlord should be able to recover litigation costs. Often the store, particularly if it is part of a chain, is in a superior financial position to the mall developer. Futhermore, both partes are sophisticated and have access to skilled lawyers. If the store is wrong, it should voluntarily act in such a way as to mitigate everyone's damages. The same, of course, is true of the landlord.

While deference to certain tacit political decisions demands that in certain classes of cases, such as personal-injury cases, a cost-allocation rule can never be applied, in other types of cases the rule should simply be that litigation expenses will be awarded where there has been no real dispute. And even in some of the rich versus poor suits, where a continued reluctance to allocate costs is ordinarily justified, we should start to penalize certain flagrant abuses. This will become more apparent in Chapter 8 in the context of my discussion of legal aid and the provision of lawyers for the poor. However, just to prefigure the point here, much of the impetus in the Reagan administration behind gutting the budget of the Legal Services Corporation (which provides free legal services

181

to the poor) came from abuses of the court system by legal-aid lawyers who expended thousands of dollars in lawyer services to help a client avoid a legitimate hundred-dollar debt.

Where people are paying their own legal fees, transaction costs often encourage just settlements. However, where someone else is paying the transaction costs, then litigation is an unmixed blessing for the wrongdoer. Legal aid, then, has many of the problems of the common itself, and it presents peculiar problems in this regard that require tailor-made solutions. The solution to gut legal aid entirely is not what I consider a tailor-made solution. But it is the type of solution that is forced on us whenever people refuse to think in terms of limited rules for specific types of problems and instead demand general rules.

While I often speak disparagingly of certain business entities, such as insurance companies, for abusing the legal process, they also are all too frequently the victims of nuisance suits, which in turn drive up the cost of premiums. There is a big difference between a real personal-injury action where the plaintiff has been badly hurt and the nuisance slip-and-fall case where there is no objective injury, and the "pain and suffering" is a figment of the plaintiff's and his lawyer's imaginations.

While attorneys' fees should not be awarded in the usual eviction proceeding or action for back rent, where a tenant fabricates some frivolous defense like "lack of habitable quarters" that proves to be an abuse of the legal process, then that individual tenant should have to pay the legal freight. It is one thing to make a political decision that tenants who fall on hard times should get the sixty days it takes a landlord to evict them to find a job and another place to live,[8] and quite another to permit a tenant—merely because he knows the legal process or has access to a free lawyer—to use abusive tactics to keep an apartment without paying rent by concocting a so-called dispute that is tantamount to theft.

Lawyers are reluctant to accept any rules that discourage litigation,

8. This sixty-day grace period is a type of social insurance. Landlords, when they set their rents, have a pretty good idea of the level of vacancies—or non-rent-paying tenants—that they will experience. Six percent is about the going rate, so all rents are predicated on this factor. In effect, all tenants buy an insurance policy for about 6 percent of their rent that guarantees them sixty days of free housing if they lose their jobs, get sick, or have other problems.

since litigation is their bread and butter. While the tragedy of the common may have a disastrous effect on litigants, it is a bonanza for the tens of thousands of new lawyers who graduate from law schools each year. But the courts themselves are not necessarily dominated by a lawyer mentality—in fact, many judges become as righteous as reformed prostitutes upon ascending the bench and are zealous crusaders against lawyer abuse. Why, therefore, have the courts done so little to engineer disincentives to frivolous litigation? The answer is really quite complex.

Preeminent among the reasons are the political considerations going to the distribution of the wealth that I have discussed above. Judges are afraid that if they monkey with the rules that allow everyone his day in court without regard to the expense he requires his adversary unjustly to incur, eventually the new rules will be interpreted in such a way as to chill legitimate claims. This is a valid approach to the problem, and it is akin to the philosophy of the temperance movement: if you never take a drink under any circumstances, you will never be tempted to abuse liquor. Drinking in moderation requires a judgment that few temperance advocates believe the average person possesses. The traditional response to the fear that a discretionary rule will be abused is to take two alternative iron-clad, nondiscretionary rules and weigh their advantages in terms of the number of correct and incorrect decisions that each will generate. The general rule that works better, on statistical average, is then selected and put in place.

However, there is another reason for lack of innovation in the allocation of costs. Determining in each individual lawsuit the proper allocation of costs requires time and consideration. These decisions are difficult to make, require complex findings of fact by either the court or the jury, and create one more appealable issue.

The *Federal Rules of Civil Procedure* and their state counterparts already have provisions for awarding costs whenever the discovery mechanisms are abused.[9] In practice, trial-court judges seldom award

9. The rules of civil procedure control the manner in which a lawsuit is brought to trial and the way it is tried. Discovery is the process by which one side can request information from the other side. Under rules of discovery one party can request to interview another side's witnesses, require the other side to produce documents from its files, or answer extensive written questions about its behavior with which the lawsuit is concerned.

costs for abuse of discovery because they don't want to spend time in hearings on whether a particular deposition was necessary or whether two hundred written questions were submitted for valid informational purposes or merely to harass the other party. If the spirit of the rules that are designed to discourage frivolous discovery were carried out in each case, the adjudication of the discovery issues might take as long to litigate as the underlying lawsuit.

I reject the argument that a rule awarding costs cannot be administered with sufficient intelligence to maintain current equitable balances in the wealth-distribution area, and I reject as well the argument that determining whether the legal process has been abused is more trouble than it is worth. If we focus—as legal scholars so often do—exclusively on the cases that are in court, it may indeed be too expensive and time-consuming for a judge to determine whether a case is frivolous. However, the real focus should be on all cases, both those in court and those settled out of court. If cost-allocation rules keep one in three new lawsuits from being filed, then there is a net gain to the overall system.

Placing the cost of frivolous litigation on the party who demands it will ultimately result in a dramatic reduction in frivolous litigation. Thus the systemwide advantage of a case-by-case determination of cost allocation will more than compensate for the time expended in the cases actually in court by the number of nondisputes that are kept out of court altogether.

The rules about frivolous litigation should still be weighted heavily against allocating costs. In the ordinary consumer-debt, landlord-and-tenant, or personal-injury case there should be a blanket rule that no costs will be awarded unless there are extraordinary circumstances of flagrant abuse. The frivolous counterclaim for lack of habitable quarters in landlord-and-tenant cases and the nuisance suit in personal-injury actions might be exceptions. In commercial disputes between business parties, however, litigation costs should *always* be awarded since there is no reason in contract matters not to require that all damages resulting from a breach be paid by the person at fault. In property damage cases where the liability is comparatively clear, the same rule should apply.

Of course, parties often do not dispute liability, but rather only the amount of the damages. If this is the case and a settlement award has been offered but refused, then taking the issue of damages to court is not frivolous. Consequently, under the system I propose, good-faith settlement efforts would become an important element in the formal legal process for the first time. Unfortunately, as it currently stands in most states, one party's willingness to settle has no bearing on any issue in a lawsuit once the parties go to trial. Yet settlement is really what civilization in general and courts in particular should be about. As Chapter 4 explained, most of our substantive and procedural rules implicitly look to settlement as the ultimate goal. It is now time to help save the common by looking to the conduct of parties vis à vis settlement as an explicit criterion for determining certain issues in court.

A rule that allocates costs to system abusers does not solve, however, the problem of competitive expenditures. During the ten years I have been a judge, lawyers' fees have been going up, computers have given birth to more complicated briefs, discovery has gotten more exhaustive, and expert testimony has become more extensive and more complex. Yet I have not noticed any substantial change in the outcome of lawsuits. Today in big cases expensive lawyers do in-depth psychological profiles of every member of a jury panel so that challenges can be made more intelligently; however, where both sides do the same thing, the outcome of these lawsuits is no different from what it would have been when jury selection was less scientific. The same is true of expensive and cumulative expert testimony.

Of course where one side is better financed or more skilled, there is a competitive advantage; however, in major litigation that is not usually the case. Clients are paying for sophisticated legal services that are valueless merely because of the inherently competitive nature of a lawsuit. What is needed is a court version of the Strategic Arms Limitation Treaty—a method for determining in advance what is a reasonable investment in a particular lawsuit, and a court order forbidding both sides from spending money for a competitive advantage that in the nature of things will be illusory. A solution to the competitive expenditure problem is difficult to engineer, particularly since in many instances competitive expenditures will be unmatched and give one side the edge. When good lawyers go up against bad lawyers, the difference is usually in the thoroughness of the good lawyer's preparation.

Certainly my discussion about the allocation of costs and competitive expenditures does not exhaust those subjects. It does suggest that a bigger and better model of a system that is indifferent to either public or private costs as some function of its use is counterproductive. It is not possible to move bull-in-china-shop-like from a rule that takes no account of costs to a rule that always allocates costs against the losing party. Yet the fact that a new structure that attempts to impose costs on system abusers is difficult to construct, or may from time to time catch innocents in its machinery, is no reason not to try to design such a structure.

Innocents are currently being caught in machinery designed to protect them, so that the real measurement of equity is not whether innocents will be caught in the new machinery but whether fewer of them will now be caught. My conclusion on that score is that both fewer innocents will be caught and far fewer innocents will be forced to go to court at all if we make court abusers pay and we limit competitive expenditures. The new system will not be perfect, but it will be appreciably better than what we have now.

Yet, as Chapter 8 indicates in greater detail, lawyers make their money by rendering services to clients. The more services they render, the greater their gross profits. Consequently there is no incentive on the part of lawyers to reduce the extent or cost of their services. It is the courts, therefore, that must undertake to formulate some rules about excessive legal costs in civil cases. Unfortunately, the argument cannot be made that by reducing excessive costs in some lawsuits legal resources will be freed for other purposes since the people who need the legal resources that would be freed cannot afford to pay for them. Nonetheless, some intelligent limitation on competitive expenditures is one aspect of any new system that is not just a bigger and better version of what we already have.

The Stepchildren 7
Courts

DURING Christmas vacation in 1981 my wife and I took our eight-een-month-old son to visit my parents near Palm Beach, Florida. The weather was unseasonably warm, so I took the family to the Hobe Sound public beach, located on Jupiter Island, the winter residence of the superrich. The approach to Hobe Sound's public beach is a tree-lined road, along which are posted signs saying: "No Parking on Road Right-of-Way." Since the beach's parking lot was crowded I returned to the tree-lined approach road and parked underneath the trees a full twelve feet off the road. I interpreted the signs as an injunction to keep cars off the road in order to avoid blocking traffic. When I returned from the beach my car had been towed away.

The police were kind enough to send a police cruiser to take me the five miles to where a free-lance tow truck operator had towed my car. I was outraged at the towing and pointed out to the policeman that the signs gave no reasonable notice that parking under the trees was prohibited. Upon arriving at the shack and junk lot owned by the old boy who had done the towing, I placed my wife and son in the car with me, locked the doors, and drove off without paying the towing charge.

A mile or so down the road the policeman who had brought me

187

pulled me over and told me that I had to pay the towing charge. I refused and told the officer that the towing operator could sue me. I pointed out that the obligation to pay towing was a civil obligation, and since the towing was illegal, the charge was entirely void. Evidently the policeman decided that helping his friend with the tow truck was more trouble than it was worth, so he did nothing further. However, there was still the problem of a five-dollar ticket for illegal parking that I was expected to pay, and that brings me to the purpose of this story.

I paid the ticket on my way home, notwithstanding that I had a perfectly winnable case before an objective judge. I could not afford to contest a five-dollar parking ticket: I would have needed to return to Florida at my own expense when the court was in session; spend several hours familiarizing myself with Florida law; and appeal from the County Court of Martin County to the next higher court in the event I lost. Not even an experienced lawyer who is able to do everything himself can spend two thousand dollars in time, effort, and travel to fight a crummy five-buck ticket. (Conversely, the man with the tow truck couldn't afford to sue me for the thirty dollars he thinks I stiffed him.)

When people think about courts and consider whether they are getting "justice," their frame of reference is often a limited-jurisdiction court like the traffic court for Martin County, Florida. The problems of these minor courts are completely different from the problems of general-jurisdiction federal and state courts, and at the heart of almost all of these minor courts' problems are the transactional costs involved in doing justice—the costs of hiring lawyers, getting witnesses (who must be paid expenses), and collecting evidence.

Limited-jurisdiction courts that handle small matters were compared earlier to general-jurisdiction courts that hear major civil cases and try serious felonies. Every state is different in the structure of its courts; no general design applies everywhere. In fact, while the terms "limited jurisdiction" and "general jurisdiction" are convenient, they do not necessarily divide the courts for our purposes here. Some limited-jurisdiction courts have the authority to decide very serious matters within one category of cases—domestic cases or criminal cases, for example—so that those courts have the same dignity, logistical support, and quality of personnel that is commonly associated with general-jurisdiction courts. In Oklahoma, for example, there is a court for criminal appeals and another court for civil appeals. Each is a limited-jurisdiction court; however, each has authority to hear all cases within its area of competence, and each is final within its own sphere.

Occasionally the opposite phenomenon occurs. In Connecticut and Idaho all state (as opposed to municipal) judges are general jurisdiction trial-court judges, but a special session of the general-jurisdiction court hears minor cases. When this happens, even a general-jurisdiction court can take on all of the unpleasant attributes of a small-claims court. But, having now made the requisite acknowledgment of state diversity, I can fairly say that in most states there are limited-jurisdiction courts that handle traffic cases, minor criminal cases, and small civil cases. These courts usually also have authority to issue search and arrest warrants and to conduct preliminary proceedings, such as bail hearings, in felony cases. As pointed out earlier, these courts are variously called magistrate courts, justice of the peace courts, traffic courts, small-claims courts, district courts, or county courts. For our purposes I shall refer to them simply as "minor courts."

It is ironic that these courts, which are considered an embarrassment by many leading lawyers and judges, handle the bulk of the nation's disputes. A survey made by the National Center for State Courts in 1975 showed that there are 21,000 minor-court judges, while there are only 5,000 general-jurisdiction judges. Relative numbers of personnel alone would imply that the volume of business conducted in these petty, embarrassing courts is greater than the volume of business conducted in the major courts by a factor of at least four. However, the quickly inferred factor of four substantially understates the difference in volume. The bulk of the traffic cases handled in minor courts is uncontested, as is the bulk of the consumer debt-collection cases and landlord-and-tenant cases. Where cases are uncontested, a higher volume can be processed. In traffic court, even when a defendant does contest a ticket, a typical hearing takes only five minutes unless a jury is demanded, which is unusual. Contested landlord-and-tenant cases take about as long. In general-jurisdiction courts defendants more frequently appear to fight about the matter.

Many people pass their entire lives without ever going to a general-jurisdiction court as either a witness, litigant, or juror. But in a world characterized by the automobile, consumer debt, and rental housing,

189

few people can avoid eventually going either to traffic or small-claims court. The result is that the courts that receive the least attention from lawyers, high-level judges, and the political process are the courts that everybody sees and does business with on a daily basis. The court system is, therefore, commonly judged by its least competent part.

Everything about traffic or small-claims courts is ugly. Only 60 percent of American jurisdictions require the judges of these courts to be lawyers. Their salaries are substantially lower than for general-jurisdiction judges, and the physical facilities are usually execrable. Furthermore, traffic and small-claims courts are typically snowed under by a mountain of paper (since each case requires its own separate file even if uncontested), and the supporting clerical staff usually cannot process the paperwork efficiently. If we ask why a system of minor courts that seemingly has greater impact on individual voters than either the federal or state general-jurisdiction courts has become the stepchild of the judiciary, we are returned to the trifling five dollars that the town of Jupiter Island extorted from my unwilling hands.

As far as I was concerned in the Jupiter Island parking episode, the transactional cost of individual justice exceeded the cost of injustice. If I had gone to the county court of Martin County with a serious intent to beat the illegal parking rap, I could have made the case as complicated as a felony trial. First, in addition to defending the parking charge on the merits, I could have argued that the system of parking regulations in all of Hobe Sound violated the federal and state constitutions because they demonstrated a specific intent to keep outsiders—particularly poor people who would be largely black and Hispanic—from enjoying public, taxpayer-supported facilities. I could raise this constitutional issue both in the traffic court and later on appeal in the next higher general-jurisdiction court, or by a writ of prohibition issuing out of the general-jurisdiction court in the first instance to prohibit the trial on the parking ticket. This prohibition action would be appealable to the Florida intermediate court of appeals, then leave could be requested to appeal to the Florida Supreme Court and even to the Supreme Court of the United States.

In order to establish the constitutional claim that the parking regulations were designed to exclude minorities from the public facilities of the rich, expert witnesses would need to be called to show that the parking scheme under which I was being prosecuted was not rationally calculated to achieve orderly parking but was intended to have an exclusionary effect. In addition, some survey would need to be made to determine the actual racial and class makeup of those who are turned away from the Hobe Sound beach because they cannot park. So far we are looking at between ten and twenty thousand dollars in legal fees, expert witness fees, and travel expenses, not to mention the value of everyone's time.

Assuming that the claims based on discrimination failed, I would still have the merits of the parking violation to litigate. Expert witnesses in the field of language usage could be called to testify about the usual meaning of the words "road right-of-way." Legal research would need to be done to find support for the proposition that the language of signs cannot be based on local usage but must be intelligible to anyone with a working knowledge of English.

"Ridiculous!" you may be exclaiming at this point. "Don't make a federal case out of a two-bit parking squabble—just go in and tell the county judge your story in the hopes he will be a reasonable person." But even if I were to approach the case that way it would still be cheaper to pay the ticket. The Town of Jupiter Island is a long, skinny affair, and the portion known as Hobe Sound is fairly close to my parents' home. The county court, however, is in the county seat of Stuart, which is over twenty miles away, and that is where I would have had to contest the ticket. The cost of gas alone would almost exceed the fine.

Any alternative to paying the fine, assuming for a moment I were living in Florida and could conveniently go to Stuart, would have involved a good two hours of my time. The rewards of beating the rap would not even pay state minimum wage. Thus, from an economic point of view, it is not qualitatively different to undertake the elaborate constitutional and factual defense already hypothesized than it is to do anything short of paying the ticket. And anyone who says, "it's not the money; it's the principle of the thing," is lying in his teeth.

As the last chapter explained in detail, while courts often appear free to the casual observer because the court itself is a public facility, courts are actually very expensive. Anyone who has served as a juror during a full term of court at the nominal compensation of fifteen to twenty-five dollars a day knows just how expensive jury service is. A housewife has a hard time finding a baby-sitter for what the courts pay for jury service. Retired people and the unemployed occasionally find jury service enjoyable or financially rewarding. But the salesman, coal miner, small business owner, or public-school teacher receives his or her call to jury duty in the same spirit that he or she would receive a news bulletin heralding the return of Attila the Hun. Witnesses feel exactly the same way about a summons.

In August 1982 a teenage boy was stabbed to death on a subway train in Brooklyn, New York. The boy was killed during the theft of his one-hundred-dollar transistor radio, and at the next stop everyone on the car scrambled out, leaving the boy to bleed to death. No one went to the police, and a day after the incident the New York police were imploring people through radio and television announcements to come forward if they had witnessed the crime. Some of the reluctance of the witnesses to come forward no doubt came from fear; nonetheless, much of the reluctance obviously came from no higher a concern than an unwillingness to sit in front of mug books for hours in a filthy police station or to have one's life disrupted for a year by repeated summonses to court, only to have the case adjourned time after time.

Only in a society as hardened to violence as New York City would citizens fail to cooperate enthusiastically with the police to apprehend a murderer. The attitude of the witnesses to the New York subway slaying is remarkable exactly because it is so rare. However, it is almost as burdensome to be a witness in a traffic case involving a motorist's disregard of a stop sign as to be a witness in a murder trial. There is no way around the fact that being a witness in any case takes at least one full day out of your life.

Perfect justice has a price, just like perfect automobiles, perfect houses, or perfect medical care. The abstract concept of justice is cherished, and admitting that justice has a price implies that justice must compete in the marketplace with automobiles, housing, and medical care. Whether or not we want to admit it, that is exactly the case on both the individual and the societal levels. The costs of justice cannot be measured exclusively by the funding received by public agencies like courts, legal aid, police, prosecutors, or public defenders. Litigant, witness, and juror costs must also be included.

Since the litigation of a petty case in traffic or small-claims court can involve as much complex lawyering and as many expensive expert witnesses as a major case in federal court, all the costs of justice can come to bear on the minor courts. What actually occurs everywhere is that expensive perfect justice is rejected by the patrons of minor courts because injustice is cheaper.

During my service as a judge I have noticed a perverse indifference by the appellate judges who run the court system, as well as by the leaders of the bar, to the complete lack of litigant satisfaction with traffic and small-claims courts. The reasons for this indifference reflect economic reality. The amounts in controversy in the minor courts are so low that few litigants can afford lawyers to represent their interests there,[1] or any of the other costs of purchasing perfect justice.

Yet certain types of specialized lawyers appear in minor courts all the time. These are criminal lawyers, debt collectors, and lawyers for landlords. The very incompetence of minor courts is often a positive advantage to lawyers who are specialized users. Criminal lawyers get to know the court system and the judges, so minor courts give criminal lawyers an opportunity to win at the amateur level while still permitting an expeditious appeal to a major court. Lawyers for collection agencies and landlords find minor courts convenient for taking default judgments, and while the paperwork processing is not very efficient for the layman who does not know his way around the nooks and crannies of one of

---

1. The one thing that lawyers and judges *have* done is to establish procedures that permit lawyers representing clients in minor courts to get out of those courts and into a regular court quickly. In many places, including West Virginia, the way a case is appealed from a minor court to a general-jurisdiction court is a trial *de novo*—a lovely Latin expression that means you do the whole damn thing over again in the general-jurisdiction court. Most litigants who are representing themselves do not know how to go to a higher court, but the lawyers do. Since the lawyers know that minor courts are not very good, they have set the system up so that lawyers can avoid these courts. When I was practicing law, if a client asked me to represent him in justice of the peace court, I would tell the client that it would be cheaper for him to go into that court and fool around defending himself and then, if he lost, to call me and we would appeal to the circuit court where we would get a whole new trial, and I could apply all of my expensive lawyer techniques.

these "people's courts," an experienced lawyer-user knows where a paper is likely to be lost and can shepherd his file through the maze. In many places the gift or tip to clerical personnel is not unknown.

I have observed an interesting psychological phenomenon among lawyers, law professors, and judges—that the amount of effort devoted to improving a part of the court system is a function not of that part's usefulness but of how interesting it is. The lion's share of any major law review is given over to an analysis of federal law and federal courts, notwithstanding that most lawyers don't practice in federal court, and federal law seldom touches the average person's life. Your next-door neighbor is far more likely to have a workmen's compensation case than an antitrust case. Yet the scholarly literature is full of commentary on antitrust and almost devoid of new approaches to the zoo we call workmen's compensation. Workmen's compensation law simply does not provide the legal scholar with any opportunity for exotic academic gymnastics.

Similarly, there is nothing very interesting in terms of legal principles about minor courts. The analysis is elementary. The more minor courts look like major courts, the higher the transactional costs become. Since litigants cannot afford transactional costs, there is no money for lawyers. The traditional approaches to improving the operation of the courts all require the active participation of practicing lawyers. Because the amounts in controversy in minor courts do not justify hiring lawyers, the traditional approaches fail. Once this problem is understood, lawyers, judges, and law professors bail out. If minor courts have any interest at all, it is to administrators, economists, mental-health professionals, and social workers.

The science of law, like any other science, is inaccessible to people who have not been trained in its mysteries. The dilemma for small-claims court reformers is that any effort to apply the "science" of law as it has been developed in the major courts to minor courts impales itself on the high wages and overhead costs of lawyers. On the other hand, informal adjudication, where the litigants need know nothing about formal legal rules because the judge resembles a tribal chief sitting under a tree dispensing justice, is also rejected. The tribal-chief system leads to arbitrary and unpredictable decisions. Lawyers and judges feel more comfortable with a system that errs on the side of expensive formality; while transactional costs may drive some litigants away, those who take a small claim or traffic ticket seriously enough to hire a lawyer will then presumably have all the advantages of a refined legal system.

Furthermore, it is not fair to say that all cases in minor courts are as petty as my five-dollar parking ticket. Some small-claims courts have civil jurisdiction up to five thousand dollars, and traffic courts can often impose a year's imprisonment and loss of one's driver's license. In many states traffic courts, small-claims courts, and misdemeanor criminal courts are rolled into one. These are the justice of the peace and magistrate courts that can send you to jail for assault and battery, fish and game violations, petty larceny, criminal trespass, and a host of environmental violations. The Supreme Court has established a constitutional right to free appointed counsel for indigents in any prosecution where there is a possibility of even brief imprisonment. Where a person faces a jail term he or she will either hire a lawyer or apply for a free one.

The Supreme Court's recognition that going to jail, even for a day, is a significant burden on anyone points up the artificiality of our distinction between "major disputes" and "minor disputes," each with its own system of courts. These categories make sense only when they are used to separate cases on the basis of whether the amount in controversy justifies hiring a lawyer and incurring other transactional costs. From the subjective point of view of the litigants, money is probably not the factor in determining whether a problem is minor. A local utility company can be involved in a multi-million-dollar rate case without anyone in the company suffering the personal anxiety that a consumer suffers when his or her car is repossessed. Similarly, a fifty-dollar fine for a traffic offense is a minor annoyance to the middle class but a major burden to the poor.

Judges and lawyers tend not to separate the concept of minor dispute as it relates to transactional costs from the concept of minor dispute as it relates to the intensity of the emotions that a case arouses. When, for example, a person is assaulted, he wants vindication and some punishment for his assailant. The assailant might be unwilling to spend several thousand dollars in lawyers' fees to avoid a thirty-day jail term, and the victim is probably unwilling to spend much money prosecuting (if the state system permits special prosecutors), yet intense emotions are

195

aroused. Where the court system fails to provide a vigorous prosecutor or is so overloaded that the case languishes a year before coming to trial or the public defender can get the case dismissed on a technicality because the paperwork was done incompetently, the victim feels the courts have let him or her down. The crime may have been a minor assault, but the case was not minor to the victim by any criterion but money. Nonetheless, this is exactly the type of case likely to be handled by the minor courts.

Lawyers in general and the organized bar in particular are uninterested in the minor courts because most lawyers do not make their living there. The policymaking appellate judges are not interested in minor courts because those courts' problems are political and administrative. Appellate judges want to work on so-called legal problems; they hate thinking about administration. The problems of minor courts cannot be solved by writing published appellate opinions. Furthermore, since the amounts in controversy are indeed minor in terms of their ability to sustain transactional costs, any improvement in the administration of the system must rely on public funds that need to be disgorged from hostile taxpayers and their legislatures.

At least in the general-jurisdiction courts the managing appellate judges can tinker at the system by enjoining the lawyers who work there to do certain things. The lawyers do what is required by the judges and pass the cost on to the clients. Where, as in the minor courts, there are no lawyers or a lawyer only on one side, the only personnel available to make the system work are the publicly paid court staffs and the litigants themselves. The current staffs are already overworked, and the litigants are ignorant. Unless the structure of minor courts is completely changed, a mere enhancement of funding for the current system will have little or no effect on enhancing consumer satisfaction.

So far I have assumed that the reader has been exposed at some time to the gallery of horrors we call minor courts. However, it is worth refreshing everyone's recollection. Unfortunately, no single profile applies to all minor courts—some are far better than others—and even within a single state quality varies from city to city or county to county. Much of the variation in quality depends on the commitment of local funding bodies, the dedication and quality of the judicial and clerical personnel, and the structure of the system. Some systems are beautifully designed but poorly funded and loaded with incompetents. Other systems are miserably designed but made to purr like finely tuned machines because of the enthusiasm and competence of the personnel. In many places, however, the system is both poorly designed and filled with incompetents who make a mockery of the word *court*.

In the latter class are contained the remnants of the old justice of the peace system. Typically justices of the peace are locally elected or appointed from among lay citizens and are paid by some combination of salary and fees based on the work of the court. Usually justices of the peace are responsible for setting up their own offices, and as often as not they hold court in their own homes. When I first started practicing law West Virginia had this system; however, it was abolished by constitutional amendment in 1974. The U.S. Supreme Court has said that a judge's compensation cannot depend on the outcome of any given case. The practical effect, however, of any fee system where compensation is based on *overall* work load is that a justice of the peace's compensation depends on the outcome of all cases taken together.

Under the justice of the peace system either the police officers or individual plaintiffs in civil cases can choose their court. Obviously the police are interested in securing convictions, and civil plaintiffs want quick judgments. Therefore, a justice of the peace who wants to make the ten to twenty dollars in fees for every case filed in his court knows that he had better be propolice and proplaintiff. Thus the judicial title "J. P." has often been thought to mean "judgment for the police" or "judgment for the plaintiff." While statutes require that court costs be paid in advance by a civil plaintiff bringing a suit (to be recovered from the defendant if the defendant loses) or by the state in criminal cases, that scheme only avoids the problem of a judge being paid according to the outcome of an *individual* case. Even an idiot can understand that the judge is still paid according to the outcome of *all* cases taken together. A justice of the peace who finds too often for criminal or civil defendants loses all his court's business. In Kanawha County, West Virginia, before the abolition of the justice of the peace system, one justice of the peace was earning over fifty thousand dollars a year by cornering the small-debt collection market.

A variation on this system occurs in small-town municipal police courts. Traffic fines can be a significant contributor to a municipality's income, and this source of revenue is particularly attractive when fines can be levied on out-of-towners. The southern speed traps along the access roads to Florida resorts have always been classic manifestations of revenue-inspired prosecution. Usually police-court judges are appointed by the mayor or city council for no definite term—thus continued tenure depends upon satisfactory performance of the revenue-gathering function.

There is one notable advantage to a system based on fees—the judges work, dispose of cases quickly, and do the paperwork correctly. When efforts are made to professionalize the minor courts by eliminating the fee system and other financial incentives to corrupt conduct, the number of hearings per judge each day slows dramatically, the quality of the paperwork deteriorates, and the docket gets clogged. This, in fact, was the experience we had in some West Virginia counties when we abolished justices of the peace and replaced them with salaried magistrates. As all labor unions understand, piecework results in higher output per worker than an hourly wage.

In many regards, minor courts are more like administrative bodies than judicial bodies. They process a large volume of uncontested cases, and their success or failure depends not on the quality of the judges but on the quality of the supporting staff. One crucial supportive function is service of process, and where minor courts are poorly funded, this is where the system often breaks down. Serving process, particularly on poor or itinerant people, requires some diligence on the part of the process server. Where salaries are low or jobs are awarded as political patronage or the work exceeds the capacity of the available employees, the system grinds to a halt.

The states are about equally divided on whether their minor-court judges must be lawyers. Where laypersons are permitted to serve as judges the variation in quality is staggering. Some of the best judges I know in West Virginia are lay magistrates. Usually these are well-educated people who enjoy court work and who quickly master the body of law that applies to their courts. Others, however, are abject political hacks who have no interest in learning the law and perceive their jobs as nothing but a meal ticket. In between are a lot of good people who are strained by the intellectual demands of the job but who perform competently and considerately most of the time.

While lawyers can run for magistrate in West Virginia, the salary range of between $15,750 and $23,625 a year (depending on the population served by the judge) is insufficient to attract lawyers. We have only four lawyers out of 150 magistrates. My own conclusion is that good, well-educated lay judges are significantly better than lazy, alcoholic, incompetent, or indifferent lawyers. Since the salary level in many states often makes this the choice, I am satisfied with lay judges. In West Virginia our four lawyer magistrates are excellent, but that is because they are either young promising lawyers or approaching retirement age. Some states, like Florida, have recognized that lawyers are easier to attract in urban areas than in rural areas. There minor county judges must be lawyers only if the population of the county exceeds a certain figure.

Inadequate or incompetent personnel combined with seedy quarters and poor logistical support exacerbate the most intractable problem of minor courts—the intensely human nature of the problems that are taken there. When IBM gets sued by the Justice Department for antitrust violations, no human issues are involved. In the words of Prime Minister Gladstone, nobody loses one moment's sleep over that *public* disaster. But when a woman goes to night court for protection from her violent husband or a teenager loses his driver's license, a human drama, and perhaps a minor human tragedy, unfolds. The square peg and round hole problem discussed in Chapter 4 becomes almost overwhelming.

Once when I was visiting a rural West Virginia magistrate court I happened to witness one of these dramas. The satellite magistrate court in Iaeger—a town of 833 twelve miles outside Welch, the county seat of McDowell County—is manned by an intelligent, hardworking lay judge in his twenties, with one assistant. On the day of my visit a young couple appeared to swear out a warrant against the man's former wife and her new husband for breaking and entering, petty larceny, and kidnapping. What had occurred was that the plaintiff husband had a child by a former marriage, and when that marriage broke up, the child had stayed with the father. A few years later, the child's mother remarried and wanted the child. She came with her new husband, took the child, who was about five or six years old, and removed him to Monroe County, which is about two hours away.

The only crime that was even arguably committed when the child

199

was taken away was criminal trespass. A mother cannot kidnap her own child; the taking of the personal effects of the child for the child's own use is not larceny; and there can be no criminal breaking and entering without the intention to commit a larceny or felony in the building after entry. The complaining couple did not understand the technical elements of the crimes they were charging; what they did understand was that they were grievously wronged and that what happened to them should have been a crime.

More to the point, however, the young couple did know that if they could mould their complaint into a criminal prosecution, the state would underwrite the transactional costs of getting the child back. If the action were criminal, the state would send a police officer to Monroe County to bring back the offending mother to be prosecuted in McDowell County, and possibly some settlement would be reached that would cause the child to be returned. However, if the couple were left to civil remedies, they would need to sue the offending mother in her own home county, hire a lawyer, and sustain travel and lodging expenses. The child's father was an ordinary laborer and his new wife, the child's stepmother, did not work but had stayed home for several years to take care of the child.

At this point I took over. I found the entire exercise far more difficult and emotionally draining than anything I had been doing in an appellate court. I explained to the couple that they must retain a lawyer in the nearby county seat of Welch who would then file an application for a writ of habeas corpus in the circuit court of Monroe County to adjudicate the respective rights to the child's custody. I had to explain the difference between a civil wrong and a criminal wrong and why their problem did not fit within the criminal law. Their case for criminal trespass was too weak to prosecute. I could not imagine any lawyer undertaking their case for less than five hundred dollars—a fee that would not make the lawyer rich—and it was difficult to get the wronged couple to accept that they would need to pay money to be put back in the position they thought they were entitled to be in by right.

While routine administrative matters like traffic tickets, bad-check cases, and eviction proceedings comprise the majority of the cases filed in any minor court, their numerical preponderance is not an accurate reflection of their relative importance. The true measure of the quality of a minor court is not how it handles thousands of uncontested administrative matters but rather how it handles the important human dramas that find their way through its doors.

The case of the kidnapped child points out that people often come to minor courts because they don't know the dimensions of their problems and can't afford to go to a lawyer. Domestic violence, quarrels among neighbors, the elderly's war against the annoyance of juveniles, actions to exact child support, and simple contract and accident cases all end up in the minor courts. Big-time law is made by big-time people arguing about big-time bucks. Big-time law interests professionals because it pays handsomely and is easier to abstract into preconceived legal categories than earthy human drama. Where earthy human drama is involved, the legal rules are seldom flexible enough to give a satisfactory human answer, yet because the minor courts are structured as "baby" major courts, litigants with human problems are usually saddled with rules developed when one multi-billion-dollar company sues another.

I am led to the inescapable conclusion that the existing system has its priorities almost upside down. In terms of human justice, the minor courts are the most important courts in the system. Instead of placing all our best resources in the courts of general jurisdiction, leaving the minor courts as the system's stepchildren, we should approach the courts from the other way around. Of course, most general jurisdiction trial-court judges would not serve as minor judges even if the pay were comparable because that is not the work they have been trained to do. Furthermore, good major-court judges would not necessarily make good minor-court judges. The skills needed in minor courts are not legal skills; they are interpersonal skills. Teachers, former coaches, and ex-military officers often make good minor-court lay judges.

While there are jurisdictions like Massachusetts where minor judges are appointed for life, in most places minor judges are either elected or appointed for comparatively short terms. Typically, in the states and municipalities with an elective system, these judges run every four years. Unfortunately, notwithstanding all the efforts that have been made to depoliticize the judiciary, in those places with elected minor judgeships, the races tend to be hotly contested. Part of the reason is economic—while a minor judgeship offers little to attract a good lawyer, it is a wonderful job for a layperson, and it is a good job for a mediocre lawyer. It offers high prestige, power within the community, interesting work, and a more than satisfactory salary for a layperson or a lawyer with no clients.

Many politically active laypersons and, where the salary is high enough, many young lawyers would like minor judgeships. Lawyers particularly seek the jobs where judgeships are part-time positions and lawyer-judges can also practice law. The result is that politics both intrudes itself and, more important, appears to intrude itself far more forcefully into the operation of the minor courts than into the operation of general-jurisdiction courts. In the general-jurisdiction courts there is little political competition for an incumbent, even where the judges are elected on a partisan ballot. Part of this is attributable to the support of incumbents by lawyers who contribute money that can be used to buy advertising and support election-day organizations. Challengers cannot raise this type of money, so they must spend their own to make a successful campaign. The cost of an election, therefore, removes much of the economic incentive to run for a major judgeship when there is already an incumbent. Large quantities of instant money are not available, however, to minor-court candidates. The lawyers don't have enough of an economic stake in the election of a minor judge.

The human drama in these courts has an intensely personal nature that not only mobilizes political influence but causes the appearance of such influence even when it does not exist. General jurisdiction trial-court judges are surrounded by a certain ceremony. Robes, titles, courtroom etiquette, and strict rules about lawyers not talking to the judge about a case without the lawyer for the other side being present all unite to reduce the appearance of corrupt political deal making. In general-jurisdiction courts litigants are represented by lawyers who know these rules. In the minor courts the litigants are largely representing themselves, and they do not understand the rules. Since election to a minor judgeship requires a person to be well known, in any contested case there will likely be a network of friends, relatives, and associates of both litigants who know the judge personally. Minor judges usually listen politely to those who volunteer information or advice merely because pomposity loses friends and votes. Thus bare politeness often gives the appearance of corrupt decision making.

Sometimes the matrix of mutual friends is an advantage. Frequently the judge is so well regarded by both sides that in a neighborhood dispute he can effect a compromise that is acceptable to both sides. When this is achieved, the ideal of an informal, neighborhood, people's court is realized. More often, however, no compromise is reached, and the side that loses is convinced that its loss was occasioned by the other side's political influence, and such, alas, is frequently the case. In the minor courts, however, it is difficult to separate appearance from reality.

The reason that judges appear corrupt is that litigants are obsessed with their own cases and watch every facet of them with an eagle eye; judges and lawyers are involved in an individual litigant's case as just one of hundreds of cases being processed through the court at the moment.[2] The litigant, however, cannot accept that the judge is not as emotionally involved in his case as he is. If, for example, a lawyer for one side in a case meets the judge in the hallway where they discuss ticket sales for the local university's athletic banquet, a litigant on the other side who observes the conversation cannot believe that the discussion was not about his case.

Politics, unfortunately, often does play a part in the decisions of minor courts. All of politics is a grand exercise in helping one's friends. In 1981 a West Virginia magistrate was forced to resign because he was giving advance notice to gamblers of impending raids by the state police after the officers came to his court for search warrants. After all, the gamblers had elected him and would contribute money in the next election. What had the state police done for him lately?

The problem of actual corruption is exacerbated, however, by lawyers and others who take advantage of the venal image that minor judges have among the general public. Occasionally, minor judges are for sale, but in my experience outright bribery is a rare occurrence. While political accommodation, including the trading of judicial favors for prospective campaign contributions, pervades the minor courts, the crass payoff by total strangers is too dangerous to be widespread.

2. I sit on approximately four hundred cases in one way or another during each of three terms of court a year. When a litigant approaches me a few weeks or months after a decision to ask why the court did something, I can't even remember what the case was about, much less the details of particular holdings.

Nonetheless, sleazy lawyers often find it profitable to require a client to pay several thousand dollars so that the lawyer can "take care of the judge." Usually in such cases, and they are almost always criminal cases, what occurs is that the police have made an obvious procedural blunder that the lawyer knows will result in automatic dismissal. The client, however, is innocent of any legal knowledge but guilty of the crime charged. When his lawyer secures a pretrial dismissal, the client thinks it a miracle and can only attribute his entirely unexpected reprieve to a judicial payoff.

Greedy lawyers are not the only culprits. The world is full of braggarts, many of whom enjoy creating the impression that they are in positions to pay off everyone and fix everything. It is common, for example, for out-of-towners who receive parking tickets in Washington, D.C., to take them to their representative or senator to be "fixed." Often a legislator or a staff member will graciously take a ticket with a sly wink and assure that "the ticket will be taken care of." Indeed the ticket is taken care of—in fact, the legislator pays the ten or twenty bucks from his campaign slush fund to buy the visitor's and his family's vote forever. Cheap! But part of the pleasure for the constituent is the thought that he has sufficient influence for a representative or senator to go to all this trouble for him. When he brags about his miraculous political power back home, the traffic court in Washington, D.C., takes a bad rap. This and related phenomena are called the "phantom bagman problem," and it is more likely to be prominent with regard to minor courts than general-jurisdiction or appellate courts.

General-jurisdiction trial judges are very sensitive to any allegation of corruption. Integrity is the only glue that holds the major courts together. The reason that major judges take allegations of impropriety seriously enough to get to the bottom of them is that such allegations are infrequent. Major courts are accused of being political whores and of deciding cases based on friendships with lawyers or litigants, but they are seldom accused of taking money. In the minor courts, however, because of the level of human drama and the sheer volume of cases, background noise is so loud that getting to the bottom of every unfounded allegation is utterly impossible. Unless a case becomes particularly prominent, minor judges tend to accept the braggart and the phantom bagman as just another annoyance, like poor quarters.

Reform in the minor courts, therefore, is severely circumscribed by both the nature of the courts' business and the inherently political way that judges secure and keep their jobs. Nonetheless, if we begin to think positively about minor courts, recognizing that the nature of their business warrants them at least as high a priority for good judges and supporting staff as the major courts, a great deal can be done to improve both real performance and public confidence.

First of all, it must always be borne in mind that minor courts are "minor" not because of their subject matter but rather because the litigants cannot afford to hire lawyers. Consequently, the organizing principle for any good minor court should be its accessibility and comprehensibility to a layperson who wants to bring or defend his or her own case. In most places minor courts are hybrid creatures—they attempt to be simpler to use than the major courts, but they still retain enough complicated rules that a layperson can be impaled on technicalities.

Among the worst of the minor courts' technicalities are the rules of evidence. Such rules in civil cases can be satisfactorily eliminated in neighborhood disputes where the judge can let anybody contribute whatever he wants. A decision based on a "catharsis" model, where everyone who wants to can talk about anything he thinks is important regardless of whether his testimony is hearsay or whether he is qualified to render an expert opinion, will be at least as just as the current system, and the litigants will be better satisfied.[3]

The secret of a well-functioning minor court is the competence, concern, and courtesy of the court's staff. Since litigants in a minor court cannot afford lawyers, the court will be successful only if staff members help litigants sort out their human problems and organize them into legal questions. The easiest way for a court to appear accessible is to print pamphlets on the law written in lay language, accompanied by a set of simple forms. But that technique does not do the job; a far higher percentage of our population is functionally illiterate than is usually imagined. Litigants need personal attention from someone who

3. I am indebted to J. Ruhnka, S. Weller, and J. Martin, *Small Claims Courts, a National Examination* (Williamsburg: National Center for State Courts, 1978) for many of these observations.

can take them through the paperwork, fill the forms out for them when necessary, and explain the process of the court. Receiving simple instructions on the operation of a court is like receiving simple instructions on the operation of a sound movie camera. The instructions may be simple to the person who writes them, but they are not simple to a person who has never used any type of camera before.

Probably the greatest litigant frustration encountered in minor courts is the constant postponement of trials. When witnesses or litigants with steady jobs come to day court, they lose a day's vacation or wages, and when they come to night court, they lose their precious leisure time. Competent staff can organize telephone procedures (similar to those employed in dentists' offices) to make sure that people will show up for court on the day set or notify everyone involved in the case well in advance when the case has been postponed.

In this regard, there are a number of specific abuses that are worth exploring. Often courts set all cases for a 10:00 A.M. docket call, which means that many litigants and witnesses must sit around the courthouse all day. This can be corrected by scheduling each trial separately and using a telephone system to assure attendance and to guarantee little wasted time. Many courts allow default judgments where plaintiffs appear but defendants fail to appear; however, the converse is seldom the case. Where a plaintiff fails to show up, the defendant should get a default. Finally, where there is a missing witness or one party has failed to bring in a crucial piece of evidence, the trial should not be adjourned but the witness called on the telephone or the evidence introduced by hearsay. In the science of judging, the tolerances are very high—while occasionally a judge will feel that additional information will help his decision, usually that is not the cse. Where the judge knows that his decision will be the same regardless of what further evidence is presented, he should decide the case. In short, every possible technique should be used before a case is adjourned so that litigants do not lose time and wages.

Much scholarly literature has been devoted in recent years to schemes for the diversion of disputes away from minor courts and into other forums such as neighborhood dispute centers or court-appointed arbitrators. While behind these suggestions is the recognition that much minor-court litigation is human drama that is hard to sort out through the application of traditional legal principles, diversion does not work as well as improving the courts themselves so that they can do what an arbitrator does. It is far better to give the minor courts authority to employ conciliation and arbitration techniques in certain types of human drama cases than to divert disputes to other forums. Other forums have no power to enter enforceable judgments.

It is easy to advocate that technical rules of pleading, practice, and evidence be discarded in the minor civil courts; it is quite another thing to discard the substantive rules of law. If a tenant doesn't pay the rent, the landlord has a right to evict him, and it confounds the rules of property for a minor judge to "arbitrate" that dispute by giving the tenant ninety days' free occupancy. Similarly, in a small accident case, if the defendant says that it was the plaintiff's fault, not the defendant's, it is difficult to see how a judge can split the damages in half, if indeed the defendant was wholly without fault.

Some classes of cases, however, like misdemeanor prosecutions for disturbing the peace—loud music or wild parties—do admit to arbitration, notwithstanding that the prosecution may be criminal. What neighbors really want is future tranquility, not punishment for past offenses. Similarly, in contract cases where both sides have some right on their side, the loss should be shared in some equitable—not all-or-nothing—way. In such instances, a regular minor court should have the authority to enter into an arbitration mode, conciliate the dispute to exact grudging acquiescence from all sides, and then enter an enforceable order. When disputes are decided by a forum other than a real court, a recalcitrant loser must then be dragged to a real court for an enforceable order. This is expensive duplication of effort.

No minor court can function without competent staff. Competence is achieved by constant training. Since I have had some very happy experiences with intelligent lay judges in West Virginia, I believe that laypeople can perform well as minor judges. In fact, I think that laypeople often make up in enthusiasm and human concern what they lack in formal legal training. Furthermore, the body of law that needs to be mastered to do a successful job as a minor-court judge is both comparatively small and comparatively simple. Constant training, by which I mean three days a month and not three days a year, will generate a competent minor judiciary and supporting staff within a short time.

Once there are sufficient officers to serve process and sufficient clerical personnel to keep track of the cases, lead litigants through the court's procedure, and contact the parties to assure their appearance or inform them of cancellations, we have the foundation of a good system of minor courts. The next step is to train these people. The human drama/human tragedy factor in minor courts must be recognized. The fields of medicine, sociology, psychology, economics, and education all have something to contribute to minor judges and their staffs. Increasingly I am coming to the conclusion that in at least one regard a good minor judiciary is like a good army. When a good army is not fighting, it is training.

The very process of training establishes an esprit de corps that professionalizes the minor courts. Among other things, a state's commitment to upgrade its minor judiciary will inevitably involve professors at local law schools, influential practicing lawyers, and specialists in related fields like medicine and sociology. This broad involvement of quality people will cause general recognition of the wide spectrum of demands that are made on the judges of the human courts. People tend to behave the way they are expected to behave. If minor courts are expected to be venal, incompetent, and indifferent, that is how personnel will respond. If an institution has a bad self-image because it has a bad public image, there is no peer pressure to improve. Once, however, the public image changes, the self-image will change, and peers will drive many of the venal, incompetent, and indifferent people out of the system or improve their level of performance.

There are no powerful political lobbies that care one way or the other about how minor courts function. Lawyers defending the poor may see a disadvantage in courts that are efficient about debt collection and eviction, but the same poor clients who would be injured by collections and evictions will benefit from improved nonsupport proceedings and better protection from domestic violence. Insurance companies that might get sued in minor courts will probably appeal to general-jurisdiction courts anyway, so they are not going to waste lobbying time fighting good minor courts. Of course, attempts to change the way judges are selected will mobilize a strong political lobby of existing judges. In some places where the remnants of the justice of the peace system are still in place, such changes are needed; in most places they are not required.

What is required is a system for policing minor judges to catch both corruption and incompetence. Most states have judicial inquiry commissions in one form or another, but their performance is usually lackluster.

While in the minor criminal courts most formal rules must be retained because they are part of a larger framework of "due process," in the minor civil courts every effort should be made to eliminate all rules that impede lay access to these courts. Nothing could be sillier than the system we have in the magistrate courts of West Virginia where the procedure parallels almost entirely the *Federal Rules of Civil Procedure*, which were developed for the litigation of major controversies by skilled lawyers in general-jurisdiction courts.

Improvement of the minor civil courts involves several distinct design changes. First, it must be recognized that litigants know nothing about how to use these courts, so court staff must be available to show litigants how to prepare and present their cases. This implies at least one lawyer staff member whose job is not to decide cases but to fill out forms and give advice equally to all. Second, all rules of evidence and almost all rules of procedure should be abolished. Third, the court should be able to handle some disputes the way an arbitrator or counselor would, without regard to many of the legal principles that apply in general-jurisdiction courts. Finally, the staffs of minor courts should always be aware of the hidden costs to litigants and witnesses of going to court. Good administration is often the key to user satisfaction, and that means devising systems to avoid adjournments after most of the people involved have come to court.

Court users should be treated like human beings. This sounds obvious, but far too often the opposite is the case. The minor criminal courts have more intractable problems than the minor civil courts—partially because they service a more difficult clientele, but the professionalization of the civil courts will affect performance in the criminal courts as well.

It all sounds very easy, but there is a long tradition of doing things in the opposite manner. In most states the highest court could make a decided improvement in the minor courts by changing their structure. Most state supreme courts have extensive rule-making power that goes to the procedures to be employed in the state's courts. The current failure of the minor civil courts is largely attributable to a design that makes them "baby" general-jurisdiction courts. The reason that scholars urge the diversion of minor cases to other forums like informal arbitrators and family dispute centers is that these forums will have less complicated rules, lower transactional costs, and greater flexibility in the solutions they can design. In other words, they can take a human drama and handle it in human rather than legal terms. But there is no reason that a system of minor courts cannot behave the same way.

Certain injustices are inherent in all minor courts, no matter how well designed or funded. For example, no minor-court system could have inspired me to contest the five-dollar Jupiter Island parking ticket—any way you sliced it, I had more to lose than to gain. Furthermore, lawyers can object that there are certain "constitutional rights" for litigants even in minor courts, including, for example, the right not to be proven liable through hearsay evidence. There are technical problems of this nature, but they are not as serious as many lawyers suppose. Due process has usually been viewed as a flexible concept that looks to some conclusion about overall fairness. So far, the Supreme Court has permitted in minor courts substantial deviations from the due-process model that prevails in general-jurisdiction courts if there is ultimately some appeal to a formal, lawyers' court.

Certainly, for every design innovation in minor courts, there is some litigant who will be treated unjustly as a result of the innovation. Yet the real measure of a court system is not whether it is capable of providing perfect justice for everyone but rather whether it provides substantial justice for the majority of its users. Since current consumer satisfaction with minor courts is very low, it is hard to imagine that radical experimentation would not be welcomed enthusiastically.

Lawyer Economics   8

L AWYERS come in all shapes and sizes. Fifty percent of lawyers who graduated from America's ten most prestigious law schools have probably never been to court for anything more serious than a traffic ticket. In Washington, D.C., alone there are 11,339 members of the bar, most of whom work for the government, national lobbying groups, labor unions, research publishing companies, or law schools. While a law degree is useful in both business and government, working as either a business or government executive is not "practicing law."

A "practicing lawyer" is a person who holds himself or herself out as capable of taking any legal problem and handling it satisfactorily. Seldom does a practicing lawyer operate without the advice of specialists, but the thing that distinguishes the practicing lawyer from others who use law training in their work is that the practicing lawyer understands enough about the whole body of law to know when a specialist is required. Large law firms with several hundred lawyers have their own specialized departments—trusts and estates, litigation, corporate, real estate, oil and gas, tax, and admiralty, for example—depending on where the firm is located. Most individuals who need legal work, however, never see a firm of this size; they use smaller, general-practice firms that may have from three to thirty lawyers. But even the small firm will have some specialists.

In 1982 there were 36,367 graduates of accredited law schools in the United States. From the number of law school graduates it would appear that the market is glutted with hungry young lawyers and that competition will bring down the cost. Unfortunately, from the consumer's point of view, lawyers are probably not overpriced since in 1982 the average practicing lawyer earned only $45,000 a year.[1] This statistical average includes both young lawyers and mature, experienced lawyers. While a few lawyers earn extraordinary incomes by anyone's standards, the majority earn only slightly more than good plumbers.

In my experience, many law-school graduates are not, and never will be, qualified to "practice law." Fortunately, most of them gravitate to work where legal training is valuable but where less intellect and stamina are demanded than in law practice. Examples of law-related jobs include insurance-claims adjuster, real estate broker, middle-management government employee, FBI agent, corporate contract officer, or hospital administrator. Often middle-of-the-class graduates from undistinguished law schools who would ultimately make fine practicing lawyers are compelled to leave law because law firms will not hire them. Had these lawyers had opportunities for further training in firms, they could have practiced law well, but they were never given a chance. Other graduates do get entry level jobs practicing law but find they do not like active practice and leave for other, related work. Lawyers who have practiced know that graduating from law school and practicing law are two entirely different matters.

Unless a person is dedicated to being a good lawyer, he will be an absolute menace to his clients—in fact, he will be worse than no lawyer at all. Law changes all the time, and a person must keep up with the changes. For example, tax law is central to almost all other law—it

1. Earnings statistics for lawyers are hard to come by. This figure was arrived at on the basis of a 1980 Iowa study showing average earnings of private practitioners; a 1980 Bureau of Labor Statistics survey indicating average salaries at the starting level, the top level, and the four grades in between; and a survey of starting salaries compiled by *Student Lawyer* magazine. Readers who want more accurate figures will find them in the IRS abstract on income, reported by occupations, due in 1983.

intrudes itself into the way we write a will, establish a trust, structure a settlement in a personal-injury case, organize a real estate venture, or merge two partnerships. While tax is the supreme specialty in law, as evidenced by the fact that it is the only area where an advanced degree, the "tax masters," is truly useful, nonetheless, it is also a field about which all lawyers need to know a great deal.

The way to keep up with the law is to attend seminars sponsored by professional organizations, and every time a lawyer goes to such an out-of-town seminar for five days, it costs about a thousand dollars. These seminars are for work and not play; classes usually meet six hours a day, and attendees are expected to read a heap of printed material. The ancillary value of such meetings is that a lawyer makes friends whom he or she can call on the telephone for a five-minute consultation. The smarter and more experienced lawyers often serve at no charge to enhance the competence of the slower and less experienced lawyers. Specialists give other lawyers advice for free when they can do so "off the top of their heads" in return for fee-generating work in cases where the specialist must take over and perform direct services.

Usually it is assumed that when a person comes out of law school, he or she understands the legal system and knows how to get things done. In fact, this is not true; unless a lawyer develops a narrow specialty, each client's problem requires extensive study of a new body of law. The result is that practicing law is grueling, intellectually demanding work. "Intellectually demanding" does not mean thinking great thoughts or producing literary masterpieces, but it does mean that the mind must be working all the time. When a lawyer writes a trial-court brief, it is the equivalent of a college term paper.

The grueling part of general law practice is the constant travel to interview out-of-state witnesses, or consult with officials at the corporate headquarters of a major client, or try a case in the state where the defendant is a resident. Even when a lawyer has a practice that does not demand travel, he or she must be available to answer client problems at night, on weekends, and during vacations. Lawyers who are interested enough in their profession to work hard at it *and* are smart enough to understand how the whole system comes together (the two abilities do not necessarily go hand in hand) are the lawyers everyone wants. Since these lawyers get the business, they also gain experience, so they become better and better; the difference between these good lawyers and young or mediocre lawyers increases geometrically.[2]

A competent practicing lawyer is dependent on expensive logistical support. He or she must rent office space with convenient access to the courts, staff the office with competent secretaries, and provide the office with a working library. My own administrative assistant (who is not a lawyer) makes $20,380 a year plus state health insurance and state retirement benefits. Books are expensive, and all law books must be updated annually either with replacement volumes or with annual supplements, so that the yearly service charge on the small, working law library of a solo practitioner may be as much as $2,500. Finally, computers have taken over law offices, and in order to be competitive a lawyer must have word processing equipment as well as trained personnel to operate it. One reason that my administrative assistant makes as much money as she does is that she can operate a computer. Altman and Weil, a consulting firm for law-office management, estimated in 1981 that in law firms of between two and six lawyers, the total overhead cost for each billable hour of lawyer time is slightly over thirty dollars.

2. The economics of law offices closely parallel the economics of large-scale manufacturing firms in terms of the positive effects of market share. As a result of work pioneered by the Boston Consulting Group, it has been observed that the larger an enterprise's market share, the stronger its continued competitive position will become as a result of a phenomenon known as the "experience curve." In essence, each time a manufacturer's total production of a given product doubles, the per unit cost drops because of improved technology associated with learning about the production of that product. The experience-curve effect is separate and apart from traditional economies of scale, such as mill run length, and is a function of the total experience of the firm from the first day it started manufacturing a product or line of products. Consequently, it appears that a company with a dominant market share will tend to expand its lead even further because both a superior product and lower costs result from greater total experience, even when no physical economies of scale are considered. In law practice there are few physical or technological economies of scale beyond a certain point; however, there is a significant experience-curve effect. A good summary of experience-curve theory as it applies to industry can be found in B. Hedley, "A Fundamental Approach to Strategy Development," *Long Range Planning* (December 1976).

Then there are the miscellaneous expenses of law practice. Travel is expensive—particularly out-of-state travel by air. Postage is expensive and so is the telephone. The continuing legal education that I have discussed must be paid for, and a lawyer who is involved with government officials all the time should make political contributions to numerous campaigns in order to sustain the goodwill necessary to get his or her clients' problems handled quickly.

Finally, I suppose, we should reflect on how much it costs to go to college and law school. At the extreme, if a person has gone to an Ivy League college and a private law school, the rock bottom price is $12,000 a year for seven years, which comes to an investment of $84,000. But money is not an accurate measure of true cost since tuition and living expenses are often paid by family, scholarships, or government grants. Going to school and being serious about it is no fun, and since being admitted to any law school is competitive, and getting admitted to a top law school almost requires coming in through the window with an "S" on your chest, the person who goes to a first-class law school has worked hard in college and probably in high school. These compulsively hard workers are the people that all the first-class firms want to hire—they do not want the kid who graduated at the bottom of his class. Since, indeed (with the exception of the very top law schools), it is the upper 20 percent of graduates who are sought after, the bidding concentrates on the top 20 percent.

Lawyers sell their services in the free market to those who can afford to pay for them. It is ability to pay, not need, that determines the distribution of lawyer services, just like other services. Since, however, both legal advice and access to the courts are now considered fundamental entitlements like food or medical care, the federal government has established the Legal Services Corporation, which provides lawyer services to the poor in certain types of civil matters.

The people who are probably most dissatisfied with their legal services, however, are the middle class who must pay their own lawyers' fees and are represented by general practitioners in small firms. The most common complaint is that lawyers do not do anything. This is a well-founded complaint since it appears to take an interminable time to settle an estate, resolve a boundary-line dispute, or recover damages for breach of a contract. While the reasons for the delay are diverse, they fall into three broad categories.

The first and by far the simplest reason for delay is that some lawyers are lazy. This hardly distinguishes lawyers from the majority of their fellows, but laziness becomes particularly vicious in small-firm law practice. Each lawyer is an individual craftsman, and most of the work he or she does must be custom produced. So far it has not been possible to organize law practice to achieve significant economies of scale. McDonald's and the other fast-food chains revolutionized the restaurant business by providing a cheap, nutritious meal of McFood through a combination of centralized processing, division of labor, volume purchasing, standardized product, and specialized management. Most people are able to eat the same thing; in the law business, however, every client's problem is unique in at least some small way. It is not possible to mass produce McLaw under a big arch at a roadside stand.

Lawyer laziness is a relative concept. Some lawyers are true layabouts who should not be practicing law but who have offices into which the uninformed frequently wander. Standards for admission to law school and bar examinations will not weed out these lawyers since willingness to work in the day-to-day struggle and academic competence are different qualities. Examinations test only academic competence. Laziness is a failure of character, not intellect. At the other extreme, however, are diligent lawyers who have so much business that in order to get it all done they would need to work fourteen hours a day seven days a week. These lawyers are not lazy in the layabout sense, but they look lazy because they undertake to handle more work than any reasonable person can do expeditiously.

The escape from this latter dilemma would appear to be to hire one or more new lawyers, but often that solution is not available. Hiring more lawyers means hiring more support staff, expanding office facilities, paying more expenses, and sometimes losing clients if the new lawyers should decide to go out on their own. Also, fees for the middle class are often reasonable exactly because a general-practice lawyer has more business than he or she can handle. What occurs is that such a lawyer quickly processes those matters that pay big money, like personal injury suits, while leaving matters that do not pay on the back burner until he or she can get around to them. In effect, then, the lawyer is subsidizing one type of client service with fees earned from other client services, but part of the price is exacted in delay—a willingness on the part of subsidized clients to allow the lawyer to handle their matters during lulls in other business when the opportunity costs are low.

The second major category of causes for delay involves factors external to the lawyer's office. In handling any but the most routine matter, like the writing of a will, people aside from the lawyer and the client are involved. In order to settle a decedent's estate, for example, it is necessary to have an audit by the state tax commissioner and a "release" of assets. If the estate is large, it is also necessary to have an audit by the Internal Revenue Service. Both state and federal agencies are overworked and understaffed, so it often takes time to get them to do their part. Particularly if there are problems, the negotiation process with government authorities can take years because the government has no incentive to settle—the IRS agents are not going to get a piece of the estate personally either way, so they hardly care how long it takes.

Rules of law are not as clearcut as usually imagined. When a client comes to a lawyer with a property dispute, it is frequently not in the client's interest to go to court immediately because the client may lose. Often what is called for is a letter to the opposing lawyer asking whether the problem can be worked out. If the opposing lawyer is conservative, such an approach may work better than going to court.

When I was practicing law, if my client had any case at all I immediately filed a complaint in court in order to convince the other side that I was dangerous. After that, however, the pace of the case was determined by a number of things beyond my control, one of which was my own caseload. In the winter term of court I was in the Legislature and in the succeeding spring term I had to try my important cases first, otherwise I could not afford to handle minor cases at a reasonable price. Other lawyers were in the same position, and even if I were able to try a particular case, often the other side was not able to try it at that time. Occasions when it was inconvenient for the other side to go to court frequently presented ideal opportunities to talk settlement, and sometimes cases were settled at that point, but whether they were was largely luck.

Judges have heart attacks, witnesses get sick or go on vacation, opposing lawyers get sick or die, or a particular court's docket gets unusually clogged because of an extraordinary occurrence like a natural disaster or a new highway going through town. All of these things exacerbate whatever delay is built into the lawyer's office itself.

The last general category of delay consists of nothing more than "the impossible case." Clients are constantly bringing cases to their lawyers that are unwinnable. Often these cases would lead to a substantial damage award if successful, so clients want their lawyers to take them on a contingency basis. Where the lawyer wants to keep the client's goodwill, as for example where the client is a member of a union the lawyer represents or has sent the lawyer other business in the past, the lawyer may take the case in the hope that he can get the client something, if only a settlement based on the case's nuisance value. What the lawyer usually has in mind is writing a few letters to the other side threatening suit. What the lawyer does not contemplate, however, is the investment of ten thousand dollars in trial expenses, including the opportunity cost of the lawyer's time, in trying a case that is destined to be a loser. Lawyers, however, are often unspecific about how bad the client's case is, and when no settlement offer is forthcoming and it becomes ime to try the case, the client is outraged that the lawyer is not pursuing it at a full gallop.

Large law firms are dedicated almost exclusively to representing business. These firms range in size from thirty lawyers in a city like Charleston, West Virginia, to 350 lawyers in cities like New York and Chicago. Except for those who are wedded to small-town practice because of its human rewards, most graduates of the country's top law schools eventually end up in one of these large firms. They may come by way of a judicial clerkship, service as a young government lawyer, or even service with the Legal Services Corporation. Yet good lawyers finally come to big firms because big firms pay big bucks, have good supporting staff and perquisites, and offer uninterrupted, long-term career advancement. I would estimate that 50 percent of these lawyers, some of whom are making as much as $200,000 a year, have never seen the inside of a courtroom as litigating lawyers. In fact, litigation is so physically demanding, because of the travel and night and weekend work to meet trial deadlines, that many qualified lawyers opt for specialties outside litigation. Elegant and refined corporate lawyers often

218

look down on litigators the way artillery officers look down on the infantry.

The structure of law practice for business users is entirely different from the structure of law practice for either the middle class or the poor. The difference in structure obviously is related to ability to pay. Business lawyers don't spend even 10 percent of their time in confrontation with others outside the business community. While businesses may deduct $24 billion a year from their tax returns for legal fees,[3] most of this money is spent for services that concern only the business community. For example, whenever a corporation issues new stock, elaborate reporting procedures must be undertaken to satisfy the rules of the Securities and Exchange Commission. Large law firms in New York City have whole departments with scores of young lawyers making between $40,000 and $65,000 a year who do nothing but securities work. This work ultimately inures to the benefit of the middle class because it guarantees that securities have been lawfully issued with full disclosure. In effect, these lawyers keep big companies more honest than they might otherwise be.

Much business law is directed to tax planning and the structuring of business deals to minimize tax liability. There is nothing illegal or immoral about avoiding taxes, and many of the best minds emerging from law schools in the last thirty years have devoted themselves entirely to this specialty. Since the bulk of business law is preventive in nature, expenditures are not competitive. There is no advantage in doing the world's most elegant securities registration statement when all that is required is a competent job. Tax advice is tax advice; either it is right or it is wrong. But once the correct answer has been discovered, it makes no sense to do any more work. Large law firms are set up to provide an orderly process for doing the routine legal work that business demands. This involves a hierarchy of talent, beginning with young

---

3. This estimate appears in an article by the eminent Professor A. E. Dick Howard of the University of Virginia Law School in the summer 1981 *Wilson Quarterly*. My own research, including conversations with the statistics office of the Internal Revenue Service, does not disclose the basis of such a figure and unfortunately Howard cannot find his original research notes and doesn't remember where he got the figure. It sounds reasonable to me, but I can't verify it from another source and neither can the American Bar Association.

219

lawyers right out of law school who can do raw research under the direction of more experienced lawyers and ending up with senior partners in their fifties or sixties who have both technical expertise and political judgment.

Business clients are always billed at a straight hourly rate, and each lawyer in a firm keeps an accurate time sheet, usually broken down into tenths of an hour, memorializing the time each day he or she spends on each client's business. The promotion of young men and women in the firm is usually related to the number of "billable hours" they generate in the course of a year.

Selecting a big law firm is like selecting a Holiday Inn. Often its lawyers are not as skilled as lawyers practicing in smaller firms, but on the other hand, it seldom does a truly incompetent job. In the same way that a traveler to a strange city chooses the Holiday Inn because its quality is standardized, a business client coming to a strange city chooses a large, established law firm.

Typically, a senior partner of a large firm will bill his clients upwards of $250 an hour; intermediate-level partners will bill about 70 percent of that; and junior lawyers will bill about 40 percent of what a senior partner bills. Consequently, an eight-hour workday, divided equally among a senior, intermediate, and junior lawyer, will cost around $1,100.

The hourly billing system, combined with clients who are indifferent to the amount of legal fees, make the income of big firms reliable. If work cannot be done quickly and competently, more people are hired and the hierarchy is readjusted. Like a Holiday Inn as compared to a small, family-run hotel, there are built-in inefficiencies. The advantage of a big firm, however, is that the client need not rely on the talents of one person. There is an organized, collective intelligence that has perpetual life and few human failings.

If we ask then why business gets such superior legal services to those offered either the poor or the middle class, the answer unsurprisingly is that business can afford to pay. If business comes to a big firm with a losing case, the firm processes that case with diligence, enthusiasm, and expedition because the meter is running just as it would on the best case in the world. There are few contingent fees, no efforts to minimize charges, no need to choose between demands of competing clients based on urgency, and, finally, no need to postpone because of the human limits of the lawyer or the demands of his family (the firm just hires more lawyers).

BIG-FIRM practice stands in stark contrast to small-firm practice—the type of practice that serves the poor and the middle class. Yet lawyers for the poor and lawyers for the middle class cannot be lumped together because they don't have the same problems. The lawyers for the poor are salaried employees of the Legal Services Corporation—they need not worry about their clients' ability to pay, but they must constantly worry about rationing their scarce time and support resources. Legal-aid lawyers cannot possibly fulfill all the client demands that come through the door. The lawyer for the middle class, on the other hand, is a small businessperson who must constantly weigh his or her clients' needs for services against their ability to pay.

This is probably as good a place as any to state a personal opinion. In my experience, the real hero of the American legal process is the small-firm, general-practice lawyer who is not usually a lightning fast calculator of his or her own best economic interests. While there are lazy, greedy, and incompetent lawyers holding themselves out as general practitioners, such lawyers are definitely a minority and prosper only in proportion to public ignorance of their reputations. The lawyers who have most of the business are overwhelmingly generous and may actually represent as many as half their clients on a subsidized basis. In addition, good lawyers advise local charities, serve on school boards, and assist community groups. Some of this helps to build a practice, but self-interest alone does not explain the hours devoted to these activities by lawyers who already have more business than they can handle.

As I have indicated earlier, practicing law is strenuous, and the people who keep at it instead of opting for comfortable salaried positions or narrow specialties are people who are excited about helping people. They take pleasure in the application of their craft to the relief of suffering. While it would be unrealistic to pretend that lawyers think first and foremost of public service rather than their own livelihoods, abject cynicism is not called for either. In my own experience, lawyers do a lot more free work than plumbers, electricians, college professors, or unionized

auto workers. What is more important, however, is that the general practitioner organizes his practice so that well-heeled clients subsidize others.

In general-practice law, big money is earned when big money changes
hands. Legal fees for individuals (as opposed to businesses) are un-
budgeted expenses that are highly resented. The average middle-class
person does not expect either to be sued or to need to sue someone
else, so when either event occurs, a middle-class person must go into
debt. In one recent contract between a criminal lawyer and a defendant
charged with election fraud, the lawyer received $25,000 up front, plus
$2,000 a day for every day in court. That means at least $50,000 win
or lose. That's as much as a cheap house! Surprisingly, the lawyer was
not overcharging the client—the lawyer is a senior member of an eight-
een-person firm backed by an expensive library with computer-assisted
legal research, and the senior lawyer is supported by numerous well-
trained young lawyers. Yet the defendant makes only $25,000 a year.
If she is acquitted, two years' salary will have been spent to prove
something she shouldn't have had to prove in the first place.

When big money changes hands, however, clients gleefully pay
their lawyers. If Great-Uncle Joe dies leaving us $100,000 we did not
expect, paying $10,000 for estate administration hardly hurts at all. If
our automobile accident case is settled for $150,000—roughly three
times what we expected—it also doesn't hurt to give our lawyer a third.
And, even if we borrow $150,000 that must ultimately be paid back to
finance a house, it doesn't hurt to borrow another $3,000 to pay the
lawyers for the closing costs and title search—the difference in payments
over twenty-five years is a few bucks a month.

Until very recently bar associations prohibited lawyers from advertising, soliciting clients, or actively competing with one another. Part
of the reason was that an ability to use the advertising media was not
necessarily an indication of an ability to practice law—recommendations
from satisfied clients provide the most reliable information. Furthermore, the leaders of the bar understood that it is unwise to encourage
lawyers to specialize in those cases that bring in big money.

A lawyer who does nothing but house closings, accident cases, and
estate administration can charge lower fees for these services; however,
because he is a specialist, he is not available to do the legal chores that
do not generate money. When I was practicing law I never charged a

client for giving advice—I sent many a woman who wanted a divorce to social service agencies because she could not care for her children if she lost the support of her husband. Sometimes mental health and church counseling worked, and sometimes it didn't, but I gave my clients the best advice I could regardless of whether that encouraged them to use and pay for more of my services. I was able to give this kind of honest advice, and not starve, because I was subsidized by rich corporate clients, labor unions, fat estates, and accident victims.

My nostalgic perception of these matters is influenced by the fact that I came from a small town where many lawyers were the sons and grandsons of lawyers. Inherited professional positions were taken very seriously. In my world the old system worked very well, but in other places under modern urban and suburban stresses the system did not work well at all. Often lawyers creamed the practice by, for example, establishing themselves with lending institutions that required all borrowers to use those lawyers' services. Costs were disproportionate to services, and there was no ancillary social benefit to offset such overcharges. Now lawyers are permitted to place dignified advertisements in newspapers and on television, and the result is that there is more competition for routine legal services like house closings, divorces, bankruptcies, and criminal defense. The old system assumed that lawyers would be imbued with the "professional" nature of their calling; unfortunately, all too often reality did not comport with the ideal.

Now legal clinics are springing up designed to operate on a pay-as-you-go basis, where each service is priced at its actual cost. A legal "consultation" costs about $15 for forty minutes; uncontested divorces are processed for $250 and court fees; and house closings are done more cheaply than before. While the legal clinic is usually staffed by young and inexperienced lawyers, it is far less forbidding and mysterious than the old general practitioner's office. In hospitality, the legal clinic is to law practice what the small loan company is to banking. A legal clinic's fees are in the newspapers, and its offices are usually storefronts. For example, the Hyatt legal clinics located in the Washington, D.C., area often share office space with H & R Block, the company that specializes in preparing tax returns. Legal clinics are also subsidized by the big accident cases that walk through the door, but they advertise slightly lower contingency fees. The Hyatt legal clinic charges a 30 percent contingency fee for a personal injury case, which is only 3¹/₃ percent less than the finest plaintiffs' firms in the world.[4]

Insurance systems have been designed to protect us from most un-budgeted expenses,[5] but such schemes have never worked very well in

4. The brochure prepared by Hyatt legal clinics to advertise their prices presents a large picture of Joel Hyatt, the founder, along with the following statement: "At Hyatt Legal Services, Reasonable fees are the Law." On the reverse side is a list of offices and the following statement of charges:

Hyatt Legal Services charges $15 for an initial consultation, which is an opportunity for you to sit down with one of our attorneys to discuss your problem. Listed below is a sample schedule of our standard af-fordable fees for handling legal problems. Call our office or consult your Hyatt attorney for fees or services not listed.

WASHINGTON, D.C. • VIRGINIA • MARYLAND
SAMPLE OF FEES

Divorce, by Agreement	$250
Divorce, Uncontested	$350
Divorce, Contested	$650
Simple Will	$ 45
Wills for a husband and a wife	$ 65
Bankruptcy (Chapter 7)	$350
Joint Bankruptcy (Chapter 7)	$450
Debt Repayment Plan (Chapter 13)	$550
Joint Debt Repayment Plan (Chapter 13)	$650
Personal Injury	30%
Misdemeanor or DWI	$450 to $950

The above fees do not include court costs. Fees may be paid by cash or check. Hyatt Legal Services will provide more detailed fee information on request.

Fees are effective from June 1, 1982. Fees may vary in other areas where Hyatt Legal Services maintains offices.

5. It is easy to insure against the cost of rebuilding a burned-down house or repairing a wrecked automobile. Almost everyone who either works regularly or is a dependent of someone who works regularly is covered by a medical insurance plan.

law. Numerous experiments have been conducted with group legal plans, but until recently they were largely unsuccessful. The Tax Reform Act of 1976 made prepaid legal services benefits available to employee groups on a tax-free basis, however, and by mid-1983 six million Americans will be covered by prepaid plans. Part of the early lack of success of insurance-type legal service arrangements came from opposition from the practicing bar, but since the Supreme Court increasingly looks with disfavor on bar rules that restrain competition, bar opposition to union or other prepaid legal plans is no longer a serious obstacle. The bar has traditionally opposed prepaid plans because they invariably imply the use of particular lawyers who are part of the plan, thus taking business away from all the lawyers in the community who are not part of the plan.

Reformers have been suggesting either prepaid legal services plans or some other type of legal insurance for years. Most people do not perceive legal insurance as an urgent need because they do not expect to use lawyers. In a way we are all insured against the most common instances when we might be sued by purchasing automobile liability insurance and homeowners insurance. Our insurance companies not only pay any judgment but also pay all the lawyers' fees. Unsophisticated people usually have no understanding of the ways in which legal advice or brief legal services, such as writing a letter to a store or a neighbor, can be useful, but everyone knows that her house may burn down or that he might get sick or injured.

A more difficult problem for legal insurance is that while many people have little appreciation of what lawyers can do for them, other people are enormously litigious. Life is full of disagreements among individuals, and almost all of these disagreements are capable of being turned into lawsuits. The difference between fire or medical insurance on one side and legal insurance on the other is the way in which "loss" is triggered. People do not want their houses to burn down so that they can collect the fire insurance, and, similarly, people do not want unnecessary medical treatment in a hospital.

While occasionally there is someone who needs ready cash and decides to burn his house down instead of selling it, and there are also those hypochondriacs who overuse medical services, both phenomena stay naturally within manageable limits. Such is not the case, however, with regard to legal services. In order for an insurance program to be actuarially sound, there must be some outside risk that triggers an insured "loss." In fire insurance, it is accidental burning and in medical insurance it is sickness. With legal insurance, however, the insured can legitimately trigger his own loss. He can either decide to sue someone, or he can allow himself to be sued under circumstances where it would be less expensive to settle out of court if legal fees had to be taken into account.

Because of this problem, prepaid legal services plans are forced to take steps to protect themselves. Most refuse to take cases that would be taken in the normal run of events by a lawyer on a contingent fee basis. Some flatly refuse to take personal-injury suits for plaintiffs. In many cases time limitations on the service or money deductibles are used to remove the incentive to "over use" the legal insurance.

Some overuse of legal services is contemplated by these plans. After all, most of the plans are designed to benefit employees and union members. Thus, where a union member can spend $1,000 worth of legal time on a $400 dispute, the plan's purpose is not defeated: it may not be efficient, but it's good for membership. Furthermore, it is in fact very likely to be efficient. The very real threat that a covered employee will be able to spend $1,000 in legal time in order to wrest his $400 back from a bloodsucker defendant makes the defendant highly amenable to reason. Thus, the illusion of inefficiency may confer the intended benefit upon the members of the plan at a real discount.

In the ordinary suburban, middle-class neighborhood there are numerous day-to-day conflicts that can lead to lawsuits. Children are a nuisance. They ride noisy "big wheels"; they play loudly on weekend mornings; they run through flower beds; they hide under porches to shoot cowboys and Indians; and they scratch parked cars with their toys and knock out windows with their balls. Older children burglarize neighbors' dwellings, drive recklessly, and can be intentionally abusive. Older people yell at children and threaten them; often they buy large and dangerous dogs; and where the neighborhood has common areas that are under joint neighborhood association control, they try to pass restrictive regulations limiting use of these areas by children. The ordinary, peaceful neighborhood is actually a seething caldron of potential lawsuits.

Parents of young children can be sued if their children's behavior constitutes a legal "nuisance." Intolerant older people can be sued for "assault," i.e., placing the children in fear of bodily injury. The children themselves can be sued for trespass, damage, and, in a few states, for insulting words. Usually these types of lawsuits never materialize because the transactional costs are prohibitive—most of the time neighbors sort the problems out themselves with only occasional intervention by the police who help compromise disputes. But if there were no transactional costs, the litigious among us would go to a lawyer every time they got angry and would torture the nonlitigious and probably uninsured among us to death.

In the normal, private lawyer-client relationship, the client tells the lawyer what he wants done, and the lawyer tells the client how much he will charge to do it. If the client is willing to pay, the lawyer will do anything that is not either illegal or unethical. Under an insurance system, however, such a lawyer-client relationship will confound actuarial calculations because of a "tragedy of the common" problem—litigious people will claim excessive "losses" and overuse the facilities for which everyone pays. The solution is to have rules that ration available services by removing the decision about whether a "loss" has occurred from the subjective judgment of the individual client. Of course, this is hardly a perfect solution, but it makes insurance against legal fees for the types of major problems people encounter—workmen's compensation, social security, failure of an insurance company to pay for insured loss, domestic relations, and criminal prosecutions—a more workable economic proposition.

Since the perceived need for legal insurance on top of the regular insurance of our automobiles and our homes is largely dependent on the individual's willingness either to seek legal advice or go to court, employers and labor organizations cannot achieve a consensus among employees or union members about the value of prepaid legal services as a fringe benefit. Most workers would probably rather have cash money than an endless supply of legal work. When, however, a need for a lawyer does arise, the cost of that lawyer is then an unbudgeted expense, and most people will exhaust the alternatives before hiring one. These alternatives include soliciting advice from young friends who are in law school, making efforts to solve the problem alone, and appealing to public officials.

Elected public officials, particularly state legislators, congresspeople, and senators, are constantly beseeched to intercede for people in their dealings with the government. Back in the days when few public employees were under civil service and when the state and federal governments were comparatively small, elected officials could often "fix" minor problems. Now an elected official is almost powerless to expedite an award under workmen's compensation, enhance the government's offering price for land threatened by eminent domain, or force a reevaluation of an adverse decision by the Social Security Administration. The changes in the last twenty years in America's political machinery have drastically diluted the ability of elected officials to, in the political parlance of West Virginia, "he'p" individual constituents who are put upon by government. Lawyers, however, can often "fix" these things through the hearing mechanisms established either in the administrative agency itself or in the courts.

Occasionally, of course, an elected official can get results that lawyers cannot get. A lawyer cannot get a new road built, a better schedule for snow removal in a neighborhood, or discretionary money put into a particular local hospital. Unfortunately, the average person doesn't know the difference between legal problems like workmen's compensation or social security, which must be processed in a craftsmanlike way through certain formal machinery, and political problems, which can be solved by political muscle.

The confusion of the two problems is exacerbated by the reluctance of elected officials to admit that they are powerless. There is an old adage in politics that if you take care of your mail, your mail will take care of you. The major source of an elected official's quality contacts with his or her constituents is through responding to written (and now telephoned) requests; any elected official wants to do as many favors for constituents as possible. Favors are the sure road to reelection since politics is mostly personal and not ideological. What an elected official is most likely to do when he or she receives a request for what amounts to a free substitute for legal services is to write a nice letter to the agency involved, with a copy to the constituent, requesting a positive result. The agencies, of course, get hundreds of such letters each day, and they have a battery of secretaries who write equally nice but utterly meaningless replies, saying in effect that the constituent will be given "every consideration." The danger is that an unwary constituent may allow himself to be horsed around for years by this type of patter. By the time he figures out the nature of this drill, enough time may have passed that the benighted constituent will no longer be able to use the agency's formal legal machinery to get the favorable results to which he may well have been entitled.

IF, indeed, the middle class, who have some options in these matters, are reluctant to pay lawyers and have difficulty doing so, what happens to the poor? Today we have a primitive legal-aid structure, providing free legal services only to individuals who meet arbitrary eligibility standards of "poverty." Unfortunately, when we are talking about a major unbudgeted legal expense, almost everyone except the rich is too poor to pay without great sacrifice.

Furthermore, all the problems that have been discussed with regard to legal insurance schemes are present in any program to provide legal services to the poor. It is, however, hard to emphasize strongly enough just how desperately the poor need access to lawyers. At least the middle class have some skills (such as the ability to understand the income-tax forms) that permit them to organize their lives competently without lawyers. The poor, however, are least able to take care of themselves, and they have the lowest level of access to free legal advice, except possibly amateur advice on criminal matters.[6]

6. Amateur advice should not be discounted entirely. Often laypeople know about the law. For example, teachers usually have expertise in school law matters, and businesspeople often know more about tax law than lawyers who do not specialize in that field. Every penitentiary has inmates who never graduated from high school who know more criminal law than recent law-school graduates. I have come to have a high regard for jailhouse lawyers, and when I was practicing law I was always interested in what my clients thought the law was. Often the client was involved in an undertaking that was covered by a certain body of law with which I was unfamiliar, and so the client's conclusions about what law applied gave me a good starting point for my own research. People of average means generally have experience working with different legal structures—some know about social security, workmen's compensation, or taxes—and the broad availability of such knowledge from friends and co-workers helps these people understand the dimensions of their problems and

It is not exactly a modern idea that legal services should be available to people who cannot afford to hire lawyers. In 1495 King Henry VII signed into law a provision that "the justices . . . shall assign to the same poor person or persons counsel learned, by their discretions, which shall give their counsel, nothing taking for the same . . . likewise the justices shall appoint attorney and attorneys for the same poor person or persons." [7]

Time passed and Henry Tudor's prescription languished. As the common law developed in England, anyone charged with a felony was denied the right to retain counsel, although that right was accorded in misdemeanor cases. Similarly, the U. S. Constitution's Sixth Amendment guarantee that "[i]n all criminal prosecutions the accused shall enjoy the right . . . to have the assistance of counsel for his defense" was historically read to mean that a person wishing counsel *and* able to afford counsel would not be denied that right. When the Supreme Court finally decided to do something about the poor's lack of access to lawyers in criminal cases, they gave a brand new meaning to the Constitution's right-to-counsel language.

Organized legal aid for the poor did not begin in America until 1876, when the German Society of New York established a program of legal assistance for recently arrived immigrants. The legal-aid industry grew slowly—it was not until 1940 that the number of cities with paid legal-aid staffs passed fifty—and the legal community's support for legal aid's growth reflected little credit on the profession.

A first blow was struck for the cause of legal aid by the Supreme Court in 1932 in the case of *Powell v. Alabama* when it threw out the convictions of eight black youths sentenced to death without proper assistance of counsel for the rape of a white woman. Thirty years later, in the landmark case of *Gideon v. Wainwright*, the Supreme Court raised on the shoulders of *Powell* and its successor cases the rule that

know when it is worth going into debt to hire a lawyer. Kenny Rogers said it all: "You've got to know when to hold them/know when to fold them/you've got to know when to walk away, know when to run." The middle-class person working in an office usually has access to executives or the company's lawyer for a quick consultation. Unionized workers have access to union lawyers. But the poor have no access at all to reliable advice other than from legal services.

7. 2 Hen.7, C.12 (1495).

in felony cases a criminal defendant must be provided a lawyer if he cannot afford one himself. This decision encouraged the creation of nationwide legal-aid societies.

By 1964 there were approximately 150 legal aid societies operating, but their staffs totaled only about 600 lawyers, and their total expenditures amounted to only $4 million. At this point President Lyndon Johnson's Office of Economic Opportunity added the provision of legal services to the poor to its War on Poverty agenda, and the Legal Services Program, later to become the Legal Services Corporation, was born. Within a decade of the program's inception, the federal government was spending over $60 million annually on legal assistance to the poor in both criminal and civil matters and had more than 2,500 lawyers working for it full time. By 1981 the responsibility for defending criminal defendants in state courts had been transferred to the states, and the Legal Services Corporation directed almost all of its attention to civil matters. In 1981 the Legal Services budget was $321 million, with 6,000 full time lawyers.

Although the legal community was less than helpful in the early years of the legal-aid movement, a majority of practicing lawyers now champion the cause of publicly funded legal services. The American Bar Association is one of the strongest advocates of the Legal Services Corporation. Yet today the Legal Services Corporation is under strong attack from the Reagan administration, which plans to cut its budget drastically. Even at its 1981 budget, however, if only 3 percent of the estimated twenty-four billion dollars' worth of corporate legal work performed each year were devoted to sticking it to the poor (and this does not include lobbying expenses and campaign contributions), corporate lawyers outgunned the Legal Services lawyers by better than two to one.

Before the formation of the Legal Services Corporation no appeal had been brought to the United States Supreme Court by a legal-aid lawyer. In the first six years of the corporation its grantees brought more than 200 appeals and won 89 of them. The successes of the Legal Services lawyers were not, however, entirely of their own making. The lawyers greatly benefited from the explosion of litigation that has taken place in America in the last twenty years. Courts were more willing than ever before to remedy claims with what detractors call "judicial legislation," and the courts embraced a number of devices, including broad readings of constitutional provisions and the "class action" suit (where small claims can be aggregated into one suit) in order to open their doors to "impact" or "test" cases. It was this willingness on the part of courts to involve themselves in the political process that set the Legal Services lawyer apart from the traditional legal-aid lawyer, guaranteed his or her success, and fomented the current condemnation that followed that success.

Legal Services lawyers won, and won big. Since legal proceedings are the zero-sum game I have previously described, others lost, and lost big. Landlords, retail businesses, state agencies, and local police departments, all accustomed to dealing peremptorily with the poor, found themselves hauled into court by competent lawyers representing traditional victims. The annoyances to the traditionally powerful were several: it was inconvenient and expensive to go to court; the "establishment" tended to lose; and when the establishment lost, case by case, strand by strand, the fabric of the law was rewoven to its detriment. Tenants' rights, debtors' rights, and extensive due-process and equal-protection rights for the poor emerged. Particularly irritating was the fact that the plaintiff poor were getting all this for free.

And there, as Hamlet said, is the rub. The representation for the poor was free to them, so they had little market incentive to avoid litigation. The court process for the impecunious plaintiff or defendant became a nearly unrestricted benefit. Defendants took an understandably dim view of a system where they had to pay for their own lawyers but their opponents did not, and they seized on their economic disadvantage (in court) as a major grievance. In fact, the complaint was largely unjustified in the great majority of cases. Although there was no incentive for the poor to settle based on legal fees alone, the natural laziness of mankind worked on the legal-aid plaintiff or defendant as an overwhelming case load worked on his or her attorney to militate against unreasonably prolonged litigation.

Occasionally a Legal Services attorney would spend $5,000 worth of time on a $400 claim and steamroll the defendant's attorney who had been told by his client that he wanted only a few dollars' worth of law. Although such occurrences may have been rare, defendants were understandably sensitive. A former chairman of the board of the Legal Services Corporation, William McAlpin, observed to a member of my staff that "the bitching didn't start when someone got steamrolled by Legal Services; the bitching started when someone got *sued* by Legal Services." The inchoate anger and resentment of these defendants coalesced around this issue and were given teeth in the Reagan administration's budget mayhem of 1982.

As is often the case when a controversy becomes emotional, a specter was called forth that, although not truly representative, cast a longer and darker image than any amount of statistical evidence could hope to clear. The specter in this case was that of the *Harvard-Law-Review*, Lexis-backed, [8] young socialist firebrand trampling local attorneys into the ground with unlimited federal money. The protestations of Legal Services attorneys that this characterization is neither accurate nor fair are correct, just as Galileo was correct in his description of our solar system. Yet, like Galileo, the legal-aid community is going to have to make an accommodation to the prevailing power structure in order to survive.

Legal Services can make a convincing case that the socialist-firebrand-attorney specter is insignificant on a statistical basis; nonetheless, that specter is the focus of attention. And the specter has materialized in more than the occasional display of extremely bad judgment in resource allocation. In fairness to the conservative enemies of legal aid, it was only the very heavy case load that prevented rare occurrences from becoming regular occurrences.

Legal Services' policy was deliberately to steamroll certain defendants. The weight of the case load demanded that where possible legal services attorneys find and try "impact" cases—cases that were undertaken not merely to win but to make new law. In a prominent recent article, two Legal Services directors write that "care would have been taken, both within states and nationally, to select cases which were appropriate for major resource commitments in order to establish precedents." [9] To a defendant in such a case the difference between a "major resource commitment" and a steamrolling would be painfully academic.

8. Lexis is a national computer service with a data base of legal material. A lawyer-user rents a terminal that is then connected through telephone lines to a central computer capable of doing both quick and competent legal research. Such an arrangement costs about $2,000 a month, depending on usage.

9. J. Dooley and A. Houseman, "Legal Services in the 80's and Challenges Facing the Poor," *Clearinghouse Review*, vol. 15, no. 9 (January 1982).

Also, regardless of official policy, there is a mentality shared by Legal Services lawyers that others in the system often find offensive. According to statistics prepared by the Legal Services Corporation in February 1982, an average staff attorney working for one of the corporation's grantees earned $17,777 a year, while a managing attorney earned $24,124 and a program director earned $32,258. Lawyers, therefore, are not usually in the program for the money—they perceive themselves as heroes, and often they are. However, the hero mentality occasionally makes them uncompromising, even in circumstances where the highest paid and most skillful private lawyer would recommend compromise.

In the summer of 1981 I attended a seminar at Columbia Law School and was in a class on bankruptcy with a Legal Services attorney from rural Pennsylvania. After class we both joined a group of students discussing the day's material with the professor, and my Legal Services friend asked how to handle a real case where his client had declared bankruptcy but had a secured creditor holding a lien for $5,000 on property worth slightly more than that. Everyone in the group exercised his or her imagination to find a way the client could beat the debt—it was the lawyer equivalent of solving the *Times* crossword puzzle—and the schemes we suggested would inevitably have involved the investment of over $5,000 in lawyer resources.

Yet the young lawyer intended to do whatever it took to beat the creditor, in spite of the fact that the creditor had done nothing improper and probably would have been happy to compromise for something less than his full pound of flesh in return for prompt payment. This was not an "impact" case; the lawyer *cum* hero just thought he owed it to his client to use every legal trick to win, and under our current system where the rich are able to hire lawyers to fight for them regardless of the cost:benefit equation, he was probably right. But the point is that a rich person would not spend more in lawyers' fees than a case was worth because he would be paying his own lawyers' fees.

From the point of view of representing the poor as a class, however, Legal Services has been highly successful. Most law now used as precedent in poverty law cases did not exist in the 1960s when Legal Services came into being. Legal Services used impact cases exactly because it did not have the funds to steamroll its opponents; in fact, it did not even have enough money to represent all its prospective clients. Legal-aid lawyers estimate that they are able to serve less than 25 percent of the needy people they have been delegated to represent. From a point of view of efficiency, Legal Services lawyers were *forced* to try impact cases—but they also enjoyed it.

A number of decisions by the Legal Services Corporation have been responsible for the breadth of the backlash against it. The corporation's decision to concentrate on services to the poor *as a class* led to the politicization of the organization. (Local Legal Services governing boards, for example, were required to include "representatives of the poor.") Advocating positions for the poor *as a class* was not necessarily a bad thing, but Legal Services was ill-suited to sustain the political heat its activity generated, as the current budget battle rout serves to demonstrate.

The poor desperately need legal help with domestic relations, bankruptcies, consumer debt, landlord-and-tenant and tax problems. A statistical breakdown of what legal services actually does demonstrates that 31.7 percent of all legal-aid work is devoted simply to giving advice. Another 14.4 percent of the work involves elementary services like writing letters, making telephone calls, or otherwise arranging some satisfactory, informal settlement of a client's problems. Only 10.9 percent of closed cases in 1981 involved decisions in court, and only 5.8 percent involved administrative agency decisions. Another 6.6 percent of cases involved a formal, negotiated settlement without litigation, and 4.1 percent involved a settlement with litigation. In 7.7 percent of the cases the clients were referred to private lawyers, which is an interesting statistic because it indicates that often clients have cases that private lawyers will accept on a contingency fee basis, but the clients don't know that or don't know how to find a lawyer who will make such an arrangement.

Even the majority of conservative opponents of Legal Services as it is currently constituted do not begrudge the poor access to lawyers for routine matters. Unfortunately, the conservative opponents find it difficult to articulate, even to themselves, exactly what it is that they oppose in legal services. However, we can list the real causes of animosity here in descending order of aggravation: (1) the hero mentality that gives to young, energetic lawyers a sense of moral superiority that makes them accusers rather than simple litigators; (2) the politicization of Legal Services into a crusading interest group that evaluates cases on the basis of their impact potential rather than their value to the individual client and frequently even solicits cases from clients who would otherwise not have sued;[10] and (3) the failure to administer the cases of the poor on some basis that takes transactional costs into account—$5,000 in legal resources may be spent to defend a case that could be settled for $500.[11]

As I am writing this, no one can predict how long a conservative administration with a conservative Senate will stay in power. If the worldwide depression of 1982-83 abates, it is conceivable that an administration hostile to Legal Services will survive until 1990. The political climate may never return to one that will permit Legal Services to flourish in its current configuration. In politics you can only choose to be a dead virgin rather than a prospering whore when you have nothing left to accomplish. The case of the unrepresented poor is too important to be martyred. Legal Services can afford the luxury of being right only so long as it does not become dead right.

Part of the problem of Legal Services, and to a lesser extent prepaid legal plans, is that they wish to model themselves on the lawyer-client relationships of the private general practitioner. Somehow it is thought to be unfair to the client for him not to be able to determine how much law he wants. Since the person paying his own lawyer can demand that the lawyer pursue a weak case, Legal Services and some prepaid plans consider it wealth discrimination not to permit a poor person or plan member to do the same. What is not understood is that the rationing mechanism in the private law office—lawyer fees—is not at work in

10. Everywhere else in the system lawyers make law only when they have to; a lawyer will generally not go all the way to the Supreme Court to make law for others if his own client can otherwise get a satisfactory result.

11. There is one mechanical problem with this objection. Legal Services has money in its budget to pay for legal services but not to pay off adversaries. Often the client does not have the $500 it would take to settle a case, which is why he or she came to Legal Services to begin with. This mechanical problem, of course, operates only when a poor client is a defendant and a judgment is brought against him. A plaintiff seeking a judgment is not so constrained.

either Legal Services or prepaid plans, so all rationing must be accomplished either by product deterioration, standing in line, or both.

Legal Services can restructure itself both to eschew pursuit of the impact case for its own sake and to make independent evaluations of the value of a client's case so that a Legal Services client must satisfy the same cost:benefit analysis concerning settlement offers as a private client. Immediately the objection is raised that it is the judge's, not the lawyer's, job to evaluate the client's case; however, that simple conclusion fails to take into consideration the discussion in Chapter 6 of the value of litigation per se. Even for the superrich, it is not judges in the system who determine the value of litigation per se but rather the lawyers and clients.

In the legal-services context, lawyers must tell clients with meritless cases that they will expend time and effort to arrange satisfactory settlements but that they will not invest valuable resources in litigation per se. This solution is no more draconian than my recommendations concerning litigation among private, well-financed parties. Chapter 6 recommended that where litigants abuse the system by using litigation per se as a weapon they be penalized by being forced to pay the other side's lawyers' fees. Yet in the legal-aid context there is no client money to pay such a sanction; only the public treasury can pay, and that is not sound policy. The only alternative is for Legal Services to police itself.

Most of the so-called impact cases that reach the Supreme Court and the highest state courts do so naturally. Thus legal aid will receive its fair share of cases where opponents refuse reasonable settlements, and these cases can quite properly go all the way. However, that is a far different exercise than going out looking for impact cases and using the courts as a political battleground for the poor as a social class. The issue is not whether the poor should get more from the system; the issue is whether Legal Services should go down the tubes because the political opponents of the poor as a class are fighting back politically and winning. A formal commitment to depoliticization will probably do far less harm to the cause of the poor than anyone currently imagines, if for no other reason than that much of the law that the poor need has already been made.

I doubt that a great deal can be done about the hero mentality of legal-aid lawyers. Psychic satisfaction derived from being a hero is probably a large part of their compensation—at least for the good ones. But good leadership can mitigate the most abrasive manifestations of "heroitis." A simple recognition that Legal Services is a publicly funded entity that requires political support from its in-court opponents should suffice. Usually private general practitioners do not get personal about their clients' cases, and it would not be amiss for the law schools to teach those who are about to graduate that a tradition of gentlemanly conduct is not immoral even among Legal Services lawyers. After all, it is an elementary and vital courtesy when you are using people's own money against them that you do it with some grace.

All efforts to deliver legal services must take account of two factors. First, legal services are unlike medical services, agricultural extension services, or higher education services that everyone hopes his or her neighbor will have. If my neighbor gets good medical treatment, that does not make me sick; and if my neighbor's son gets a good education, that does not make my son any the less well educated. But in the zero-sum game of litigation, the winners profit at the losers' expense. While the constraints on providing publicly funded medical services, agricultural services, and educational services are budgetary, the constraints on providing publicly funded legal services are budgetary and political. In addition, legal-services expenditures are competitive. Unlike both industry and commerce where greater investment leads to higher productivity, the cost of litigation can be bid up without improving the end result of the litigation process.

Our tradition of permitting the client to determine whether he or she wants to litigate *and* the exact amount of competitive litigation costs to be incurred arose from a world in which every litigant paid his or her own lawyers' fees. Increasingly, however, we are building a society where it is not possible for a majority to pay their own lawyers' fees except through tax-supported services or group plans. This direction of society, arising as it does from our increasing complexity and the more universal need for legal advice, obviously implies that we are creating a legal "common" with attendant rationing problems. The next step in history, therefore, is to focus on intelligent systems for rationing scarce legal resources—systems that involve neither product deterioration nor standing in line and that seek to minimize the waste inherent in a costly, competitive, zero-sum game.

If, for example, in the cases handled by legal aid the same type of cost:benefit decisions were made that are made in privately financed litigation, much of the political hostility to legal aid would abate. Creating such alternatives is certainly a better fall-back position in an era of conservative administrations than any other course. It will be hard to revitalize legal aid after it has been effectively gutted by being relegated to state control. It is better to keep the federal program intact in a slightly changed form.

Conclusions   9

THE first requirement for getting the right answers in the area of court reform is to ask the right questions. The focus of this book has been to explore why courts do not work as well as we would like them to work, with particular attention to how the courts affect and are affected by society-wide political battles. Obviously, where the courts become involved either wittingly or unwittingly in political battles, those same courts will either become the target or the ally of the combatants in those battles.

Through at least the past decade, no public problem has worried Americans more persistently than crime. When people are asked in opinion surveys to list the problems that concern them most, the threat of crime typically comes at or near the top. But when the same people list the issues on which they will decide which candidate to vote for, crime usually comes behind half a dozen other subjects. The explanation they offer most frequently is that a candidate's statements about crime are unimportant—no one can do much about the problem.

The reason for this hopelessness is that voters do not know the questions and therefore cannot evaluate the political answers. Furthermore, many officeholders are liars—while they talk a good game about crime control, they are in fact the political proponents of special interests that actively seek mediocre, if not downright incompetent, court performance. Yet it has never occurred to most voters that any organized interest (other than a crime syndicate) would be against good courts and the efficient enforcement of the laws. Voters do not expect the baldfaced political lie in this area of concern.

It is as naïve, however, to assert that all the problems of the courts and related agencies come from behind-the-scenes political battles as to assert the converse. Actually the problems of the courts and related agencies can be divided into three broad categories. At the top of the list are indeed political battles, which is just another way of pointing out our lack of consensus about distribution of wealth, moral responsibility, and which laws are just. But immediately below political battles come budgetary considerations. While budget constraints are often used to justify positions motivated in fact by the political battles of the first category, nonetheless, all government agencies must compete with one another for funds. Finally come the courts' structural problems. The judiciary has no hierarchy that lends itself to political leadership; judges are largely independent, which reduces opportunities for quality control; and the personalities and age distribution of the appellate judges who manage the system make them uninterested in overall administration.

All of these problems are exacerbated by the structure of state legislatures and Congress. Legislatures are interested in economic rather than social issues, because economic issues deliver the money or votes to win elections. Unfortunately for the frustrated voter who recognizes that political rhetoric about courts is seldom translated into action, courts are a social issue for the proponents of better courts but an economic issue for the opponents of better courts. If poor court performance were either entirely an economic issue or entirely a social issue, more might have been done in court reform.

Furthermore, there are many different types of courts, and each of them has its own mix of problems. For example, the biggest problems of the federal courts are political. A host of special interests do not want a proliferation of "activist" federal judges who will intrude themselves into traditional state matters like the running of schools or mental hospitals. Judges, as I pointed out, have the capacity to constitute an alternative government; the only limit on their ability to run things is the absence of personal stamina or supporting manpower.

241

Yet the problems of the domestic-relations courts and the minor, limited-jurisdiction courts, are almost entirely budgetary. There are no active political lobbies that want to slow down the granting of divorces or impede full and fair consideration of issues like alimony or child custody. The overwhelming problem in domestic-relations courts is the expense of lawyers and the difficulty of collecting alimony or child support awards. To do something about the domestic-relations courts' problems it is necessary to transfer certain functions that are currently being performed by private or legal-aid lawyers to salaried public officials. Where one parent violates a court order and takes a child, the other parent should not need to spend thousands of dollars to get the child back. Similarly, a mother should not have to spend more money than alimony or child support is worth trying to collect it. While these problems can be solved, the solutions involve the transfer of costs that are currently borne by private litigants to the government treasury.

The minor courts can be improved 100 percent by higher quality staff, more commodious quarters, and a complete revision of the adjudicatory model. But all of this is costly, especially at a time when little real income growth is expected from the American economy. While in absolute terms the money involved in the management of a state court system is small in comparison to total state expenditures, there are still thousands of other competing demands for government money where the amounts involved are also small in absolute terms.

The problems of the general-jurisdiction civil and criminal courts are in one regard different and yet in another regard the same. Different lobbies for different reasons oppose expansion of civil and criminal courts respectively. However, since in most states and in the federal system the civil and criminal courts are the same institution, lobbies that oppose greater capacity in one perforce oppose greater capacity in the other.

The reader may have noticed that throughout the course of this book I have avoided the term *justice*. That is not because I am a cheerful cynic who believes the term has no meaning other than as a political conclusion; it is rather because the term has a defensible objective meaning only at the extremes. It is unjust to send an innocent person to jail, and it is unjust to decide a court case because of political influence or other corrupt motives. However, when we move away from the extremes, one person's justice is another's injustice. Older people, for example, who are terrorized by antisocial adolescents demand justice for themselves, the victims. The mental-health professionals who work with disturbed children all day point out the horrible conditions under which many of these children live. The uniform conclusion among social workers is that the majority of children who commit serious crimes have had their share of society's vengeance in advance. Justice, then, the social workers conclude, does not involve more and better punishment but rather the provision of competent social services to compensate for lack of justice in both home and neighborhood. Thus the courts are as often in the business of deciding between right and right as they are in the business of deciding between right and wrong.

Our perception of justice in the enforcement of civil matters such as consumer debt or landlord-and-tenant cases is some function of our conclusions about society's distribution of wealth and the fairness of the economic system. The vigorous enforcement of an existing law is not necessarily synonymous with abstract justice because the law itself may be unjust. Since everyone's definition of justice is largely subjective and related in some way to his or her own self-interest, it should not be surprising that none of us gets our own personal expectation of justice from the courts any more often than we get our own personal expectations of "good government" from the legislature or executive branch.

The courts do not do a very good job of protecting our own self-interest because that is not their job. Courts are in business to reconcile conflicting self-interests, although the problem is not usually stated in those terms. Often courts fail us simply because they and their supporting agencies are incompetent. But another reason for our shattered expectations is that we can't agree on what we want the courts to deliver. Older people expect juvenile offenders to be sent to prisonlike facilities for long terms; parents expect judges to refer antisocial children to a host of social-service agencies for rehabilitation. Both are right, for as the poet Hart Crane once said: "There is the world dimensional [only] for those untwisted by the love of things irreconcilable."

IF I could convey only one message in this book, it would be this: courts are to be avoided at all costs. To the maximum extent possible, people should rely on their own private systems for self-preservation rather than courts and their supporting agencies. While the ideal of conflict avoidance and self-reliance cannot always be realized, it can be realized more often than is currently the case. Part of court avoidance inevitably involves having access to legal advice. Unfortunately, the extent to which one can opt out of court protection is usually some function of income, so that the middle class has a better shot at self-preservation than the poor.

Starting with simple things, a cheap burglar alarm is better protection against thieves than the police. The object of a burglar alarm is not to alert the neighbors or the police but to frighten the hell out of the burglar in order to induce a precipitant departure before he does any damage. The ringing of a loud bell has a chilling effect on a burglar's incentive to browse through the bureaus and closets of a house. It is a more effective deterrent than the cop on the beat.

In many communities, volunteer neighborhood watches seem to be successful in deterring crime and enhancing apparent safety. Where people must live in a high-crime area, a little community initiative can bring substantial returns. Far better, however, is to get out of high-crime areas whenever possible. In the absence of a compelling economic reason related to income, employment, or family circumstances, it is silly to live in a sewer.

On the civil side, it is very difficult to avoid domestic-relations courts (although a majority of divorcing couples more or less settle their differences amicably), and if a person is poor, it is difficult to avoid being sued (except by the less attractive alternative of paying one's debts). Yet it is possible to avoid being a plaintiff in court by being careful with whom one does business. No one should rely on a written contract as a guarantee of satisfactory performance. A personal relationship with the people with whom one does business, the reputation of the company for satisfying its customers, and the expectation of mutually profitable business relations in the future are what good business relations depend upon. Anyone with good credit need not pay for goods in advance, and a person should tactfully bargain about who has the burden of a lawsuit in the event there is a dispute about whether goods delivered conform to the contract.

Felix Frankfurter once observed that the best way of resolving conflict is to avoid it. That is the type of remark that any judge will make after a few years on the bench; judges understand better than anyone else the degree to which real life is meaninglessly abstracted into legal principles during the course of any lawsuit. I have watched numerous businesses go bankrupt because the respective parties to a business controversy hired lawyers who were skilled in courtroom litigation instead of lawyers who were skilled in business. A skilled business lawyer usually understands that his client will come out ahead in the long run if he meets other parties to a controversy more than halfway and effects a settlement where at least part of his investment is preserved. Going to court should always be the last, not the first, resort.

I am not unmindful of the class-biased nature of suggestions about self-preservation. The lower a person's socioeconomic position, the less he can organize his affairs around avoiding courts. Nonetheless, the fact that not everyone can protect himself does not mean that no one should protect himself. The point to be made here is only that the inherent inefficiencies of courts and supporting agencies is one factor that must be constantly borne in mind in the arrangement of one's daily life. But having made what I consider an obligatory observation on the desirability of avoiding courts, it is now time to summarize what can be done to improve them. Obviously, improvement of the criminal courts and their supporting agencies has a higher priority in the minds of most individuals than the improvement of the civil courts.

IN the course of writing this book I was asked to serve on the advisory board of the National Victims of Crime, Inc., a Washington, D.C., based national lobbying group for better criminal justice. Initially the focus of National Victims of Crime (which was started in 1981 after Congressman Hamilton Fish, its founder, was mugged outside the Capitol) was on *national* legislation that would further traditional conservative positions on crime control. Thus the goal was more police, stiffer mandatory sentences, more prosecutors, more prisons, and possibly a death penalty.

When I began my service on the advisory board I pointed out, and with some apparent success, that the action in crime control is not at the national level but at the state level. While a national lobbying group is important for fund raising, quality staff work, and national publicity, a citizens' lobby will work only if at some point it selects a target state and begins the political dialogue. To do this requires a lot of money, which must be raised from broad-based contributions from business, foundations, and individuals.

In general I am reserved in my enthusiasm for think tanks and other research groups. Most of the government or foundation money is spent to employ university professors, lawyers, and miscellaneous bureaucrats to prepare poorly written papers that no active, high-level politician will ever read. Yet, notwithstanding these reservations, if any progress in criminal law is to be made, a team of experts from active law practice, penology, the judiciary, mental health, and social work must be organized to write a comprehensive state statute for a particular target state.[1]

The pure research that would bear on the development of a comprehensive state statute has already been done—there are thousands of studies on penology, criminal motivation, treatment programs for juveniles, and all the related problems. What is needed now is not more research but the application of existing research to construct a working document in the form of a statute a state legislature can pass. Such a statute must include not only structural reforms but also specific budget bills to fund the program. Once a lobbying group has drafted a statute for a particular state, we have passed the talking stage and entered the doing stage, which is what everyone wants.

The construction of a politically acceptable package to improve criminal courts and their supporting agencies must be done very carefully, bearing constantly in mind society's diverse opinions on criminal justice and the compromises that will need to be made to secure a working coalition. The fact that a lobby is militant and well financed does not mean that it will, for those reasons alone, be successful. The militant and well-financed opponents of abortion have had very few legislative successes exactly because they cannot secure majority sup-

1. My own suggestion for the target state has been Massachusetts because its court system is particularly poor, and it is small enough that lobbying efforts using the media are not prohibitively expensive.

port. Before undertaking to write the model statute (or, really, statutes), care must be taken to touch only the areas where there is broad agreement, leaving the political hot potatoes that do not relate to the prevention of violent street crime for another day.

Opinion about how we should handle crime breaks down into four major positions. On the far right are those who believe that more police, more prosecutors, plenary police powers, longer mandatory prison sentences, and capital punishment are the only morally correct responses. On the far left are those who believe that all criminality is the product of society—this is an unfair, corrupt, and decadent culture to which crime is a perfectly acceptable response by the poor, minorities, or those who cannot compete. Between these two extremes are what can be called the "moderate right" and "moderate left" positions.

The moderate right recognizes that many criminals are driven to crime by social circumstances; however, the moderate right despairs of getting at the "root causes" of crime. Therefore, it demands symptomatic relief and endorses proposals to expand the engines of enforcement. Yet the moderate right does not oppose rehabilitation programs, creative systems for probation, or nonpunitive approaches to juvenile offenders where any of these techniques will work. The moderate right is not ideological; it just wants results.

The moderate left also wants results that reduce violent crime, but it rejects proposals that rely heavily on giving more authority and manpower to police and prosecutors. The moderate left expects that enhanced police power will be abused. While many members of the moderate left are terrorized by crime, their response is ambivalent because they fear a "police state."

In my experience, the majority of Americans fall into the moderate left or moderate right camps. The more likely a person is to be a victim of violent crime, the higher his or her likelihood of joining the moderate right, but the correlation is not perfect. In order for a lobbying group at the state level to develop the breadth of consensus needed for success, some alliance of these two groups must be achieved. The primary bones of contention between the two groups are the extent of police powers and the method of punishing offenders.

The moderate right is made up of largely law-abiding citizens who are optimistic about the integrity and moderation of the police. The moderate left are often less law-abiding citizens—they more frequently violate the drug laws, the vice laws, the drunk-driving laws, and the economic regulatory laws. These transgressions are minor in comparison to the crimes that terrify us—murder, armed robbery, rape, burglary— but many members of the moderate left are not enthusiastic about an across-the-board enhancement of police power. What, for example, would happen if the police were given power to stop and frisk suspicious people and used these new powers in upper-class Beverly Hills by nabbing movie producers with cocaine in their pockets?

The majority of moderate-left adherents aren't concerned just with their own immunity from prosecution. Many understand that the activities of the police tend to follow closely the geography of political power, and since historically the police have been used as a weapon against the poor and minorities, the moderate left is unwilling to provide new opportunities for such oppression. Consequently, any citizen lobby must have heavy representation from groups like blacks and Hispanics who are the traditional victims of both crime and of police harassment.

Part of the dilemma for the moderate left and the moderate right is that it is difficult to assess how well the traditional answers to crime control—more cops, stiffer sentences, more prisons—actually work. West Virginia, for example, has the lowest crime rate in the United States, and we abolished capital punishment by statute in 1965. Doubling the police force in rural areas where police aren't relied on in the first place to control crime will have no effect on the crime rate. On the other hand, in urban settings such as New York City's subway system where the police are the primary deterrent to crime, increasing police will drastically lower crime. In between these two extremes is approximately half of America in cities as diverse as Springfield, Massachusetts, Racine, Wisconsin, and Wheeling, West Virginia.

We do know that in both upper-middle-class suburban developments and urban, low-income housing projects citizen patrols are reducing crime. Therefore, more police and more patrolling will reduce crime in urban and suburban areas. The real question to be answered is the extent of the powers that are to be given to the police. The moderate right complains bitterly about the exclusionary rule that requires guilty criminals to be released whenever the police violate technical rules about interrogation, search, and seizure. Yet it is the exclusionary rule that protects the less law-abiding moderate left when they use drugs, solicit prostitutes, or have poker games in their basements.

What has happened is that the civil-liberties aspect of the criminal law has become the battleground where people fight about the justice of minor regulatory laws. What the moderate left would really like is a system that gives the police more power to prevent violent crime, while maintaining the status quo in the area of drugs, morals, gambling, etc., but this is a difficult position to articulate. However, if such a scheme is what it takes to make progress in preventing violent crime, then theoretical harmony must be sacrificed on the altar of practical politics.[2]

The far right and the moderate right together do not have the votes to change our current criminal-justice system. They need the active support of the moderate left. But since the moderate left is also concerned about personal safety, it is possible to reach an accommodation and present a united front. Notwithstanding the lack of consensus concerning the enforcement of a wide spectrum of criminal laws, there is at least a strong consensus that something should be done about violent crime. It is this consensus, combined with the fact that most adults consider violent crime an urgent problem, that makes the National Victims of Crime or any other action-oriented lobby potentially effective.

A well-financed lobby does a number of things that unorganized citizens and amateur do-gooders cannot do. The first is to raise money.

2. This lack of theoretical harmony can actually be justified pragmatically. A society can quite comfortably tolerate private poker games, a little prostitution, and even some drug use. However, the levels of these activities when they are legal and when they are illegal differ dramatically, even when the law is hardly ever enforced. For example, once prostitution is legalized, prostitutes can be recruited from the local high schools. Newspapers can carry advertisements that say: "Earn a little money in your spare time doing something that's fun. Come in after school and set your own hours." While some women will turn to prostitution as a way of making a living regardless of the law, the fact that prostitution is illegal discourages many more who might try it if it were a more respectable job. The same applies to gambling and drugs. The existence of easily available legal casinos encourages gambling, and legalizing marijuana would immediately increase its consumption.

Without money to hire qualified staff, nothing else works. While occasionally at the local level where people are dealing with simple issues volunteer staff can be politically effective, serious lobbies know that high-quality professional staff involved with legislators on a long-term basis are essential to get legislation passed. Volunteers either do not have the technical expertise in bill drafting and legislative mechanics or cannot devote the time necessary to sustain a long-term effort.

From my own experience, any time a proposal is submitted to legislators it must be in the form of a complete piece of legislation. Legislators, particularly state legislators with limited staffs, do not have time to work on the initial design of comprehensive legislation. Once such legislation has been prepared, however, legislators do have time to bang out the budgetary and other compromises necessary to get the bill passed. And it should be borne in mind that efforts to improve the criminal courts and their supporting agencies are not a one-shot deal. Almost any bill is better than no bill at all, and if only a part of a program is passed in one year, more can be added the next year and the next. It is sustained effort that pays off in the end, but initially there must be a comprehensive plan to shoot for.

Technical staff is not the only productive use to which money can be put. As Chapter 3 explained, bills are either passed or killed in the Byzantine legislative committees where the decisions of legislators have low visibility. Skilled lobbyists understand what goes on in the committee process—the committee room and legislative corridor are the lobbyist's natural habitat. Money permits publicity when committee-room maneuvering kills a bill. Where lobbyists are representing special-interest groups with small constituencies, such publicity is liable to generate hostility from legislators and do more harm than good. However, where the issue is one of general concern and the constituency is both large and militant, legislators will avoid adverse publicity and turn their negative activities to killing other, less visible, legislation.

Publicity involves several separate components. At one extreme, a well-financed lobby can actually purchase prime-time television advertisements describing the actions of hostile legislators. At the other extreme, newsletters explaining the nature of the legislation submitted and the performance of individual legislators can be sent to members of the lobbying organization. In between are formal press releases and televised press conferences by the lobby's leaders.

Of course, the lobbying process is greatly facilitated if the local newspapers and television stations adopt the cause of better criminal courts and supporting agencies as their own. In that event the press itself magnifies the return to every publicity dollar spent. However, active press support is a two-edged sword. If a crime-control citizens' lobby appears to be too one sided—in other words, if it stresses only the police powers and punitive side of crime control—it will lose the press because, in my experience, young reporters usually are members of the moderate left.

The reform of the civil courts presents far less opportunity for citizen participation than reform of the criminal courts because there is no broad-based constituency with identical interests. There will, of course, be some spillover from efforts to improve the criminal courts that will affect the civil courts. But since the wisest course for people primarily concerned with criminal courts is to separate the two systems whenever possible to minimize political opposition, the spillover will be modest.

While we are all confronted with the danger of crime every day, the average person is at most an occasional user of the civil courts. Of the adult population who have been to a civil court, by far the greatest percentage have been there for domestic-relations matters. Outside of domestic relations, the most frequent visitors to civil courts are specialized users like insurance companies that already have active lobbies concerned with courts. Unfortunately, what these lobbies want is usually at odds with what nonspecialized users want. As noted throughout this book, delay and incompetence often serve the interests of specialized users quite well. The occasional, nonspecialized user will never join a lobby or contribute money to improving an institution he hopes to avoid at all costs. After all, most people are optimists.

There is one development that augurs well for increased attention to systemic improvement in the civil courts. The 1982–83 economic depression has focused our minds on this country's slipping competitive position in the worldwide economy. If the Reagan administration's experiment in revitalizing laissez-faire free enterprise fails, the torch will then pass to the Democrats, where the neo-liberal wing emphasizes government guidance to enhance our competitive position in international trade.[3]

Between 1970 and 1980 our imports increased from 9 percent to 21 percent, while our exports increased from 9 percent to 17 percent. Obviously, America has entered a worldwide economy and is subject to being outgunned by foreign competition. We must now, therefore, adopt strategies that make us competitive in the international market or lose jobs. Since we are up against other nations like Japan and France that have "corporate state" structures where the government actively encourages the export sector, we must adopt similar government policies in order to compete.

Our competitive disadvantage was once explained to me in jest, but succinctly, by an international lawyer: "In France the central bank is part of the government, and in Japan the government is part of the central bank." America, however, lacks such felicitous relationships and is inherently unsuited to any quick conversion to a guided economy. Not only do we lack existing institutions capable of enhancing our competitive position, but we have a host of institutions that are antithetical to such an undertaking. Preeminent among such institutions is the civil court system, with court power to review administrative agency decisions at a leisurely pace that delays action to the point where agency decisions become obsolete. The courts are not unique in their lack of suitability to modern times. The United States does not even have a central bank. The Federal Reserve is to a central bank what chicken feathers are to chicken salad.

All countries are prisoners of their history. France is a prisoner of its years of class warfare; Japan is a prisoner of its stoic philosophy; and America is a prisoner of its love of adversary relationships. In labor relations, for example, we have the highest number of workdays lost as a result of strikes per employee of any developed country. Great Britain is close behind us with 10 percent fewer, but the next highest country, France, loses only 40 percent of what we lose to labor disputes.

If the United States decides on a program of active government

3. The preeminent statement of this position can be found in a brilliant work by Ira Magaziner and Robert Reich, *Minding America's Business* (New York: Harcourt Brace Jovanovich, 1982).

involvement with industry to sustain American jobs in the face of foreign competition, then attention will need to be given to the problems of delay in the courts and the power of the courts to frustrate legitimate economic decisions by other private and government power centers. When and if the courts become the focus of our attention because they need to be improved to enhance our competitive position, we will have an opportunity to redesign a substantial portion of the civil court litigation system. Yet here again it is important to separate what an overwhelming majority of people want changed from all the things about which there is no consensus.

Unfortunately, few of the people concerned with courts are familiar with court management. Lawyers usually understand the problems of the courts only to the extent that they observe particular problems in pursuit of their clients' interests. A corporate lawyer, therefore, is likely to be ignorant of the problems facing a domestic-relations litigant, while a general practitioner doing domestic and criminal work is unlikely to be familiar with the problems corporations face in getting judicial review of administrative agency decisions.

Nor are most people in the system aware of how mechanical problems, such as delay in getting jury trials, are designed to offset other things like outrageous jury verdicts. We cannot tamper with the incentive to settle that delay provides to a plaintiff without also tampering with its offset, the potentially enormous jury award. Systems engineering of this magnitude, repudiating as it does the jury-rigged contrivances that were hundreds of years in the making, is likely to be forthcoming from only the most imaginative of appellate courts.

There is no common language for discussing court reform. Yet lawyers and litigants in the current civil-court system should be able to use the concepts advanced in this book to urge systemic changes as appropriate cases arise. Good cases can force appellate judges, and even trial judges, to consider systemic issues. After all, appellate judges consider any argument placed before them in a case. While they may reject suggestions implying systemic reform when those suggestions are argued in cases before them, they must at least give explicit reasons for the rejection.

Consequently, it is not amiss, for example, for lawyers to begin to urge new rules concerning the allocation of costs when litigation per se is used to oppress one side of a lawsuit. Nor is it amiss for a domestic-relations lawyer to urge a local trial judge to use the court's inherent powers to devise a system by which alimony and child support can be paid to a public official who can hire a lawyer to enforce the awards. In a similar vein, appellate courts should be made aware of the burdens the system places on industry by the delay inherent in litigating about environmental matters. Again, in my experience, lawyers seldom argue the judicial system's administrative problems in briefs or at oral argument, which is often why appellate judges give so little attention to systemic reform. If appellate judges are interested only in those things that arise in traditional lawsuits, we can accommodate them by presenting our questions about the court system that way.

Throughout this book I have attempted to explain rather than condemn. My editors have been disappointed that I am not a militant advocate of across-the-board reform (which implies current corruption) or, at least, reorganization (which implies only incompetent administration). Perhaps because I am a practicing politician I understand that the true reformer or reorganizer must be satisfied with modest gains. One modest, yet important gain is to understand the nature of the courts' problems. In this regard I am put in mind of Gertrude Stein's hospitalization and operation. On regaining consciousness, she asked the doctor, "Well, what's the answer?" Told that the case was hopeless, she replied, "In that case, what is the question?"

Index

INDEX

INDEX

INDEX

About the Author

Justice Richard Neely is a graduate of Dartmouth College and the Yale Law School. He was elected to the West Virginia Supreme Court of Appeals in 1972, where he was Chief Justice in 1980. Between his graduation from Yale and his election to the Supreme Court, Neely served as an Army artillery captain in Vietnam and practiced law in his own one-man office in Fairmont, West Virginia. In 1970 he served one term in the West Virginia Legislature. In addition to his judicial duties, he is professor of economics at the University of Charleston and he is the author of *How Courts Govern America*.